Iskren Ivanov
Pandemics Among Nations

De Gruyter Contemporary Social Sciences

—
Volume 12

Iskren Ivanov
Pandemics Among Nations

U.S. Foreign Policy and the New Grand Chessboard

DE GRUYTER

ISBN 978-3-11-152368-2
e-ISBN (PDF) 978-3-11-074086-8
e-ISBN (EPUB) 978-3-11-074101-8
ISSN 2747-5689
e-ISSN 2747-5697

Library of Congress Control Number: 2022934828

Bibliographic information published by the Deutsche Nationalbibliothek
The Deutsche Nationalbibliothek lists this publication in the Deutsche
Nationalbibliografie; detailed bibliographic data are available on the internet at http://dnb.dnb.de.

© 2024 Walter de Gruyter GmbH, Berlin/Boston
This volume is text- and page-identical with the hardback published in 2022.
Cover image: MicroStockHub/iStock/Getty Images Plus

www.degruyter.com

"Power positions do not yield to arguments, however rationally or morally valid, but only to superior power."
Hans Joachim Morgentau

"Mastering others is strength; mastering yourself is true power."
Lao Tzu

Preface

History ends where the new world begins. Power is the eternal driving force of our time. The structure of the international system undergoes a profound transformation that liberalism refuses to accept. Liberal scholars miss the essential aspect of international politics, which determines how the world will look in the future years – anarchy. This book is about the post-pandemic structure of world politics, and I have come to the point of writing it due to the theoretical myth that realism is insufficient to explain political relations among nations. Thirty years after the end of the Cold War, the world is on the brink of another bipolar confrontation between the most powerful nation on the earth – the United States and its rising adversary – China. The prospect of Asian power taking over the global leadership horrifies the Western world, although the legacy of the liberal world order still inspires the considerable optimism of its proponents. The liberal paradigm truly believed that power no longer serves as a driving force of politics. The collapse of the Soviet Union and the short period of unipolar peace favored the liberal dreams of eternal peace. However, with the USSR defeated, the struggle for power did not end. It was a radical simplicity to believe that the unipolar world offers the universal pattern of peaceful coexistence and geopolitical consensus. The remarkable optimism of liberalism turned out to be its greatest weakness.

History has come to the point where international realities no longer correspond to the everlasting structure of the unipolar world. To realize the consequences of the Pandemic is to accept that the struggle for power never ends. Conflicts between nations emerge as the United States and China seek to reshape the balance of power. International organizations and institutional bodies fail to intervene in global crises. The ideal of peace seems to decline, and the dictate of realism is on the rise. The readers of this book might object that no great power will risk a war with another. History shows that peace had failed many times when great powers fought and succeeded when they tried to survive. Our world should get to the point that peace and war serve the national interests of the most powerful nations. The success or the failure of peace thus is not a privilege of humanity. Peace is the best way to guarantee our survival. Yet, in the nuclear age, war often prevails due to the natural desire of nations to seek power and the anarchic nature of the international system, which makes conflicts occur. Therefore, there can be no peace without confrontation.

My first gratitude goes to the team of *De Gruyter* for being so patient with a bookish scholar like me and for granting me the opportunity to publish my work. Their labor was essential for this book, and I sincerely appreciate it. I owe deep gratitude to my U.S. Foreign Policy Professors Muqtedar Khan and Daniel Bottomley from the Joseph Biden Jr. School of Public Policy and Administration at the University of Delaware. They inspired me to elaborate my studies on International Relations and sharpened my expertise in American politics. I am liable to debt to my academic advisor, Prof. Tatyana Dronzina, for her professional support, without which I would not be able to refine this book. I am also deeply thankful to Professor Mary Neuburger from the University of Texas at Austin, who invited me to teach a course on U.S./Russia Foreign Policy at UT. Her advice on different points of my writing motivated me further in my research. Finally, I was deeply inspired by the works of the realist scholars cited in this book, some of whom I had the opportunity and privilege to meet in person.

Contents

Introduction —— 1

Chapter One
The problem of power and peace at the beginning of the twenty-first century: peace through confrontation —— 6
    The puzzle of Kenneth Waltz —— 7
    The security dilemma of Robert Jervis —— 9
    The offensive realism of John Mearsheimer —— 11
    The offshore balancing of Mearsheimer and Walt —— 14
    The Thucydides's trap of Graham Allison —— 18
    The Long Haul of Robert J. Art —— 21
    The hegemonic war of Robert Gilpin —— 23
    Getting coercive —— 25
    Six pillars of coercive realism —— 31

Chapter Two
Bound to cheat: liberal foreign policy in a realist world —— 34
    Anarchy and the illiberal end of history —— 35
    Coercion and the limits of American power —— 43
    Sovereignty and principled realism —— 53
    Polarity and the unipolar syndrome —— 60
    Endurance and misperceptions on power —— 70
    Powershifting and wishful thinking —— 82
    Six lessons from the pre-pandemic world —— 91

Chapter Three
China: The Silent Cultivator —— 102
    Mao's dialectics —— 104
    The power of cultivation —— 114
    Sinocetrism: Tributary Diplomacy vs. Military Paternalism —— 123
    Marxism and liberalization —— 136
    Strategic culture and the realist paradigm —— 143
    Why should we expect China to act differently from Washington? —— 151
    Is Beijing less concerned about its survival than Washington is? —— 155

Chapter Four
The Post-Pandemic Structure of International Politics —— 159
    Setting the model: the pyramid of balance —— 162
    Assessing the primary variables —— 167
    Assessing the secondary variables —— 169
    Defining the aspects —— 172
    Inferring the postulates —— 174
    Confrontation under the security dilemma: four worlds —— 202
    World 1: Offshore containment —— 207
    World 2: Bellum omnium contra omnes —— 209
    World 3: Scorch War —— 211
    World 4: Nuclear apocalypse —— 213
    Objections to my approach —— 217
    Three-Check Chess: The Grand Chessboard Revisited —— 221

Conclusion —— 225

References —— 229

Index —— 240

Introduction

What are the geopolitical consequences of COVID19? How will the Coronavirus Pandemic affect international politics and great power competition? Is Beijing moving to dethrone the United States as a global leader in the post-pandemic security architecture? Could smart power have maintained the U.S. global dominance without risking a war between the U.S. and China?

These questions have been vaguely discussed in either international relations or security studies. Complementing the problem of the Pandemic theories that are not developed to assess this impact is the difficulty of mustering empirical data. The collection of such data involves two methodological challenges. First, there is no compatible approach to determine the origins of the Coronavirus. It is deeply misleading to employ conspiracies by tracing COVID's roots in biological warfare or China's secret labs. It is also hard to define what the American preventive strategy was and even harder to examine if there was any. The second difficulty is that even though we have probable scenarios for the post-pandemic security architecture, we cannot draw general conclusions about what the world will look like through 2050. We can probably search for some implications on the balance of power or the security dilemma, but this will not shed light on the long-term impact of the Coronavirus Pandemic.

This book introduces an original explanation of the post-pandemic security architecture, which I call *coercive realism*. I do not use the word "theory" for two reasons. First, to design a theory of international relations requires a profound knowledge of international politics and plenty of empirical data that the author of this book, as a young scholar, does not claim. Second, constructing a theoretical explanation of international politics requires analyzing case studies such as various international conflicts or historical precedents. Although this book explores a limited number of such cases, their operationalization aims to provide an explanative and evidentiary framework of the post-pandemic world rather than position coercive realism as a source of general theoretical knowledge. Third, although I do not purport to offer a theory, I have employed the standard methodological approach to IR studies by defining the variables in my research and testing my assumption by explaining world politics. That is to say, that I believe my study deserves a plausible and proper research design to provide further explanations of what we will face in the next ten to fifty years.

The assumption that U.S. Foreign Policy under the Trump administration provided a test for many international relations theories (Jervis 2017, 3–7) provides a logical starting point for my concept. Most of the existing theories assert that the state is its decision-makers because state action is the action taken by those acting in the name of the state (Snyder, Bruck and Sapin 2002, 4). However, foreign policy decision-making diverges from external geopolitical realities that not all decision-makers can detect and analyze. In this book, I offer a structural analysis of the post-pandemic world order instead of following the institutional approach of the liberal paradigm. My assumption is that the post-pandemic structure of international politics will evolve into a complex shape, which I call the *pyramid of balance*. Thus, I believe that more profound knowledge of existing realist theories could better explain the evolving structure of international politics and clarify our expectations for the post-pandemic world order. In addition, this book introduces a methodological approach that seeks to explain the future of polarity.

Although there is a growing body of literature by liberal scholars discussing the essential relation between power and politics in international relations, most of the contributions in this field are barred by four methodological weaknesses, which, I assume, undermine their theoretical validity. First, liberalism usually pays more attention to soft power instead of focusing on military interventions, coercive diplomacy, and economic sanctions to enforce national interests (Campbell and O'Hanlon 2006, 67). Strategic use of tanks, aircraft carriers, and nukes could justify a preemptive strike or mass retaliation. However, diplomacy and attraction cannot explain why even the most educated and hawkish decision-makers would go to war without having any reliable information about the existence of a particular national security threat.

Second, most of the case studies that liberal scholars assess in their writings derive from unipolarity without discussing the structural perspective of realism. It is hard to determine which of these cases will apply to the post-pandemic world and even harder to predict if they will be reliable enough. The Coronavirus Pandemic is a major test for all schools of international relations because simple forms of cooperation and international agreements can no longer prevent conflicts among nations. Liberal decision-makers, who reject the realist theories about resource distribution, even failed to provide a unified response to the need for scarce resources such as COVID vaccines and medical logistics.

Third, the geopolitical consequences of the Pandemic, the challenges, and the opportunities for U.S. Foreign Policy are either overlooked or misunderstood. For some, post-pandemic America is a troubled and unequal society, further weakened by the Coronavirus and destined to return to isolationism (Heisbourg 2020, 20 – 22). Because such claims view American democracy as a gradual process rather than a part of the Anglo-Saxon tradition, they are incorrect in assuming that U.S. Foreign Policy is declining. One should not confuse the decline of the liberal world order with the popular but inconsistent assumption that the United States experiences its decadence. U.S. Presidential doctrines can lead either to war or peace, but the struggle for global domination has always been present in Washington's foreign policy since the Spanish – American war in 1898. Another group of scholars succumbs to the temptation of theoretical absolutism by employing idealistic rhetoric for the future of Sino-American relations, neglecting that the Chinese geopolitical strategy rebukes the hawkish instincts of Neocons and Eurasian nationalists.

Finally, most liberal theories, particularly those that rely on institutionalism, do not provide us with an explanation of how international bodies could help the most powerful nation on the earth confront rising China. In truth, international organizations and soft power matter in world politics. However, in overstressing values, culture, and institutional cooperation, the United States faces the danger of colliding incommensurate resources with mismatched realities. Therefore, it is reasonable to assume that the winning strategy for American policymakers would be to manipulate the balance of power by confronting their counterparts rather than struggling for hegemony at all costs. For example, the Bush doctrine opened Pandora's Box in the Middle East by mobilizing massive military force that could have been used later against Iran. Preemptive strike originates from the assumption that the enemy is about to attack and that striking first will be better than allowing the enemy to do so (Mueller and Castillo 2006, 6–7). Preemption was successful in regime change but failed to maintain permanent stability in the region. Paradoxically, the quick fall of Saddam Hussein and the two-decades-long presence of American troops in Iraq did not contribute to liberal hegemony.

This book is limited in two aspects. First, my explanation incorporates the neorealist school as its theoretical core and rejects the neo-liberal approach to international politics. My empirical concern with neo-liberal theories is that international bodies turned out to be a false promise established by the most powerful states in the international system so they can maintain and increase their share of world power (Mearsheimer 2009, 23). Moreover, proponents of liberalism have compromised the empirical robustness of the liberal paradigm, which seeks to explain the future of international politics in less consistent and less definitive concepts. The fundamental problem with the liberal theories is that the Pandemic and the rise of China delegitimize their theoretical validity. For example, state actors have been far more effective in fighting the Pandemic, while international organizations failed to provide a unified response to COVID. Second, instead of preventing the rise of regional hegemons after the end of the Cold War, the United States followed the liberal temptation and endorsed a policy that advocated the spread of democracy. Thus, I have found it reasonable to focus my review on concepts that explain the realist view of China's rise. I discuss some of the basic neo-realist theories, although my research does not cover the entire body of realist literature relevant to the topic.

The research roadmap of this book includes four steps. The first chapter presents a methodological review of the most influential realist writings. In this part of my research, I discuss the theories of Kenneth Waltz, Robert Jervis, John Mearsheimer, Graham Allison, Stephen Walt, Robert Art, and Robert Gilpin. This is not to say that I neglect classical realist scholars like Hans Morgenthau. However, discussing all realist theories will require another book. In the last section of this chapter, I outline the variables in my model and operationalize them to construct my explanation. Then, I summarize a short conclusion about the pillars of coercive realism.

The second chapter of this work analyzes the post-pandemic implications of U.S. Foreign Policy. I argue that the liberal concept of power is ineffective against China for two reasons. First, with the transition from U.S.-dominated to Sino-American contested world order, hard power, and more particularly, nuclear weapons will become central to the post-pandemic structure of international politics. Second, Western perceptions of Beijing's Grand Strategy are not relevant to the Chinese comprehension of hegemony and global leadership. The chapter offers a critical review of the liberal view of China's foreign policy. My assumption is that European Union and Russia have duplicated and reproduced the American behavior of unipole while struggling over their ultimate purpose – to become global actors. China, quite the opposite, developed a unique pattern of foreign policy that will dominate the Chinese grand design in the post-pandemic world. The chapter explains why liberal concepts failed to maintain the unipolar world order and why, instead of favoring the United States, liberalism benefited the rise of China.

Chapter Three explores Chinese realpolitik. I begin with a theoretical review of Mao's dialectics and then I examine the philosophical aspects of Confucianism and Taoism. I argue that China's Grand Design embodies the policy of silent cultivator, which Beijing follows on its rise. I also discuss other aspects of Chinese foreign policy, such as Sinocentrism, China's Strategic Culture, and tributary diplomacy. My conclusion is that the Western misperceptions of Beijing's foreign policy led to the bipolar structure of the post-pandemic world order.

In the final chapter of this book, I try to explain the post-pandemic structure of international politics, which I define as the pyramid of balance. I operationalize the variables in my concept to infer the aspects of my model and its corresponding postulates. Then I proceed to calculation of the security dilemma in the post-pandemic world. Chapter Four also offers answers to the eventual objections against the theoretical validity of my concept. My conclusion of the chapter involves three revisions of Zbigniew Brzezinski's Grand Chessboard.

Finally, some experts might criticize this book as exceedingly ambitious because it challenges the conventional and predominant understanding of international politics. The reason for this is that this research revives the classical realism of Hans Morgenthau or the warnings of Henry Kissinger, which the neoliberal scholars have indirectly disguised as compromised and outdated. Knowing that Morgenthau's theory and Kissinger's concept of great power competition shape the modern understanding of international politics, liberals prefer to avoid offering a complete revision of realism. However, with the Coronavirus Pandemic still present, it is pretty evident that the optimistic view of human nature and the institutional approach to political relations among nations cannot provide a reasonable explanation of international politics.

Chapter One
The problem of power and peace at the beginning of the twenty-first century: peace through confrontation

I begin with a theoretical review of the fundamental neorealist theories, which provide a plausible starting point for my concept. Why choose the realist school? Liberals justify each other's paradigms by operationalizing the balance of power, non-state actors, decision-making, and ideology. Their passion for exploring and explaining politics among nations favors the operationalizion of variables such as international organizations, *suis generis* communities, individuals and prioritizes security challenges such as attraction, values, distribution of power, and environmental degradation. The result of this theoretical clash presents us with the inability to resolve the post-pandemic puzzle, which most liberal scholars claim to unravel. Even Francis Fukuyama admits, "The Pandemic has shone a bright light on existing institutions, everywhere, revealing their inadequacies and weaknesses." (Fukuyama 2020, 30).

It is challenging for liberals to consider the impact of a widespread disease like COVID19 on great powers competition, the global balance of power, and the decision-making process. Many of the most prominent liberals have reached a consensus that the Coronavirus Pandemic is a major challenge to international security. Yet, instead of giving a plausible explanation for state behavior and global distribution of power, they invoke high-end scenarios for the end of the Coronacrisis. This approach is one-sided and misleading because it is limited to one basic assumption, which is, by its very nature, neither realist nor liberal – when will we get back to normal? By overstressing the Pandemic's end, liberals confine their paradigms to an extent beyond which their assumptions are consistent *only* with the short-term geopolitical effects of COVID19. Therefore, their theoretical suppositions have been limited and redesigned to exclude long-term scenarios and ignore other variables such as WMD proliferation and offense/defense balance.

My criticism of the neo-liberal theories is not absolute, as it challenges only paradigms that fail to explain the post-pandemic security implications. Although such concepts are not entirely deprived of methodological peculiarity, they no longer assist scholars in developing further explanations of the post-pandemic world order. However, to reject the theoretical validity of neo-liberalism entirely is unreasonable and incoherent. Liberal ideas are central to international relations and U.S. Foreign Policy, which indicates that they will survive the Pandemic. In addition, instead of criticizing individual liberal scholars, I have chosen to employ a more comprehensive approach. Primarily, my theoretical review seeks to explain how the realist theories succinctly capture the transformation of the post-pandemic international system in contrast to the inability of liberals, who failed to predict the rise of another potential hegemon – China. Finally, it is important to highlight that the scope of my review is limited to the aspects of the aforementioned theories that, I believe, will be of most relevance to the post-pandemic world order.

The puzzle of Kenneth Waltz

Realism owes a big debt to the prophetic writings of Kenneth Waltz. In *Theory of International Politics*, Waltz argues that anarchy is central to international politics and that states are sovereign political entities responsible for developing their security strategies (Waltz 1979, 88–89). After the end of the Cold War, what passes for security architecture was challenged by China long before the Pandemic. Two decades of war on terror and Sino-American interdependence have culminated in a trade war between the United States and China. The doctrine of President Trump provoked high tensions with Beijing, while Chinese military activities in the Asia-Pacific shifted the balance of power in the region in favor of China. Finally, the Coronavirus outbreak fractured the pre-pandemic status-quo and escalated into a global Pandemic that blocked political relations among all major powers. In other words, COVID19 brought to an end a process that began shortly after September 11 – the emergence of bipolar world order: neither America nor China was powerful enough to defeat the other without risking mutual assured destruction, both powers had their grand design in search of power and resources. International organizations were helpless to prevent the emergence of Sino-American bipolarity. Thus, the international system today embodies an *anarchic* security architecture that corresponds empirically to Waltz's theory.

Waltz assumes that the balance-of-power system is unstable with two great powers and that four powers are required for its proper functioning (Waltz 1979, 163). Can we say that a world dominated by the United States and China will be less secure than in the Cold War? What will happen if Europe strengthens its political, economic and military potential and becomes global actor? The Pandemic reflected the inability of great powers to accept the reality and the lack of moral standards in the international system. The post-pandemic world order relies on America and China's primary state actors, still refraining from war. Washington and Beijing, however, do not abstain from challenging each other and involving their allies in their strategic competition. With its purpose accomplished partially, China will seek to surpass the U.S. in the next 30 years and establish a Sino-dominated world order based on what Waltz calls "maintaining one's autonomy in the face of force that others wield." (Waltz 1979, 194). Polarization and division in the United States, on the contrary, indicate that future Presidential administrations should prioritize the Nation's unity and U.S. national interest over hegemonic ambitions to domesticate public opinion for further interventions. Yet, this book argues that their ability to co-design the post-pandemic world order is limited. Europe excluded the opportunity to create its armed forces within NATO, while Russia failed to reconsolidate Eurasia politically and militarily. My claim originates from the assumption that the bipolar Sino-American order will be much more unstable than a multipolar model, dominated by four major powers with their abilities to sustain the balance-of-power system.

Another assumption of Waltz that provides a plausible explanation of the post-pandemic security architecture is his theoretical assessment of war. In *Man, State, and War: A Theoretical Analysis*, Waltz coins the vision that the locus of the important causes of war results from selfishness, misdirected aggressive impulses, and stupidity (Waltz 2001, 16). However, his structural explanation adds to theories of war another variable, which presumes that conflicts emerge from the structure of the international system. The idea that war is a necessary evil has been prevalent among decision-makers – it is a pattern through which they could justify their actions. This is precise because global leadership requires scarce resources that soft power cannot usually acquire. With no means of confronting each other and with no intention to launch a competition, the United States and China established diplomatic relations during the Cold War. Even so, both actors viewed themselves as *Manifest Destiny*. This aspect still embodies U.S. Foreign Policy in contrast to the Chinese perceptions of Beijing's role in the post-pandemic age. Waltz even cites the Confucian phrase: "There is deceit and cunning and from these war arise." (Waltz 2001, 16). However, as Henry Kissinger points out, at the opposite end of the Eurasian landmass from Europe, China was the center of its own hierarchical and theoretically universal concept of order (Kissinger 2014, 10). The Chinese cultural perceptions of selfishness and aggression initially differ from the Western Original Sin. It could be best described by the words of Sun Tzu, who states if your opponent is of choleric temper, seek to irritate him. Pretend to be weak, that he may grow arrogant (Tzu 2008, 5).

Finally, Waltz argues that states will display characteristics common to competitors: namely, that they will imitate each other and become socialized to their system (Waltz 2014, 122). I argue that this assumption serves as a relevant explanation of the post-pandemic world order because history shows that the international system embodies a paradox of anarchy and wars fought in the name of sovereign rights of states. Mansfield specifies that polarity and concentration refer to the distribution of power, while wars are less likely to occur when power is balanced among the major powers than when it is imbalanced (Mansfield 1993, 116). The Pandemic will change nether of these, and thus, the realist concept of international politics will continue to dominate the international relations theory. Great powers will establish a post-pandemic world order, not through cooperation and integration – the United States and China will continue their struggle for global dominance, while peace will be identified with balance-of-power. In China, communism constitutes the political formula of the regime, but each military strategy originates from pre-communist concepts of war and peace. Therefore, the idea of a China-dominated Asia Pacific, ascending as an independent political and cultural entity, serves as a logical starting point for Beijing's Grand Strategy.

The security dilemma of Robert Jervis

In his prophetic article *Unipolarity*, Robert Jervis claims that unipolarity is no guarantee against economic shocks, widespread disease, or environmental degradation (Jervis 2009, 193). Twelve years later, China shifted the balance of power in the Asia-Pacific by conducting military exercises over Taiwan and challenged the U.S. dollar dominance by piloting its digital currency. It turned out that, as Jervis had predicted, unipolarity contained the seeds of its modification: everything about China – its communism, its military, its economy, stands as a straight challenge to the American concept of a globalized liberal order built on democracy and human rights. In short, the Silk Road begins where the American dream ends.

If, however, major powers in the post-pandemic security architecture are so antagonistic, what will be the future of their competition? In his dissection of the international system, Robert Jervis claims that depending on whether the offense or the defense has the advantage and whether offensive postures can be distinguished from the defensive ones, the great powers interaction could result in "four worlds" (Jervis 1978, 211). In this chapter, I operationalize the security dilemma of Jervis to provide a robust empirical foundation for my theory. I begin with the variables which shape the four-dimensional model of the author.

The mutual distrust between the United States and China emerges from their desire and potential to dominate the anarchical post-pandemic world. In his Cold War article, Jervis assumes that "it would be harder for the U.S. and the Soviet Union to cooperate even if both support the status-quo." (Jervis 1978, 209) I believe this assumption is valid for the post-pandemic security architecture because, as Mearsheimer points out, "the United States is likely to behave toward China largely the way it behaved toward the Soviet Union during the Cold War." (Mearsheimer 2016, 19). China, quite the opposite, has little to do with Soviet Russia. Some Western or even Russian decision-makers could argue that China, despite its socialist market economy, embodies the same despotic amalgam of communism and the one-party state as the USSR before it collapsed. Such perception of China is misleading because Kissinger predicted clarifies that "Beijing possesses the ability to pose unacceptable risks in a conflict with Washington and is developing increasingly sophisticated means to negate traditional U.S. advantages." (Kissinger 2012, 45). In my explanation, I define this ability as *strategic manipulation*.

Jervis operationalizes two variables to explain the security dilemma – whether the offense or the defense has the advantage and whether offensive postures can be distinguished from defensive ones (Jervis 1978, 211). In the final chapter of this book, I will explain why that cooperation will evolve into confrontation under the security dilemma. Although the United States and Russia have been trying for years to integrate China into arms control agreements, this has proved futile. The status-quo states can follow different policies than aggressors, but all major power coexist in a condition of constant warning. Washington and Beijing can procure defense systems, but tensions over Taiwan could easily escalate into a military conflict. Relations between NATO and Russia rely on a system of post-Cold War agreements, which will transformed into sanctions when Moscow decided to annex the rest of Ukraine. It is then empirically correct to conclude that the post-pandemic security architecture is dichotomous. It could evolve into an open military confrontation, in which the status-quo state, which has enough offensive advantage (America), may attack China and then wait to be surpassed economically and politically by the latter. However, the post-pandemic security dilemma could also result in a less hostile environment if Washington reshapes its defense strategy instead of striking Beijing first. In conclusion, the art of China's strategic manipulation is that Beijing seeks to convince the world of Washington's desire to prevent China's rise through a war in which America is fighting to strengthen its hegemony, not the defense of its allies. In short, as Kissinger highlights, "on the Chinese side, the confrontational interpretations follow an inverse logic." (Kissinger 2014, 46).

The offensive realism of John Mearsheimer

In his research, *The Tragedy of Great Power Politics*, the notable realist scholar John Mearsheimer rejects the neoliberal understanding of international politics and argues that great powers are always searching for opportunities to gain power over their rivals, with hegemony as their final goal (Mearsheimer 2001, 16). This section will stress his vision of China's rise by testing whether the five bedrock assumptions of offensive realism are relevant to the post-pandemic security architecture. The anarchic nature of the international system permits military conflicts to occur and challenges state actors that are tempted to sacrifice hard power in the name of their national interests. This first assumption is valid for the post-pandemic world order, where the United States and China would prefer to establish a more regulated security environment in which all major powers have their spheres of influence. International bodies such as United Nations and World Health Organization failed to provide an adequate response to the Coronavirus Pandemic and thus, reaffirmed the realist assumption that institutions have minimal influence on state behavior and hold little promise from promoting stability in the post-Cold War world (Mearsheimer 1994, 5–49).

Mearsheimer's second assumption is that great powers inherently possess some offensive military capability, which gives them the wherewithal to hurt and possibly destroy each other (Mearsheimer 2001, 20). If the vaccine distribution can be described as security cooperation between major powers, then the bedrock assertion of offensive realists will not be valid. But if the relations among state actors are strained because of insufficient supplies, there is little place for international agreements or predictive behavior. Although great powers should cooperate to minimize the global impact of the Pandemic, their behavior is more relevant to the assumption of Mearsheimer. Both United States and China still spend more money on weapons than vaccines. Furthermore, did any state actor propose the establishment of an international institution to regulate the distribution of COVID vaccines? On the contrary, U.S. President Donald Trump slammed W.H.O. for being China's puppet and withdrew Washington from the organization.

Offensive realism argues that no state can be sure that another state will not use its offensive military capability to attack the first state (Mearsheimer 2001, 21). The lack of certainty leads us to the old Latin phrase *Si vis pacem, para bellum* (If you want peace, prepare for war), which reflects the contemporary Western understanding of warfare. The assumption that the United States should have the right strategy and weapons to fight a limited nuclear war dominates the post-pandemic U.S. Foreign Policy, and thus, the main point remains although Russia and China know that they have a common purpose, they will not be able to reach it together. Chinese President Xi Jinping rejected the idea of a Sino-Russian alliance because Moscow's multipolar design does not correspond to Xi's vision of China-dominated world order. Even when Russia and China act together, the point of uncertainty over the strategic outcome of their behavior exceeds the expectations of the leaders in Moscow and Beijing.

Mearsheimer claims that survival is the primary goal of great powers (Mearsheimer 2001, 21). Why might America fear that China may have used the Coronavirus as a biological weapon? Why did President Trump call COVID19 the "Chinese virus?" Would a nuclear holocaust have become a reality if Trump had won reelection in 2020? Washington might underestimate the probability of such a scenario, while Beijing might not react timely to a potential preemptive strike due to internal disagreements within the Chinese Communist Party. However, if both United States and China raise such suspicions, Europe and Russia are highly likely to prepare for a military confrontation, thus prioritizing their survival. Even if there is a peaceful solution to this simple case, decision-makers can be changed, public opinion could shift, and allies might invoke bilateral or multilateral agreements. No matter how great powers coexist in the international system, they will not reject their right to self-preservation in the post-pandemic age.

The final assumption of Mearsheimer is that great powers are rational actors that are aware of their external environment and their behavior (Mearsheimer 2001, 30). To protect their national security, the United States and China seek to maintain control over scarce resources such as COVID vaccines and medical supplies. This strategy became visible when Pfizer, Moderna, and Sinopharm launched the global distribution of vaccines. China adopted a selling strategy to spread the Sinovac in Asia-Pacific. Russia started a campaign to promote Sputnik V in Europe. The United States provided Mexico and Canada with ample vaccine supplies. However, the further expansion of "vaccine diplomacy" brings more responsibilities that require rational behavior and long-term strategies on behalf of all major powers. If a supranational institution could supervise the proportional distribution of vaccines, national strategies would not be necessary. But since there is not, and since the W.H.O. lacks such capacity, it is a primary responsibility of the states to elaborate their approaches to fighting COVID19. Therefore, rational behavior that will be recognized as constructive and praiseworthy if demonstrated by a great power during the Pandemic will be taken as a routine decision if manifested by a minor actor.

Another important face of offensive realism is Mearsheimer's assessment of China's rise. In *The Gathering Storm: China's Challenge to US Power in Asia*, he asserts that China will try to dominate the Asia-Pacific region much as the United States dominates the Western Hemisphere (Mearsheimer 2010, 389). This assertion involves two aspects: whether Washington and Beijing will go to war and whether the Dragon imitates Uncle Sam. In this book, I argue that China will not attack the United States but rather tempt Washington to launch a preemptive strike. The line of my first argument can be found in the assumption that, in contrast to Western military theorists like Clausewitz, Chinese military strategy takes a more strategic view of warfare (Holmes 2001, 10). Suppose the United States is ready to cooperate in the post-pandemic world order. In that case, China can increase the chances of a peaceful bipolar competition by showing that Beijing accepts the challenge. However, suppose Washington insists that China has little choice but to cooperate. In that case, it can seriously shift the balance of power and lead to a hawkish-inspired appeal for a military confrontation. A potential U.S. preemptive strike against China may result in a military triumph for the former, but it will also be an ideological victory for the latter. Although such a scenario is highly unlikely, American decision-makers know that China might fear a further U.S. intervention in the Asia-Pacific. Therefore, Washington would not benefit from a war with China but somewhat corrupt its charisma of a global leader with that of a ruthless hegemon.

Mearsheimer also claims that Confucian Pacifism is a problematic paradigm in foreign policy decision-making and security (Mearsheimer 2014, 36–38). The claim joins another realist belief that the *parabellum paradigm* is dominant in Chinese strategic thought is linked to the belief that China behaves aggressively like other great powers (Johnson 1995, 212). Although I assume that Mearsheimer and Johnson are correct in assuming that Confucian Pacifism does not rule out employing war as an instrument of statecraft, Chinese decision-makers develop a smart strategy that advocates *strategic cultivation* over weapons and tanks. China is not an exceptional great power, but its *parabellum paradigm* starts with the central point of Sun Tzu's treaties that "when using our forces we must seem inactive." (Tzu 2012, 4). In contrast to the *Art of War*, *De Re Militari* depicts war in terms of principles, legions, and superiority, stating that "He who aspires to victory, should spare no pains to form his soldiers." (Flavius Vegetius Renatus 1996, 40).

To conclude, I presume that the bedrock assumptions of Mearsheimer's offensive realism are entirely relevant to the post-pandemic security architecture, which makes them a logical starting point for my explanation. Following the Coronavirus outbreak, great powers acted unilaterally regarding the insecurity they felt, which killed the neoliberal expectations of cooperation. Even if China and Russia continue to develop their partnership, Beijing and Moscow can disagree on what kind of alliance they seek and the compromises they are willing to make to deter America's influence in the post-pandemic security architecture. The more actors strive for multipolar world order, the more they are unlikely to accept the return to the globalized "old normal" and struggle to revise the U.S.-dominated liberal order.

The offshore balancing of Mearsheimer and Walt

Stephen Walt is clear when claiming that the Coronavirus Pandemic is a world-shattering event whose far-ranging consequences we can only begin to imagine today (Walt 2021). Although most neo-realist scholars have discussed the global impact of COVID19 in their predictions for the post-pandemic world order, Walt has focused on state control and nationalism as primary outcomes of the Coronacrisis. The empirical evidence of his assumption has become visible globally: the Capitol Insurrection, far-right extremism in Russia, human rights violations in China, the rise of the right-wing parties in Europe, the height of the populist elites in Brazil. Should we blame COVID19 for the global rise of nationalism? This book joins the academic debate by supporting Walt's assertion that some of the worst forms of populism around the world tend to be associated with older populations rather than young populations (Walt 2020, 1). My concern is that the Pandemic has provoked populist attitudes among the older generation, not simply because of the chaos and obstacles to freedom of movement. Another important reason for this crisis is the rise of left-wing ideologies supported by the younger generation. The question of this ideological cleavage has global dimensions. It can be seen as a major challenge to the post-pandemic world order because, as Robert Jervis concludes, there are significant variations in the ways people see the world that affects how they act (Jervis 2017, 14).

In *The Case for Offshore Balancing: A Superior U.S. Grand Strategy,* Walt and Mearsheimer anticipated that "if China continues its impressive rise, it is likely to seek hegemony in Asia" (Mearsheimer and Walt 2016, 81). This prediction originates from the robust assumption that China used the American strategy of staying out of foreign wars and building a world-class economy. However, the most important limitation of China's foreign policy in Asia is that it cannot rely on non-rational actors like North Korea and thus, fails to establish a stable system of alliances in the region. More generally, nobody trusts Pyongyang. The "cooperation" between China and North Korea is explained by how their partnership activates each time when Washington reminds of its military presence on the Korean Peninsula. The most significant challenge to U.S. Foreign Policy in the Asia-Pacific, on the other hand, arises from Beijing's desire to colonize economically strategic U.S. allies like Australia. Just as the United States expanded in Latin

America after the Spanish-American war in 1898, China elaborated its own *Roosevelt Corollary*, claiming the South China Sea as its backyard. For example, cooperation within the Big Five and the establishment of AUKUS enhanced the mutual commitments of the United States and its allies in the APAC. Kissinger, however, warned that "the challenge China poses for the medium-term future will, in all likelihood, be political and economic, not military." (Kissinger 2005). Therefore, Chinese economic diplomacy, combined with manipulation of political and historical narratives, could lead actors in Asia to distance themselves from each other and develop hybrid attitudes, which will transform their cooperation into mutual distrust. The Pandemic might further make such transformations irreversible.

This book is generally optimistic about the *offshore-balancing* strategy. Mearsheimer and Walt suggest that instead of policing the world, the United States would encourage other countries to take the lead, intervening only when necessary (Mearsheimer and Walt 2016, 74). Before the Pandemic, both United States and Russia had developed regional strategies that could trigger a hot conflict in Eastern Europe. Moscow's purpose was not to allow Ukraine to join NATO, and Washington's was to contain the Russian influence near the Alliance's borders. Structural shifts in European security began after the outbreak of COVID, which, according to Walt, reinforced nationalism (Bieber 2020, 10). Although the NATO Member States have reached a consensus in their support for Ukraine, they also have concluded that the latter should also join the Alliance in the near future. The other side of the coin is that, in contrast to the United States, United Kingdom, and Canada, European allies are willing to compromise vital interests of the Alliance in the name of their energy dependence on Moscow. This dependency, to some extent, restrained Germany, France, and Russia, and thus, no actor in the region could gain dominance. Here, I will join Mearsheimer and Walt in their belief that the offshore-balancing strategy does not prohibit Washington from giving friendly states in the key regions advice or material aid (Mearsheimer and Walt 2016, 77). However, my primary concern is that the struggle for a post-pandemic liberal hegemony could be detrimental to the U.S. national interests as the complete withdrawal from key regions. Robert Jervis justifies such concerns, presuming that a more significant threat would be the failure of Europe to unite coupled with an American withdrawal of forces, which could lead to a security competition within the Old Continent (Jervis 2013, 25). Therefore, I assume that the post-pandemic offshore-balance strategy should better combine husbanding U.S. strength with enhancing Washington's intelligence capabilities. Military presence, of course, should be limited only to regions of crucial importance to the U.S. national interests, which, as Walt admits, include mutual issues of partnership such as climate change, counterterrorism, the management of the world economy, or containing U.S. adversaries like China (Walt 2019, 32). Thus, America will be able to sustain its global leadership and to cheat the imperial overstretch that, as Jack Snyder points out, propelled that security could be achieved through further expansion (Snyder 2003, 31).

Another theoretical aspect of Walt's realism, which provides a starting point for my theory, is his concept of alliance formation. Walt operationalizes three essential variables: threat response strategies, ideology, and foreign policy instruments. (Walt 2013, 5). Security cooperation, sovereignty, and informal arrangements are also central to Walt's concept of alliances alongside his assumptions that balancing is far more common than bandwagoning; ideology is less powerful than balancing, and that neither foreign aid nor political penetration is by itself a cause of alignment (Walt 2013, 5). In this book, I will operationalize Walt's variables, investigating alliance formation in the Asia-Pacific considering that in 2011 U.S. President Barack Obama announced that the United States would "pivot to Asia" given the Sino-American security competition in the region (Mearsheimer 2014, 27).

Walt argues that balancing is more common than bandwagoning or, in other words, allying with others against the prevailing threat dominates alignment with the source of danger (Walt 2013, 17). Most hypotheses on balancing are based on the assumption that alliances are easy to create when a state is powerful and aggressive enough to threaten other state actors. To explain the system of alliances in the Asia-Pacific is more complex than analyzing the historical and cultural reasons for its formation. However, external challengers like China could make yesterday's enemies most trusted allies. If one asks what could lead to the formation of an alliance between Japan and South Korea, the answer is China and its nuclear pet – Pyongyang. Beijing's military capabilities and economic rise increase the chance of military confrontation in the region and thus, further necessitate U.S. allies to align with each other. The purposes and priorities of U.S. Foreign Policy in the region vary. The Pandemic, however, triggered another strong anti-Chinese sentiment among all actors in the Asia-Pacific. As the offensive capabilities of China and North Korea continue to improve, Tokyo and Seoul face a strategic dilemma: to enhance their cooperation or reshape their foreign policy. The former will strengthen balancing, while the latter could provoke tensions between the American allies. In the post-pandemic world, the core of the U.S.-led system of alliances in the Asia-Pacific will consist of several less powerful state actors. Their willingness to cooperate and contribute to each other's security will be of critical importance to all U.S. allies because even a minor crack of one would make the rest of them vulnerable. My assumption is that, in the post-pandemic security architecture, balancing will benefit U.S. Foreign Policy, while bandwagoning will serve as a cornerstone of China's smart strategy. In other words, balancing should remain central to alliance formation in the Asia-Pacific because it will allow the United States to provide security for its allies. Bandwagoning, on the contrary, will provide China with a more sophisticated strategy to make other states actors economically dependent on Beijing. This is not to say that traditional U.S. allies like Australia and Germany will abandon Washington and join Beijing. However, the more economically dependent Australians and Europeans become on Beijing, the more their foreign policy and national interests diverge from those of the United States despite the existence of AUKUS and NATO. In the chapter that follows, I will further explain the evolution of balancing and bandwagoning in the post-pandemic security architecture.

In his theory, Walt demonstrates that ideology is less powerful than balancing as a motive for alignment (Walt 2013, 5). Although ideological solidarity can occur when both sides share political and cultural traits, money and weapons always play a more significant role, especially in a world recovering from the Pandemic. However, American allies do not underestimate the benefits of U.S. military support, and much of the political the debate is limited to the discussion of how intensive the American military involvement should be in the region. In Japan, debate on Article 9 is still on the rise. Since Japanese decision-makers, however, understand that a potential Chinese or North Korean aggression against Japan would be destructive, Tokyo remains a reliable U.S. ally under Article 9 of the Japanese Constitution. I assume that Walt is right in his claim that similarity in domestic ideology leads to alliance formation. However, cultural dynamics could cause policy-makers to reshape their attitudes and present alliances as necessary, and thus, to percept commitment as the inevitable behavior to contain external threats. Moreover, the U.S.-led system of alliances in the Asia-Pacific is highly hierarchical, with Washington as the primary source of collective security, further proving Walt's conclusion that ideological impact and solidarity coexist depending on centralization and security perceptions (Walt 2013, 40).

Finally, Walt concludes that neither foreign aid nor political penetration is a powerful cause of alignment (Walt 1988, 5). Walt's conclusion provides a methodological starting point for calculating the balance of power in the Asia-Pacific. In my book, I define this methodology as *Walt's equation*. The equation contains the United States (single variable) and its allies (multiple variables). The more security America provides to its allies, the greater the control by the former over the latter. The greater America's influence on the political system of its allies, the greater the solidarity within the alliance. In other words, Walt is correct asserting that foreign aid and political penetration are of crucial importance to alliance formation (Walt 1988, 46–49). China's military modernization is of primary concern to the United States and its allies when combined with North

Korea's nuclear ambitions. Japan and South Korea are unlikely to launch a preemptive strike or retaliate without American strategic interference. Moreover, America's monopoly on the Asian-Pacific security presumes asymmetrical dependence and motivation between Washington, Tokyo, and Seoul. It is argued that a potential conflict in the region would favor the United States in its ambition to prevent the rise of Beijing. However, one should remember the words of Robert Jervis, who warns that it is neither surprising nor evidence of misperception that those who start wars often lose them (Jervis 2017, 679).

Misperception of the Coronavirus weakened the decision-making apparatus of the U.S., triggering a wave of Sinophobia, in which epithets like "the China virus" dominated the political rhetoric of the Trump administration. Japan's belief that the time to resume the Article 9 debate was linked mistakenly to the South Korean fear of Japanese military revival. Less remarked on is the dilemma of the dependent and independent variables in the post-pandemic security architecture of the Asia-Pacific? Is political penetration of the U.S. shaped democracy strong enough to maintain alignment among American allies such as Japan and South Korea? My assumption aligns with Walt's hypothesis that penetration is most effective when other causes contribute to the alliance (Walt 1988, 50). Neither liberal democracy nor Chinese communism is consistent with the political traditions of major U.S. allies in the Asia-Pacific. After World War II, Japan and South Korea's path to self-determination and survival went through an alliance with the United States. Proponents of liberalism believe that promoting democracy secures the U.S.-led system of alliances. However, Walt proves that the validity of such arguments is highly ambivalent unless we accept that democracies always win wars.

The Thucydides's trap of Graham Allison

In his notable book *Destined to war: Can America and China Escape the Thucydides's Trap?*, Graham Allison identifies the outcome of the Sino-American competition with the military history of Ancient Greece. Allison's theory is unproblematic and robust because it takes into account the historical inheritance of the Greeks and the military rise of China. Although his understanding of U.S. Foreign Policy towards Beijing is coherent and systematic, the assumption that the United States and China share portentous similarities is challengeable (Allison 2018, 8–10). To define why and how, I will further outline three premises that justify the post-pandemic relevance of Allison's theory.

The first and the most substantial claim of Allison's theory concerns the comparative approach of his concept. Allison presumes that classical Greece represented the first great steeple of civilization and that Thucydides was the first to focus exclusively on capturing history (Allison 2018, 25). What is essential about this presumption is not the indisputable contribution of the Ancient Greek philosophy but the claim that the Greco-Roman political and cultural inheritance dominates the conceptual understanding of history and politics. Although Thucydides is primarily accepted as the legendary predecessor of realism, able to explain the eternal struggle for power, his chronicles are not unique to military history. The Chinese treatise *The Art of War* dates back to the Warring States period in Ancient China (5th Century BC), making it the oldest military classic (Holmes 2000, 10). Thucydides's *History of the Peloponnesian War* provides a plausible starting point for explaining power competition and war. Yet, as Allison notes, this definitive account of the conflict between Athens and Sparta is one of the greatest works of Western civilization (Allison 2018, 27). Thucydides's perception of war as a military conflict that inevitably sparked after rising meets rule is relevant to the Western military theory but inapplicable to the Chinese comprehension of warfare.

Another thoughtful aspect of Allison's theory concerns his historical approach to great power competition, as demonstrated by the sixteen case studies in his book (Allison 2018, 42–43). Two cases involve the Asia-Pacific: the Russo – Japanese war (1904–1905) and the Attack on Pearl Harbor during World War II. However, the Shinto-inspired military doctrine of Imperial Japan is irrelevant to Sun Tzu's concept that specifies: "All warfare is based on deception." (Tzu 2012, 70–71). The Japanese military tradition denounces deception but advocates death and honor over humiliation or defeat (Morgan 2003, 3). The rest of the cases include military conflicts between European empires and Great Britain, and a few examples of the Eurasian tradition that still inspires Russia. By separating the state actors into two groups – land and sea nations – Allison's theory becomes persistent with the theoretical influences of Chinese scholars, who advocate a different concept of power (Weigert 1942, 20). The practical result of those methodological transformations is that the concept of Thucydides's trap encloses variables from sixteen cases, but overemphasizes on four traditions (European, Ango-Saxon, Eurasian and Japanese), that are less relevant to the Chinese military observances.

Finally, Allison defines Thucydides's trap as a natural, inevitable discombobulation that occurs when a rising power threatens to displace a ruling power (Allison 2018, 1–2). Therefore, a war between the United States and China is a confrontation over the redistribution of power and resources. The basic claim of Allison originates from the well-established realist assumption that military conflicts are *natural* and that state preferences are fixed and conflictual (Powell 1994, 313–344). I believe that Allison is correct in his belief that

President Xi Jinping's primal ambition is to restore Chinese dominance in the Asia-Pacific (Allison 2018, 108). If Donald Trump had won the 2020 Presidential election, Allison's presumption would have been empirically tested. On the contrary, President Biden's doctrine is more linked to the orthodox foreign policy of the U.S., an approach closely resembling that of Barack Obama. The use of universal doctrinal explanations and the lack of distinction between Chinese Art of War and American Neoconservatism may thus generate multiple contradictory assertions that challenge the theoretical cogency of Thucydides's trap.

To sum up, Allison's theory has two essential contributions. First, Allison's vision of China as "The Biggest Player in the History of the World" is an original base for explaining Beijing's smart power (Allison 2018, 3–4). The arguments presented in favor of his assumption differ entirely from most realist theories in their nature and validity. Unlike the rest of the neorealist scholars, Allison's theory is designed primarily to test the geopolitical externalities arising from China's rise and to challenge the hawkish-inspired belief that Beijing will not dethrone Washington as a global leader. Although most international relations theories pretend to outline a China-dominated world order scenario, only a few have ever projected it.

Second, the distinctiveness of Allison's theory lies in its assumption that there are twelve clues to peace that can prevent the United States and China from a large-scale military conflict (Allison 2018, 187). In the case studies, where different conflicts have been examined and their outcome – analyzed, including variables such as nuclear diplomacy, factor timing, or cultural commonalities, Allison has designed a complete strategy for avoiding Thycidides trap. Therefore, his theory is theoretically and methodologically robust to explain the post-pandemic security architecture. However, the primary dilemma is whether America and China would endorse a doctrine of confrontation, the purpose of which is to reshape the globalized world order in an unprecedented way since World War II? To answer this question, Allison follows the traditional realist approach that advocates geopolitical accommodation, redefines Sino-American relations and human rights coercion by undermining the communist regime and encouraging independent movements in Taiwan, Xinjiang, Tibet, and Hong Kong (Allison 2018 224–225).

I assume that two of the strategic options suggested by Allison are relevant to the post-pandemic security architecture: accommodation and redefining U.S. – China relations. The undermining strategy proposed by Allison advocates covert American support for separatist insurgents in Tibet and ideological deterrence of China (Allison 2018, 222–224). However, what will happen if China recognizes Palestine? Will Washington be willing to send a Nimitz-class carrier to the South China Sea? Besides, the significant difference between Communism in

China and the USSR is that Beijing had begun a through-going reform and opening, while the Soviet economy had stagnated in centralized control, enforced egalitarianism, international isolation, and ideological dogmatism (Garver 1993, 26). Negotiating a long peace between Washington and Beijing would mean a global military competition. South Korea and Japan will explicitly reject a possible recognition of China's authority over the Paracel Islands or a potential withdrawal of U.S. troops from the region. Tokyo will most likely modify Article 9 of the Japanese Constitution, provoking further tensions with Seoul. From this perspective, Beijing will seize the opportunity to undermine the U.S.-dominated system of alliances in the Asia-Pacific. The long peace, thus, will shortly transform into a second Cold War.

The Long Haul of Robert J. Art

To say that the U.S. system of alliances provides security and stability in the Asia-Pacific is to state the objective realities in the region. In his notable work, *A Grand Strategy for America*, Robert Art argues that the United States produces the same buffering effect in East Asia, where the jockeying among the powerful regional actors – Japan, South Korea, and China – is much more pronounced (Art 2013, 141). However, it is harder to prove that the U.S. presence in Northeast Asia is similar to the NATO-dominated post-pandemic security architecture in Europe because, as Mearsheimer highlights, "the geography of Asia is fundamentally different from that of Europe in the Cold War." (Mearsheimer 2016, 30). Unless China's strategy in the region changes radically, the future of the U.S. – South Korean – Japanese alliance could be expected to develop to an extent beyond that of NATO. Moreover, if Beijing seizes control over the South China Sea, U.S. Foreign Policy will switch to containment. Some might argue the American allies will try to project their deterrence strategy, especially Japan, which has the option to defend unilaterally. However, without the United States, the post-pandemic balance of power in Northeastern Asia is doubtful to become stable even after a successful deterrence against China. Looking at a potentially unified Korean Peninsula or Japanese-controlled Senkaku Islands, such scenarios seem unrealistic because a few could assert how radically the Asia-Pacific region will be shattered by the eventual reunification of the two Koreas.

Art gives a prescient explanation of the post-pandemic reality in *The United States and the Rise of China: Implications for the Long Haul*, arguing that the country best positioned to challenge America's preeminence, first in East Asia, then perhaps later globally, is China (Art 2015, 260). What makes Art's theory robust and relevant to the post-pandemic security architecture is his research design, which originates from three benchmarks. In my theory, I use those assumptions sequentially to explain the post-pandemic world order.

The first benchmark of Art states that China will shape the international environment in ways that are conducive to its national interests (Art 2015, 362). When strategic vacuums emerge in regions empty of a global actor, another major power expands, challenging the former's primacy. This process is visible in the Asia-Pacific, where Beijing builds artificial islands in the South China Sea, contesting the U.S. dominance in the region. However, the Chinese expansion in the Asia-Pacific brings new responsibilities and a wide range of commitments to actors such as North Korea. Although Robert Art is right in claiming that China seeks to establish a Sino-shaped international environment, my concern is that such a scenario is seen as an opportunity by European countries like Germany, which have become economically dependent on Beijing. Therefore, strategic vacuums exist in Europe as well.

The second benchmark involves Art's explanation of China's inexorable rise (Art 2015, 264). Although international relations experts have discussed the long-term impact of the Pandemic on Sino-American relations, a lot of them have ignored this topic. Art and Mearsheimer have applied a more detailed approach to the future of the U.S. – China competition, but their concepts challenge each other's perceptions of containment. Mearsheimer explicitly deals with the classical doctrine of containment, while Art operationalizes the same concept in a compound view, suggesting that it involves two central ingredients: stalemating a power militarily and waging economic denial against it (Art 2015, 265). The concept of compound containment has affected a vital aspect of U.S. Foreign Policy that has not been examined since the end of the Cold War: the post-bipolar relevance of the deterrence theory. The first Presidential administration to test Art's theory was that of Trump. The Trump administration rejected President Obama's smart power and endorsed a harder approach toward China. Art's concern is containing the Chinese rise in terms of military power and economic growth. To protect the U.S. global dominance, Trump attempted to hold Beijing's economic growth. The compound strategy involves an export ban of Chinese production, but as Art points out, waging unilateral economic warfare against China when it appears unprovoked by Beijing would backfire politically against the United States (Art 2015, 265). Trump's attempts to confront China alarmed the European allies, who feared that American sanctions would create a vulnerable spot in the European Union's economy. In other words, Art's claim that the United States could shoot itself in the foot if it tries to stop China unilaterally corresponds to what Kissinger calls the *increasingly sophisticated means* of Beijing to negate traditional American advantages (Kissinger 2012, 45).

In his final benchmark, Art operationalizes Jervis's security dilemma to explain power transitions in the international environment. Art builds his theory on three variables and four case studies, including the Sino-American competition. (Art 2015, 366). Economic interdependence and ideological confrontation are central to great powers competition, but another variable is present in U.S. – China relations: political culture. Although scholars like Mearsheimer and Allison are skeptical of the *Confucian paradigm*, Xi Jinping's foreign policy proves the assumption of Kissinger that military imperialism is not the Chinese style (Kissinger 2005). The Coronavirus Pandemic drove Beijing to manipulate the security environment by expanding its influence in the Asia-Pacific and thus, verifying the claim of Robert Jervis that many of the means by which a state tries to increase its security decrease the security of others (Jervis 1978, 169). China will act depending on the extent to which it can challenge America and regardless of the mutual assured destruction scenario. Beijing, however, will not strike Washington but rather tempt it to retaliate.

To conclude, the Long Haul theory of Robert Art provides us with a plausible starting point for a further explanation of the Sino-American competition. I assume that the six principles of policy suggested by Art could serve as a cornerstone of the post-COVID U.S. Foreign Policy in the Asia-Pacific. (Art 2015, 384). Washington could not afford to lose its influence in Taiwan or allow a nuclear apocalypse. The Trump Doctrine, on the other hand, has shown that creating tensions with allies and waging economic warfare unilaterally can be detrimental to U.S. national interests. The demand for collective security in East Asia is higher than in Europe. Yet, the mutual distrust between major U.S. allies such as Japan and South Korea will undermine Washington's efforts to promote and establish any form of multilateral cooperation. The most substantial possible evidence is the Senkaku Islands dispute. However, institutionalizing security multilateralism in the region is possible only if the Korean Peninsula unites under Seoul. United Korea, with American troops at the Chinese border, will give little place for territorial disputes, but such a scenario depends on unpredictable variables such as Pyongyang's nuclear program.

The hegemonic war of Robert Gilpin

Wars are an indivisible part of international anarchy. In *War and Change in World Politics*, Robert Gilpin defines Thucydides's concept of *hegemonic war* as the basic mechanism of systematic change in world politics (Gilpin 1981, 209). Gilpin's theory is particularly relevant to the post-pandemic security architecture, considering the Sino-American tensions over Taiwan. The balance of power in the Asia-Pacific favors Washington because, as Mearsheimer concludes, Chinese military forces are inferior to those of the United States. Beijing would be making a huge mistake to pick a fight with the American military nowadays (Mearsheimer 2014, 29). The real question is what will happen in a post-pandemic world in which the United States and China struggle for power and global dominance and in which Russia and Europe confront in the post-soviet space.

One of the most prophetic assumptions of Gilpin is that resources are central to great powers competition (Gilpin 1981, 189). The stagnation of the Roman economy and the technological innovation of China are clear symbols of power structures: the former declined after centuries of conquests, while the latter survived to see communism consume its political culture. I argue that Gilpin's vision for China's economic growth and resource exploitation corresponds to the evolving military strategies of Beijing. Kissinger explains this evolution and clarifies that Sun Tzu focuses on the psychological weakening of the adversary, not on hard power (Kissinger 2005). Therefore, China *manipulates* warfare as a primary mechanism of major changes in the international system with the world economy. The fundamental question is how the United States will counter this strategy in the post-pandemic age.

Gilpin suggests that an innovative solution involves rejuvenation of the society's military, economic, and political institutions (Gilpin 1981, 189). Most Chinese and Russian scholars assume that the United States is a declining power like Rome in its last years. This theory is also popular among some European and American scholars, who suggest that Washington should become "first among equals" instead of sustaining the U.S.-led system of alliances. My book rejects this view. I assume that U.S. Foreign Policy could follow two of Gilpin's strategic lessons and counter Beijing's smart strategy: increasing resources and decreasing costs (Gilpin 1981, 197). However, even if America successfully deters Beijing's post-pandemic strategy, foreign policy decision-making in Washington will face two significant difficulties.

The first challenge here arises from China's rise. The United States will have to generate enough military, economic, political, and cultural resources to sustain the U.S.-led system of alliances established after World War II to maintain its global leadership. Failure to do so will expose America to unprecedented downsides of a post-pandemic world, in which China will become more powerful and influential. The second challenge is the possibility of a hegemonic war between the United States and China. Gilpin stresses that hegemonic wars are characterized by the unlimited means employed and the general scope of warfare (Gilpin 1981, 200). There is a growing body of literature about the possibility of a military confrontation between Washington and Beijing. I assume that a Sino-American war is not a necessity for future presidential administrations but rather a Chinese temptation for Uncle Sam. My assertion follows the logic of Kissinger, who explains the manipulative strategy of Beijing and concludes that in an actual conflict, both sides possess the capabilities and the ingenuity to inflict catastrophic damage on each other (Kissinger 2012, 47). Therefore, the Sino-American confrontation in the post-pandemic age could bring the world to the brink of a hegemonic war, but the United States alone will have the final word on whether to attack or not. If Washington succumbs to the temptation to fight a conventional war with China, both major powers risk mutual assured destruction being nuclear deterrents. Suppose the American decision-makers, however, resist Beijing's pressure. In that case, the post-pandemic world order will transform into a cold bipolar confrontation, which Mearsheimer defines as a Sino-American security competition (Mearsheimer 2016, 27).

In conclusion, Robert Gilpin's assessment of hegemonic war raises how Western perceptions of warfare and competition differ from the Chinese. When both United States and China confront, other major actors like Europe are expected to choose sides. A prolonged Sino-American arms race could lead Washington and Beijing to fight a hegemonic war, even facing the alternative of MAD. On the other side, the mutual understanding of each other's perceptions and attitudes could avoid the nuclear holocaust and further stabilize the balance of power in the post-pandemic security architecture. What decision-makers expect from their counterparts and how the former interpret the latter's reactions is detrimental to foreign policy. If the United States thinks that China wants to achieve a bipolar world order, Beijing will respond by elaborating more tools of psychological weakening and strategic deception. If Beijing does not threaten Washington and its allies directly, there will be no reason for the latter to use hard power. However, there is still a corresponding risk of war because no matter how strong the two actors are, the Chinese deception could easily provoke the U.S. to retaliate.

Getting coercive

In this section, I introduce my explanation of the post-pandemic world order, which I call *coercive realism*. My concept purports to join the neorealist family for two reasons. First, coercive realism derives its theoretical arguments from the previously discussed theories. Second, although coercive realism is influenced by offensive realism, defensive realism, and the hegemonic theory, it offers an original structural approach to international politics. Therefore, in the chapters that follow, I test my concept through abstract theoretical judgments and by providing empirical explanations and logical assumptions. I begin with a short review of my methodological approach.

First and foremost, I build my concept on seven theoretical pillars. My methodological approach follows Kenneth Waltz's argument that theory embodies theoretical assumptions (Waltz 1979, 10), and thus, each pillar of my concept corresponds to a theoretical statement. Furthermore, by employing Waltz's approach, I infer the driving arguments and essential factors which compose the structure of coercive realism. An example of such an argument is the realist assumption that anarchy is the natural state of the international system and my assertion that war and peace serve the national interests of great powers. Therefore, in a system of competing great powers, state actors prefer confrontation and weapons versus dialogue and diplomacy. However, I do not limit my explanation to state behavior and foreign policy. My theory moves beyond methodological interpretation to an empirical explanation of why potential hegemons need more than a deadly nuclear arsenal and a strong economy to sustain the balance of power in international relations.

The definition of my concept leads us to the second purpose of my work – to test the explanation by providing empirical explanations of international politics. I have chosen to focus on U.S. Foreign Policy and China's Grand Design for three reasons. First, there is a consistent consensus that the Sino-American competition will dominate the future of the international system. Many decision-makers and scholars have consistently neglected Henry Kissinger's warnings about China's rise. In the light of wishful thinking, most of them forget the lesson of Morgenthau, who explains that China has been for at least a millennium great power of a peculiar kind in that its outlook upon, and relations with, the outside world have been different from those of other Great Powers (Morgenthau 1968, 34). Moreover, many pointless strategies have been developed because the basic implications of Beijing's political and military philosophy that should be analyzed in advance have been completely ignored. Second, the mechanisms by which Beijing expands its influence are not entirely familiar to the Western perceptions of *realpolitik* and *containment*. Kissinger reminds us that U.S. Foreign Policy in Asia must not mesmerize with the Chinese military buildup (Kissinger 2005). The very nature of Beijing's foreign policy expresses a specific type of universalism, which differs from the Western *Manifest of Destiny*. In this context, my theory explains why China's policy of silent cultivator could be more detrimental to U.S. Foreign Policy than military tensions and trade wars. Third, the Coronavirus Pandemic proved Mearsheimer's historical prediction that U.S. Foreign Policy would be best served by slowing Chinese growth (Mearsheimer 2001, 46). In 1991, Washington was at the Cold War ended while Beijing could not even detect a U.S. aircraft carrier in the South China Sea. In 2018, deep concern over China's technological advances was the centerpiece of the National Cyber Strategy (The White House 2018, 2). In 2021, America was on the verge of a sustained increase in its military budget, and Beijing acted as one of Washington's largest trading partners. The tools of U.S. Foreign Policy vary, but the ultimate purpose remains the same – sustaining the American global dominance. In truth, promoting human rights and democracy is still useful to uphold the U.S.-led system of alliances and deter Beijing. In a world of Sino-American competition, however, Washington should demonstrate that it could either defend democracies from China or deter China from undermining democracy.

In the final chapter of this book, I apply my theory to explain the post-pandemic structure of international politics and discuss four scenarios about the future of the international system. Zbigniew Brzezinski's notable book, *The Grand Chessboard*, provides an academic inspiration for my explanation, and thus, I have decided to entitle my study *The New Grand Chessboard*. My concept, however, is *not* a challenge to Brzezinski's work. I use coercive realism with the intent to refine, not revise Brzezinski's concept. In addition, I offer a structural explanation of the post-pandemic world order, which involves a geometric vision of the post-pandemic world, which I call *The Pyramid of Balance*.

Finally, I assume that liberal and realist scholars will criticize my explanation for being methodologically challengeable and empirically irrelevant. Some will certainly tempt to challenge it as pandemic-centered or even futile. However, it is important to highlight that, like most realist explanations, coercive realism follows two golden rules, which Kenneth Waltz summarizes in *Theory of International Politics*.

First, Waltz indicates that theory is an edifice of truth and reproduction of reality (Waltz 1979, 8). My explanation envisions three plausible realities, which, I assume, embody the true nature of the international system: anarchy, power, and politics. For example, the United States and China explicitly challenge each other, and international institutions are helpless to unite the world in the face of COVID19. While investigating the origin of the virus is a desire of Washington and its allies, Beijing's efforts are directed not at assisting the international community as at expanding China's influence worldwide. In such conditions, it is hard to imagine that any international actor could possibly bring the world out of anarchy. In addition, two concepts are central to my research: war and peace. Both depend on what Morgenthau calls greatest accumulation of power: the existence of powerful state actors, which are hostile towards each other (Morgenthau 1985, 8).

Second, a theory should give a positive answer to three questions (Waltz 1979, 12). The first one concerns the examination of the variables. Realism, the best-known approach to international relations, provides an empirical identity for my concept. The realist paradigm seeks the forces which determine political relations among nations and to comprehend the ways in which those forces act upon each other (Morgenthau 1985, 3). In addition, Robert Jervis proves that our understanding of the actor's images and beliefs affects the further question that we ask about the behavior that we expect of the actor in other cases (Jervis 2017, 30). Perceptions and misperceptions about the Pandemic have generated plenty of external and internal sources of behavior for all international actors. Therefore, to argue that the Coronavirus Pandemic affects the behavior of great powers is to assume that the latter will enter into another stage of the competition. For me, however, to consider the Coronavirus Pandemic *itself* an independent or dependent variable is methodologically irrelevant. Morgenthau is clear when stating that testing rational hypothesis makes a theory of politics possible and that, in politics, it is possible to distinguish between objective truth and subjective judgment (Morgenthau 1985, 34–35). The former relies on evidence and reason, which originates from prejudice and wishful thinking. In this book, I use the terms *post-pandemic* to present my predictions about the future of the international system and give an objective, rational and reasonable explanation of the Pandemic's impact. I assume that COVID19 is a force, which affects political relations among nations, but it cannot serve as a central explanation of how political forces act upon each other.

The second methodological emphasis of Waltz is about the application of statistics. My approach involves a larger number of variables, which I operationalize by offering a multi-level approach that presumes a structural analysis. I have employed a straightforward methodology to construct my explanation by utilizing mathematical calculations. I have then outlined the empirical results of my research by inferring postulates and predictions about the future of the international system. This book incorporates three primary variables, which correspond to the realities that I mentioned above: power (independent variable), politics (dependent variable), and anarchy (intervening variable). By *power*, I refer to the ability of the most powerful state actors to control political relations among nations and to manipulate the balance of power in the international system in favor of their national interests. For instance, the United States still enjoys political, economic, and military domination, which allows Washington to control the actions of other international actors and to exercise power over the conditions of peace and war for decades to come. Democracy, human rights, and collective defense, on the other side, are psychological relations of control and influence that exist between America and its European allies. Although U.S. Foreign Policy tools vary, the ultimate purpose remains: defending the vital national interests. When I talk about *politics* in my research, I speak of the short-term and long-term material purposes of foreign policy. Since international politics is a struggle for power, each international actor's foremost purpose is to become a *great power*. Non-state actors do not possess the protosource of power: sovereignty. Through their foreign policy, international entities embody the collective will of all member states, which, under critical conditions, would rather defend their national interests than the common good. Finally, *anarchy* intervenes to demonstrate that moral categories in international politics are personal attribute of each nation, and thus, the struggle for power in international politics do not follow codes of universal validity. Paradoxically, religion has become the most recent example of that alignment. Right-wing extremism, political Islam, and Hindu nationalism are all expressions of power for their acolytes but false prophets for the rest of the international community.

Secondary variables refer to the pyramidal structure of the post-pandemic world and involve state actors, resources, and imperfect rationality. *State actors* include the United States, China, and states with nuclear weapons. I define them as the *nuclear concert*. Thus, in contrast to the U.S.-Soviet bipolarity from the Cold War, I assume that the post-pandemic world will exist in a state of *nuclear bipolarity* with America and China as predominant great powers, shaping but *not sharing* world politics with the rest of the nuclear concert. *Resources* include all the resources available to the mentioned actors to affect international politics. *Imperfect rationality* is a term I coined to indicate that in the post-pandemic world, the possibility of mutual assured destruction would be far greater than during the Cold War. Although state actors are primarily concerned with their survival, they could become far less rational when realizing that they are losing to their adversaries. The reason is that, after the end of the Cold War, state leaders of the nuclear concert have become even more obsessed with power than their predecessors. Sophisticated weapons, emerging technologies, the possession of WMD, and most of all – the desire for power have made decision-makers of the nuclear concert less rational and more reckless.

In his third clarification, Waltz stresses the necessity of a systematic approach (Waltz 1979, 12). Three questions are central to my theoretical approach: is anarchy still central to international politics, how the struggle for power determines the problem of peace in the first half of the twenty-first century, and how great powers competition will determine the post-pandemic structure of international politics. The systematic approach presupposes that I indicate the methodological difficulties I have faced and define the limits of my theory. The first problem arises from the huge body of literature, which is difficult to review with precision. To systematize the inherited legacy of realism will require another book. Instead, I have chosen to review the writings of six neorealist scholars. My review is not critical but structural. In addition, I consider only the aspects of those concepts which provide a plausible starting point for my theory while also using other works to infer robust hypotheses. The second challenge involves the global scope of my research. It is very difficult to infer empirical data about the Coronavirus Pandemic and its future impact. The conclusions derived in the final chapter of my book are but predictions. I do not claim to give prophetic explanations of the post-pandemic world order. Thus, I have abstained from general perorations such as the end of history, the decline of America, or the Chinese new era. Moreover, my book does not deal with conspiracies or biopolitics, and it is an international relations research. The final consideration and its corresponding limitation refer to my study's historical record.

I have paid much attention to the United States and China for three reasons. First, my concept seeks to avoid the temptation of Western-centrism. European powers have dominated international politics, and the United States still holds a predominant position in the international system. China, however, is what Stephen Walt calls *suis generis* region (Walt 2013, 14). Therefore, examining China's Grand Design will provide us with a better understanding of political relations among nations. Changes in Chinese foreign policy lead to changes in world politics, and thus, assessing Beijing's doctrines is as important as explaining U.S. Foreign Policy. It is also worthwhile to compare the former to the latter and explore both images through the perceptions of other international actors. My second argument concerns the balance of power in international relations. From the end of the Cold War until now, China has become the only great power that could effectively challenge the primacy of the most powerful nation at this moment – the United States. Russia and European Union seek to duplicate the American foreign policy approach in their struggle for power, while Beijing has elaborated its own Grand Design that makes China resistant to the psychological relations of the Western influence, as discussed above. Russia lacks the economic strength to maintain global leadership, and Europe has not yet built its military forces. Therefore, only the United States and China are in possession of what Morgenthau calls self-sufficiency in strength (Morgenthau 1985, 8). My final consideration refers to polarity. Since the end of the Cold War, Washington's primacy in the international system has evolved three into three stages. The first stage began immediately after the dissolution of the Soviet Union. America's global dominance flourished on the ruins of the bipolar world, and U.S. Foreign Policy tended towards maintaining unipolarity and acquiring more power overseas to become the world's policeman. Each change in the U.S. Grand Strategy at that time was produced by the ambitions of the Clinton administration to intervene in regions where human rights have been violated. The second stage marks the September 11 attacks. Following the events of 2001, the war on terror became the cornerstone of U.S. Foreign Policy. The primary tools used by the Bush administration involved military interventions in the Middle East and imposing economic sanctions on rogue states. Preemptive strikes dominated the U.S. military strategies, but after the election of Barack Obama, conventional warfare slowly transformed into dumb war. It was the period when the United States faced the limits of its power: Washington could not rebuild broken governments. Another factor was also central to this second period. The Obama doctrine created a strategic vacuum, which allowed many international actors to claim the status of great powers: China, Russia, the European Union, India, and Brazil. This leads us to the third stage, which started in 2016 with the election of President Donald Trump. The Trump doctrine provided a valuable test for all candidates: America first. The purpose that all of the mentioned actors pursued was multipolarity, but the tools of their strategies vary considerably. Despite their differences, however, all but China followed the U.S. example of becoming a great power without considering that America is a unique experiment and that plagiarizing America's model creates psychological relations of control and influence among Washington and the rest of the candidates. Instead of becoming great powers, all proponents remained regional actors. All but China.

Six pillars of coercive realism

I will proceed with the pillars of coercive realism. I will define and discuss each pillar by providing examples in support of my assertions. Finally, I will test my theory in the following two chapters of this book.

Anarchy. Coercive realism presumes that anarchy is the natural state of the international system. My theory follows the assumption that in international politics, anarchic does not mean chaotic (Mearsheimer 2001, 16). What liberals call "world order" is a manifestation of anarchy for a simple reason: political relations among nations are subject to human decisions and thus, reflect the endless struggle for power between humans. However, people need political actors to restrain the struggle. Otherwise, anarchy will evolve into chaos, and the latter will result in mutual assured destruction.

Coercion. My concept claims that war and peace serve the national interests of the most influential actors in international relations – the great powers. My claim originates from the statement that war results from the selfishness of human nature and the structure of international politics (Waltz 2018, 16). Therefore, decision-makers have the natural disposition to exercise coercion over other counterparts' actions and thus wage wars or sustain world peace in favor of their national interests. Coercion presumes conventional or non-conventional strategies like military interventions, alliance building, offshore balancing, or strategic manipulation, which Kissinger describes as the sophisticated strategy of negating traditional offensive advantages.

Sovereignty. I assume that sovereignty is the proto-source of power, and thus, state actors are the central entities in international relations. The sovereign status of each state actor empowers it to develop its security strategy and operate under the security dilemma. The actions of the most powerful state actors – the great powers – shape the international system, which exists in what Robert Jervis identifies as offensive/defensive balance (Jervis 1979, 210). Great powers shape the balance-of-power according to their perceptions and misperceptions, apart from universal categories such as international law and ethics. International institutions, including *suis generis* communities, have limited power to affect the offensive/defensive balance for two reasons. First, they are but a collective expression of the offensive/defensive postures of their Member States. Second, international bodies often become a tool of influence for the state actors.

Polarity. Coercive realism identifies the struggle for power in international relations with manipulation of polarity. I utilize the term manipulation to indicate the ability of a global actor to exercise offensive or defensive coercion and thus, to sustain the balance of power in its favor or to challenge the primacy of another major power. Whatever the tools of a foreign policy, such as alliance-building, territorial claims, or acquisition of resources, a great power's strategy always aim to manipulate polarity in favor of its national interests. Robert Jervis gives a perfect example by stating that bipolarity was in part the product of the Soviet and American decisions to mobilize national resources and rally allies (Jervis 2001, 44–45). On the other hand, minor actors stick to the established status quo or seek to increase their power.

Endurance. I assert that endurance and self-preservation are central to state actors, and therefore, coercion is a product of rational decisions. Here, I join Mearsheimer's bedrock assumptions that great powers are rational actors, which seek to maintain their territorial integrity and autonomy (Mearsheimer 2001, 16). However, the degree of self-preservation, especially when a state acquires nuclear weapons, varies depending on the actor's perception of power. I assume that four basic perceptions of power correspond to the foreign policy of global actors: preserving, maximizing, demonstrating, and exercising power. Self-preservation and survival are central to all of them. A detailed analysis of a nuclear warfare scenario will show that the Chinese moves towards strengthening Beijing's presence near Taiwan have been described as another Cuban missile crisis. However, the United States and China have abstained from demonstrating or exercising power in the region not for the purpose of preserving or maximizing power but in a term of preventing a nuclear holocaust.

Powershifting. My concept suggests that the anarchic nature of the international system is subject to historical transformations of power, which I call *powershifts*. The sources of powershifts are state behavior and objective material conditions. The first one refers to military conflicts, and imperial overstretch, which Jack Snyder explains by discussing preventive use of force and its potential to spark endless wars and internal rebellions (Snyder 2003, 30). Snyder is clear when stating that great powers, which have husbanded their power, avoided the imperial overstretch. The second group emerges from objective preconditions, which Robert Jervis summarizes in his analysis of unipolarity: economic shocks, widespread diseases, and environmental degradation (Jervis 2009, 193). Therefore, military conflicts, shocks, and even pandemics could become forces that lead to powershifting and, thus, determine politics among nations.

My explanation could be criticized on the ground that its pillars represent a hybrid theory and that most of my assumptions lack empirical validity or simply reinvent older theories. Therefore, in the following chapters, I will discuss my concept to prove that it could pass the ultimate test: to explain events in the real world (Mearsheimer 2001, 4). I do not seek to challenge or revise the realist theory but enrich it. It is impossible to make theoretical contributions or give plausible explanations without reviewing and employing previous theories. Therefore, I try to explain the contemporary political relations between two nations, which I believe are the most powerful international actors at the moment of this writing – the United States and China. I also provide different historical examples to demonstrate the validity of my concept. Henceforth, I will operationalize my explanation in three steps: explaining the rise of the United States, exploring the Chinese Grand Design after the communist revolution, and constructing some predictions about the future of the post-pandemic world order.

Chapter Two
Bound to cheat: liberal foreign policy in a realist world

In the following chapter, I explore the basic implications of U.S. Foreign Policy after the Cold War. Although my analysis draws some parallels with the Cold War, it is limited to the post-bipolar period for three reasons. First, to understand the post-pandemic world order, it is necessary to explain the pre-pandemic balance of power. Some might argue that the term *pre-pandemic* could incorporate not simply the period from 1990 to 2020. My concern, however, is that overstressing the Cold War will enlarge the scope of my research. The history of U.S. Foreign Policy proves that the end of the bipolar confrontation marks the geopolitical peak of Pax Americana. Thus, unipolarity and the subsequent powershifts after September 11, 2001, could provide a better starting point for explaining the post-pandemic balance of power.

Second, the post-Cold War period poses for the United States two fundamental issues Washington has never faced before. The first issue refers to the limits of American power, which I will discuss further in this chapter. The most complicated predicament for the U.S. global dominance is similar to the one Britain faced after World War II – to divide its cultural domination from its world power status. Although the Allies defeated Nazi Germany, Britain could not sustain its colonial system. London modified its foreign policy when the British realized the risks of gripping their colonies were out of proportion to the chances of rebuilding Pax Britannica. Instead, Britain has chosen to transform the Empire into a Commonwealth of Nations. The second concerns the transition from unipolarity to bipolarity – a process that started after September 11 and finished with the U.S. withdrawal from Afghanistan. Although the transition period did not deprive the United States of its superpower status, China finally gained the position to challenge the American primacy. These processes and powershifts are the results of Beijing's strategy to transform the international system from Pax Americana to a China-dominated political universe, in which all nations are under the tributary obligation to offer their economies as impost to the Chinese state.

Third, the Sinocentrism of Chinese foreign policy, combined with Chinese communism, provokes ideological and political clashes with the United States and its allies. However, the confrontation between America and China does *not* reflect the Cold War in economic and ideological competition. As relations between Washington and Beijing deteriorate, China has already created feudatory economic dependencies with Europe. By feudatory, I mean a system of economic dependences that could be detrimental to the Euro-Atlantic solidarity. The Soviet Union simply lacked the economic potential to build feudatory dependencies outside the socialist camp. Politically and militarily, the world was bipolar, but economically, the United States was the most powerful nation. Another predicament Washington faces in its relations with Beijing originates from a less, even poorly analyzed aspect of the Chinese foreign policy strategy: supporting state and non-state American adversaries such as Russia, North Korea, Iran, and the Taliban. In other words, China does not limit its support to communist regimes and does not seek to build or export communism. What Beijing wants is to replace the globalized liberal democracy with the Sinocentric world order and social harmonious society.

I begin by explaining the transition from U.S.-dominated world order to nuclear bipolarity. One might reject that the international system has already undergone a process of transformation and that the balance of power has shifted in favor of Beijing. The empirical validity of such arguments stands in solid contrast to the geopolitical realities, which reveal that anarchy is still central to the post-pandemic world and that only the United States and China are in possession of the military, political, and economic power to shape world politics. Kenneth Waltz is clear when concluding that in peacetime, the bipolar world displays a clarity of relations that is ordinarily found only in war (Waltz 1964, 884). In other words, to consider the post-pandemic world a multipolar entity, as many international scholars still do, is to fail to understand that the Sino-American competition today shapes what Morgenthau calls forces, determining political relations among nations (Morgenthau 1985, 3).

Anarchy and the illiberal end of history

Realism believes that great powers are rational actors. Thus, the end of the Cold War presented the United States with the opportunity to learn from the Soviet mistakes and adapt foreign policy decision-making to the unipolar system. Instead, under the slogan for the end of history, liberals declared the realist paradigm "in trouble" and made it possible for the post-Cold War generation of U.S. policymakers to place U.S. national interests under the flag of liberal hegemony. With the Soviet Union defeated, it was useless for Washington to abandon realism and endorse a strategy that advocates international institutions and promotes peace through global governance. The truth was that liberal scholars neglected the historical warning of Waltz that the American aspiration to freeze historical development by keeping the world unipolar was doomed (Waltz 2000, 36). Military interventions, cultural overstretch, and the struggle for liberal hegemony exceeded Washington's resources. The real trouble with liberal proponents was that, regardless of their ideological differences with realists, they believed in the false promise that international institutions push states away from war and promote peace (Mearsheimer 1994, 7). That has proved to be untruly due to many institutional weaknesses such as lack of military capabilities and inadequate political consensus between the Member States. Once the United States realized that it could not rely on international bodies to defend human rights and resolve crises, the liberal paradigm fell into the trap of *hawkism*, which advocates messianic struggles against authoritarian regimes in the name of democracy (Snyder 2004, 5). Hawkism, combined with the struggle for liberal hegemony, called forth a non-rational foreign policy strategy and thus, deformed American global leadership into preventive use of force.

The post-Cold War anarchy presented three temptations to U.S. Foreign Policy, which liberalism failed to overpower. First, the struggle for liberal hegemony has undermined both vital interests and the national security of the United States. The most evident expression of this subversion is the presumption that multilateral cooperation within international institutions will promote peaceful coexistence, and thus, the struggle for power will step down to a world order of global governance. At the outset, the pursuit of liberal hegemony had an exclusively utopian purpose: it sought to promote democracy and human rights for all state actors regardless of their national interests. Following September 11, however, the peaceful nature of liberal democracy took a strong military connotation. For the Bush doctrine sought to globalize Washington's vision and act preemptively against non-state actors, that challenged the U.S. global dominance, the end of the history turned out to be the establishment of what Robert Jervis calls U.S. hegemony, primacy, or empire (Jervis 2003, 83). It is for this reason that the liberal paradigm failed to predict the lack of support from the United Nations for the U.S.-led military interventions in Iraq. The opposition began to reject the U.S. argument of self-defense, which was a refusal to recognize the sovereign right of the United States to defend its national security. Although Washington invoked Article Five of NATO, European allies confronted the Bush administration with the intent to minimize their commitments and avoid war with transnational terrorist networks. In 2013, immediately after the chemical holocaust in Syria, NATO tried to make its presence in Afghanistan counterweight to President Obama's intervention, thus undermining its political and military solidarity. While the Alliance was hesitant in its support for the Obama administration, Russia launched a military intervention in Syria, further shifting the balance of power in the Middle East. Thus, instead of serving as a counterweight to Kremlin's global aspirations, NATO favored Russian foreign policy. Some might argue that the allies realized that the remnants of the Assad regime could probably join the emergent ISIS and imperil the southern border of the Alliance. At that time, U.S. Foreign Policy in Syria relied on the Obama doctrine, which proclaimed that Assad should be punished because credibility and the future interests of the United States and its allies were at stake (Goldberg 2017, 5). Before the intervention, President Obama had drawn a red line and moved towards an alliance with the Peshmerga Kurds, intending to pursue a policy of co-operation and multilateralism. The objective realities, however, did not envisage robust commitments on behalf of the U.S. allies. European Union considered Syria the last bulwark of Moscow's post-Soviet presence and thus, imposed sanctions on the Assad regime. However, the French commitment came in response to the Paris attacks in 2015. France realized that a potential NATO intervention in Syria would provoke tensions with Moscow and aggravate the Ukrainian crisis.

Although the Obama doctrine was popular in Europe, the institutional solidarity within the Alliance thinned for another reason: the prospective accession of Ukraine to NATO. In a thoughtful warning, John Mearsheimer argues that the United States and its allies should abandon their plan to westernize Ukraine and instead aim to make it a neutral buffer between the Alliance and Russia (Mearsheimer 2014, 87). It is precisely the intention of liberal apologists to westernize Kyiv through membership in the Alliance. Realism, however, believes that political positions are not subject to moral codes but simply to superior power. Ukraine falls under the unenviable position of a hostage, dependent on the U.S.-Russia competition in Eastern Europe. Following the Russian annexation of Crimea, the United States responded to Moscow's intervention with a smart strategy. Washington's sanctions were to close relation with financial support for Kyiv, combined with expectations of its future integration into the European Union. By supporting the independence of Ukraine and increasing NATO's military presence in the Balkans, America expels Russia from what the Soviet Union once considered its backyard. This policy succeeded in deterring further Russian aspirations in the region but created perilous preconditions for the future of the Alliance. Even if Ukraine becomes a NATO Member State, Article Five from the Washington Treaty will survive if it passes the ultimate test-launching collective defense against Russia. Moscow, however, enjoys stable financial and commercial relations with many Ukrainian pro-Russian oligarchs, and it is the United States, which might become a victim of Ukraine's westernization. Although most Ukrainians are in support of their country's accession to the Alliance, anti-liberal attitudes in Kyiv could escalate into a political crisis. Therefore, a neutral, U.S.-backed Ukraine would better favor Washington's national interests, while a less favorable outcome could be expected if NATO overstretches again to the Russian borders.

Another problem arises from the functioning of global international organizations, which purport to perform the sacred duty of sustaining the balance of power in the international system. Waltz clearly states that the collective-security system of the United Nations depends on the ability of one powerful state at the moment of serious threat (Waltz 1979, 163). The structure of the UN Security Council provides us with empirical proof of Waltz's statement. A crucial point in the decision-making process within the organization is voting, where the national interests of the five permanent members clash. The motto "It's your world" represents the efforts of the United Nations to build a "better" world. However, history shows that state actors tend to abandon the mission of the UN founding fathers and trade it for its sovereign right to defend. Waltz reminds us that mutuality of dependence leads each state to watch others with wariness and suspicion (Waltz 2019, 132). Peacekeeping operations and binding resolutions are not a universal formula of interdependence, which could accommodate or limit great powers competition to an extent beyond which they should give up their national interests and the security of their citizens. Similar concerns apply to the mission of the UN. The promise of the United Nations for a shared world carries out a preclusion of what realists believe to be international anarchy and reflects the liberal creed of international order. The ultimate test for each international institution would be to resolve anarchy and maintain order. However, the limited ability or the complete lack of enforcement mechanisms prevents international bodies from constructing a system of interactions with other actors. In short, such institutions do *not* make foreign policy. They look at foreign policy not as behavior with foremost purpose but as a structure, embodying the collective will of the Member States. To pass a resolution or decision without a foreign policy strategy could even escalate the tensions and inevitably pass the stick to state actors. When China and Russia vetoed the draft resolutions on the Syrian Civil War in 2011, the United Nations failed to resolve a conflict, which later escalated into a chemical holocaust. If the Security Council were to avert Assad from using chemical weapons, Beijing and Moscow should overcome their differences with the United States on this issue and prevent genocide. Both states rejected the draft, and thus, interdependence among the Security Council permanent members triggered suspicion instead of reconciliation. In the aftermath, the threat that U.S. Foreign Policy faced in Syria was military and political. The concerns that Assad would side with the Russians and that America would lose Syria to Moscow were so realistic that the United States intervened to back the Syrian opposition. The situation, however, escalated when Russia maintained a military presence in the region, which excluded the Iraqi scenario. The United Nations failed to protect Syrians from domestic oppression, and the security architecture in the Middle East became a projection of the U.S.-

Russia competition. Thus, it turned out that the UN could not order the anarchic international system.

The second temptation refers to the use of force. Liberals admit that military forces might be necessary to protect liberal states and societies and to advance liberal aims (Greener 2007, 295). In the aftermath of the Cold War, the Clinton administration believed that protecting human rights and exporting liberal democracy, which served the United States well during the bipolar confrontation, would continue to benefit U.S. Foreign Policy under unipolarity. However, that promise failed and, even worse, degenerated into hegemonic hawkism, which Robert Jervis also defines as imperial temptation (Jervis 2003, 388). Proponents of liberal hegemony succumbed to the allurement of imperializing U.S. Foreign Policy for two reasons. First, the threat that America faced after September 11 was unconventional by its nature. It was a shocking picture of the transnational terrorist networks attacking the heart of democracy and unipolarity. Behind Al Qaeda's ideology, which the Bush doctrine summarizes as the crossroad of radicalism and technology, there was a non-state actor, highly centralized and able to defend itself against the conventional American strategies. However, the threat of global terrorism was simply military and ideological. Hegemonic hawkism provided an opportunity for its enemy – to exhaust the United States economically and compromise the core liberal assumption that promoting human rights and democracy would secure peace. Therefore, military interventions in Iraq and Afghanistan were relevant to the threat of demonstrating power and irrelevant goal setting. Preemptive strikes against Iraq benefited U.S. Foreign Policy only in terms of prestige and retribution, but the latter had no bearing on regime building. The acolytes of hegemonic hawkism intended to use force for the sake of America's protection. Yet, they misjudged that purpose, seeking to build liberal democracy in the Middle East. Thus, global terrorist networks, even being non-state actors, proved the realist assumption that in international relations, the use of force applies only for a state's protection and advantage.

Another issue that the use of force poses for U.S. Foreign Policy after the Cold War involves the fraud assumption that protecting American national interests aligns with Western cultural predominance. Historically, the strategy of President Carter to deter the Soviet Union by replacing *realpolitik* with *moralpolitik* presents us with an excellent example of a non-rational strategy. An enduring aspect of moralpolitik was the view that promoting and protecting human rights was central to U.S. Foreign Policy (Schweigler 1978, 85). However, the Soviet intervention in Afghanistan proved that the use of military force had more significant repercussions than the moralist appeal of the Carter doctrine. America could not contain rogue states and spread radical ideologies by fighting in Afghanistan or arming the Syrian opposition. If the Obama administration convinced the majority of the Americans that Washington should withdraw from Afghanistan, the grueling burden of democracy-building in Kabul forced President Biden to withdraw the U.S. troops from the county. Therefore, there is no rational logic in believing that the Western cultural predominance is vital to U.S. national interests and that converting regimes to liberal democracy benefits the U.S. global dominance.

The practical judgment of the Afghanistan war also stands against proponents of liberal hegemony and favors the realist paradigm. Although the Taliban were no match for the United States militarily, their tactics were immune to the conventional American strategies. Washington held the power to invade Afghanistan again and dethrone the regime in Kabul. However, the use of force did not defeat the Taliban – it pushed them back to the mountains. To defeat ultimately, such a non-state adversary America had to, quite literally, beat it. The actual conquest of the Taliban would require another intervention. I hope that no American policymaker would risk the lives of thousands of soldiers in a military operation with incalculable risks and unpredictable outcomes. Another scenario could involve what new liberals consider the spread of national self-determination and democracy (Moravcsik 2013, 250). Promoting democracy in the Middle East, however, failed for two reasons. First, the United States sought to export liberal democracy during the Arab spring – a purpose that could not be attained with the tools U.S. Foreign Policy applied – regime change. Instead, Washington should adapt its strategy to the political and cultural specificities of the Middle East and North Africa. It is important to highlight that failed states in the region – such as Libya – recognized political Islam, not liberal democracy, as an alternative to dictatorship. On the other hand, Egypt that embodies a political amalgam of military autocracy and the secular state, has become an outpost of the coalition against ISIS. Therefore, the all-catch liberal approach of exporting democracy through global American commitments turned out to be counterproductive.

The second reason concerns the U.S. support for Israel and the recognition of Jerusalem by President Trump. The most trusted American ally in the Middle East, upon which Washington's strategies depend, is Israel. The fact that the political culture of the Jewish state differs from that of the Arabian states is a logical factor that predetermines the distinct position of the former in that region. It is nonsensical to argue that the strategic importance of Israel in 2021 is not what it was in 1951. When exploring the alliance between America and Israel, it is essential to highlight that oil is a less important factor than in relations with the Kingdom of Saudi Arabia, which also enjoys Washington's support. The cultural, political, and historical profile of Israel remains a fundamental aspect of importance, which American foreign policy takes into account, although Washington's support varies from one administration to another. Israel is an ally that the United States could not afford to lose. One of the most important factors, which exercised an influence upon the U.S. Foreign Policy before the Pandemic, was the political flirt of President Trump with Israel and the subsequent recognition of Jerusalem as the capital of the Jewish state. It is for this reason that the very existence of Israel, which did not enjoy President Obama's support, now depends not only upon its ability to maintain powerful military and effective defensive capabilities but also upon the status of Jerusalem. For Israel, whenever its security and sovereignty are threatened, the very idea of Zionism is challenged, and the survival of the Jewish people is left in jeopardy. Thus, Zionism and Pan-Arabism reflected the natural deterrence in the Middle East between Israel and its Arab adversaries. What gave both ideologies their actual importance to the United States was the Palestine struggle for independence. The fate of the Palestinians is unclear and provokes tensions between Europe and the United States, for which both are unable to offer a general solution to the Jerusalem problem. Washington carried its strategy on the rhetoric of confronting antisemitism, while European Union relied on its soft power to resolve the Arab-Israeli conflict. So far, no international body has offered a peaceful solution.

Therefore, do American national interests align with Western cultural predominance? Challenged at home by domestic tensions and social polarization, the United States was unwilling to further use force against the Taliban and withdrew from Afghanistan. It is, however, a fallacy to call the American withdrawal defeat. Proponents of liberal hegemony might consider it as such. By believing so, they prey on the third temptation of the post-Cold War period: confusing domestic with international politics. Kenneth Waltz reminds us that international politics is the realm of power, struggle, and accommodation (Waltz 1979, 113). Decentralization and power dominate the international realm, while hierarchy and justice hold the national arena. Therefore, Washington's struggle to sustain U.S. global dominance presumes the use of force or containment of China. Although unipolarity implied that universalization of domestic politics and values could reshape international politics, in a world where nuclear powers interact and accommodate the objective realities of the international system, there is little place for justice. If China tries to annex Taiwan and threatens America with nuclear retaliation in case of U.S. interference, Beijing will be successful. Taiwan does not possess the military capability of countering potential Chinese interference. For this reason, China could invade Taipei if the United States strengthens its military presence in the South China Sea. If Taiwan requests help from Washington, America becomes vulnerable to a nuclear strike because Beijing has already developed weapons of mass destruction and thus, could retaliate. The sole restraining factor that would save the world from the nuclear holocaust is the fear of mutual assured destruction. Therefore, politics serves the most powerful state actors, which exercise power to reshape the balance of power in international relations according to their perceptions of justice, whether it will be Make America Great Again or Serve the People. To say that the international system is anarchic and that power dominates the political realm determines the political action is to state a fact, that will continue to shape the driving forces behind political relations among the nations in the post-pandemic world order.

The struggle for cultural predominance turned out to be disastrous for domestic politics in the United States and quite unjust for the American national interests overseas. However, the Biden administration has a very effective way of influencing the Chinese strategies to match the vital American interests. To counter Beijing's conventional war-fighting capacity, it has become evident that Washington should abandon its pre-pandemic behavior. While for China, it might have been relevant to pursue a policy of prestige in Afghanistan that approach could no longer benefit Washington in terms of military spending. The importance of the Chinese support for the Taliban government in Kabul reaffirmed Washington's intentions to pursue a double strategy of ideological containment by preventing the spread of the Taliban ideology. In assessing the Chinese strategy, which pretends to respect the civilizational choice of Afghanistan, a post-Cold War communist power as China finally abandons the orthodox Soviet dogma that exporting communism would contain democracy. Beijing found that each conflict, regardless of the ideological intentions of the parties, could benefit the Chinese foreign policy. An enduring aspect of Beijing's Grand Strategy is that maintaining the parabellum paradigm of China will secure the Chinese global influence. The American intervention in Afghanistan proved that military power could serve as retribution for September 11, but promoting democracy and regime building through the long-term deployment of American troops in Kabul had quite detrimental consequences for U.S. national interests.

To conclude and better assess the post-Afghani syndrome, it is helpful to remind the conclusion of Robert Jervis that it is neither surprising nor evidence of misperception that those who start wars often lose them (Jervis 1988, 679). An analytical assessment that ignores this conclusion and misjudges the Biden doctrine would have limited usefulness. American individualism and liberal democracy are incompatible with Afghanistan's political culture and traditions. Therefore, promoting domestic values through regime change will not remodel the natural state of the international system – anarchy. Instead, attempts to elaborate a multipurpose approach to international politics that advocates justice and global hierarchy will transform anarchy into chaos. Not only such an approach is irrelevant to U.S. vital interests, but it also runs counter to them. Yet, suppose the competition between the United States and the Soviet Union has transformed into peaceful coexistence as President Carter. In that case, liberal scholars could have proclaimed the end of history in 1980.

Coercion and the limits of American power

Is American power unlimited? The United States represents an exclusive example of a superpower that embodies omnipotent resources and a favorable geostrategic location. If we assume, however, that American power is unlimited and that it is destined to bring peace and justice, we could easily succumb to the liberal temptation of the post-Cold War Manifest Destiny. Human decision-making predetermines U.S. Foreign Policy, and thus, peace and war are justified only when they serve the U.S. national interests. Kissinger draws the dividing line between national interests and domestic issues when stating that foreign policy begins where domestic policy ends (Kissinger 1966, 504). One should not confuse the justification of peace and war with moral aspirations or philosophical expressions of good and evil. Nor to jump beyond the natural predisposition of fear, which drives human nature to defend when there is an immediate threat to national security. Peace and war are but tools through which state actors struggle for power. History shows no better parallel for that than the post-Cold War period.

Coercion, in general, means that a state actor possesses the power to punish transgressors of the rules (Art 1996, 11). In international politics, coercion is necessary for three reasons. First, it is impossible for a sovereign state to protect its national security without possessing the power to coerce. After the dissolution of the Soviet Union, the nations in Central Asia went independent and endorsed a policy of cooperation with Russia. Although Moscow had planned further to integrate the post-Soviet republics into the Eurasian Union, independent states like Kazakhstan rejected the Russian projects for mutual defense.

This leads us to the second sovereign need for coercion – maintaining offensive capacity. International organizations and, in particular, military alliances possess limited capabilities to coerce and gain legitimacy from what Waltz calls the image of a common enemy (Waltz 2000, 25). Following the collapse of the Soviets and the enlargement of NATO, the ultimate threat to collective security switched from Moscow to Iraq and Afghanistan. For two decades, global terrorism has predetermined the Alliance's strategies according to the foreign policy of its largest financial and military contributor – America. Shortly before the American troops left Afghanistan, the allies acknowledged that the sophisticated military technologies of Russia and China threatened the collective security of NATO (Mattis 2018, 47). Eventually, if the purpose NATO pursues is realistic, the Member States can rely on their own cyber and military capabilities to counter the Chinese technological advantages. However, if Article Five from the Washington Treaty does not apply to nonconventional threats such as cyberwarfare and hybrid warfare, one arrives at the conclusion that NATO needs reform.

Coercion, in terms of diplomacy, can achieve a limited and positive outcome in short-term than to manage a number of competing goals over more than a decade (Alterman 2003, 277). The policy of isolating Putin's Russia and the policy of sanctions on its partners are relevant responses to the annexation of Crimea. Since the expansion of the Russian influence westwards threatens European democracies, proceeding by political and ideological tools – sponsoring far-right movements and extremism – Washington should also contain Moscow by political means. For that purpose, the United States should exercise a policy of sanctions without demanding further military alignments against Russia. If Washington abandons that policy, NATO will find itself at war with Russia.

Before further discussing the nature of coercion, it is necessary to refute the liberal misjudgment that Waltz's theory of international politics is insufficient either for explaining foreign policy decisions and outcomes or for conducting foreign policy (George 1997, 45). At this point, theoretical definitions of power overshadow the dichotomous nature of coercion. As we analyze U.S. Foreign Policy in the post-Cold War period, liberal scholars argue that the concept of power embodies hard, soft, and smart aspects (Nye 2021, 199–204). For liberals, hard power behavior presumes coercion, manipulation of structure, and payment, soft power includes positive attraction and persuasion, while smart power refers to the successful combination of both (Nye 2021, 201–205). The explanation of Waltz is much more refined because it relates to the fundamental purpose of U.S. Foreign Policy – to defend the American national interests in the complex puzzle of international politics. Waltz argues that each state pursues its interests, however, defined, in ways it judges best. Force is a means of achieving the external ends of states because there exists no consistent, reliable process of reconciling the conflicts of interest that inevitably arise among similar units in a condition of anarchy (Waltz 2018, 238). Therefore, if the use of force (power) predetermines state behavior (politics), the international environment (anarchy) intervenes to relate and bind them in a constant struggle to protect national interests. Although liberal explanations provide us with a solid empirical basis and exquisite definition of what power is, it still tends to neglect three realist assessments, which reflect the limits of American power and could explain why the struggle for liberal hegemony does not benefit American national interests.

The first assessment concerns the third principle of political realism, which postulates that the concept of interests in terms of power is an objective category (Morgenthau 1978, 10). Morgenthau further argues that circumstances of time and place do not affect interests. Therefore, it is incumbent upon U.S. Foreign Policy to protect American national interests and defend U.S. national security whether or not the international system is unipolar, bipolar, or multipolar. Liberal scholars, however, tend to advocate coercion for hegemonic purposes. Under the hard stick of military interventions, soft power has dominated U.S. Foreign Policy since the Spanish-American War in 1898. Thus, the most logical question arises from the dilemma of the United States is destined to be the patron of human rights and democracy.

Furthermore, to what extent does the spread of liberal democracy and the promotion of human rights benefit U.S. Foreign Policy? History of International Relations shows that, in terms of state behavior, American Foreign Policy could pursue a successful course if it is determined by commitments to the U.S. allies rather than by the export of values. U.S. national interests may not always coincide with the interests of Europe, Japan, or Turkey, but benefits from security cooperation exceed losses from disagreements between allies. It is essential to highlight that the primary objective of most alliances is to combine the member's capabilities in a way that furthers their respective interests (Walt 2009, 90). The United States, for example, cannot look with composure at the French overtures in NATO. When French President Emanuel Macron declared that Europe experienced the brain death of the Alliance, his words were but a manifestation of the forthcoming triumph from Brexit. President Trump, who threatened to reconsider Washington's commitments to NATO, blasted Macron for his words and later insisted European allies increase their defense spending to at least two percent. With the election of President Biden, Euro-Atlantic tensions deescalated, and Washington reconfirmed its commitment to Article Five. Although American support for NATO varies from one Presidential administration to another, the Alliance itself remains among the primary tools of U.S. Foreign Policy, and as such, it benefits U.S. national interests in countering Russia. If Moscow added to its influence in Eastern Europe security cooperation with Western Member States through gas policy and bilateral agreements, it would threaten the vital American interests in Europe.

Exporting democracy, on the other side, had disastrous outcomes for U.S. Foreign Policy in the post-Cold War period. There was a chance for Washington to pursue a foreign policy that, although interventionist and coercive by its nature, to advance U.S. national interests and maintain the balance of power in international relations. America, however, chose neither of those strategies and pursued a policy of prestige, combined with coercive diplomacy and military interventions. In 2001, Washington intervened preemptively in Afghanistan and toppled the Taliban rulers in Kabul. Two years later, President George W. Bush dethroned Saddam Hussein without limiting the American commitment to the post-war recovery of Iraq. Although the preemptive strategy of Washington was successful and the retaliate response to September 11 was decisive enough, the United States tried to rebuild the governments in Kabul and Baghdad, which, if it had succeeded, would have led to the absorptivity of religious extremism and military dictatorship by liberal democracy. It was a just war, which sent an explicit warning to all U.S. adversaries: do not confront the United States unless you have nuclear weapons. The U.S. decision to prolong its stay in Iraq and Afghanistan and to reconstruct the broken governments of Baghdad and Kabul exceeded the very purpose of the military interventions in MENA. It transformed them into a global war on terror. Post-war commitments to the region did not benefit the American national interests. Instead, Washington's continuous presence in MENA triggered a wave of anti-Americanism, which Muqtedar Khan and Sara Chehab describe best as transformation from a promise of change, to moments of euphoric optimism, and then to drab pragmatic realism (Khan and Chehab 2012, 180).

The U.S.-backed protests during the so-called Arabian spring ended with Civil War in Libya, a military coup in Egypt, and political commotions in the Middle East and North Africa. Washington's strategy of promoting human rights and spreading democracy by exercising hard, soft, or smart power partook the same universalization of liberal hegemony, which upheld U.S. Foreign Policy after the Cold War and compounded it by misconceptions of the political culture of MENA countries. Proponents of liberal hegemony grounded their arguments on two misleading presumptions. One is that promoting human rights, which are indeed primordial to all people, would secure peace. The other is that liberal democracy could serve as an effective and reliable tool for alliance building. Instead of securing peace and building a system of alliances, the United States got involved in the longest war in American history. In truth, Washington still has the power to change regimes and topple corrupted governments. Although America is the most powerful nation in the world, capable of defeating rogue states and containing the global influence of other major powers, it has become impossible for Washington to rebuild states, fix governments, and convert them to democracy. The realist prophesies of Hans Morgenthau that the United States has become vulnerable, taking the risk of being powerful but not omnipotent, marks the first limit of American power – *producing global democracy.* Kenneth Waltz further warned about Morgenthau's prediction coming true by concluding that if the world is now safe for democracy, one must wonder whether democracy is safe for the world (Waltz 2000, 13).

The second realist assessment refers to the U.S. national interests. A year before September 11, 2001, The Commission on America's National Interests issued a report that summarized U.S. Foreign Policy in four priorities: vital, extremely important, important, and secondary interests (Allison 2000, 5–8). This document had a strongly positive aspect: it keeps American foreign policy out of the imperial temptation, which Jack Snyder later describes as imposing peace on the tortured politics of weaker societies (Snyder 2003, 29). In their report, Allison and his team limit the promotion of democracy, prosperity, and stability in the Western hemisphere and advocate the post-Cold War commitments to all American allies. Did Washington succumb to the temptation? Aside from the domestic impact, September 11 attacks had two negative results: the war on terror created tensions between Washington and its European allies and blurred the prism of American national interests. Russia and China have not been slow to exploit the checkmate position in which the United States found itself after the misjudgment of Iraq's programs for WMD (Jervis 2010, 123). While Washington struggled to define the limits of its commitments in Iraq and Afghanistan, Beijing and Moscow formally recognized the global threat of terrorism and thus, got the better of the Bush doctrine, which considered Communists and Eurasians partners in the war on terror. From President Bush's point of view, it was much more favorable to let Russia and China increase their global influence and focus U.S. Foreign Policy on fighting terrorism than to prevent the rise of Russian nationalism and Chinese aspirations for regional hegemony in Asia. China was aware of the complications that Washington faced in its efforts to rebuild the regimes in Kabul and Baghdad. The Chinese understood that the balance of power sloped towards Beijing when the global financial crisis of 2007–2008 forced the Obama administration to cut the U.S. defense budget. China then became a global factor in international politics. The real trouble for hawkism was dualistic: the rise of far-right nationalism and mutual dependence between America and China. Paradoxically, support for unipolarity among American allies grew weaker as the Russian and Chinese struggle for multipolarity grew stronger. The main strategic issue for the United States was no longer whether Beijing could pose a challenge to the American global dominance. It was rather how Washington could prevent China from threatening the U.S. national interests.

A rational look at U.S. Foreign Policy towards the Middle East and North Africa would show that the temptation of imposing peace in the region led to results that are even more detrimental to American national interests. The Iran Nuclear Deal from 2015 and the subsequent U.S. withdrawal from the agreement confirmed the prediction of Robert Jervis, who, stressing the discouraging record of coercive diplomacy, suggested that the United States should not rely simply on carrots and sticks (Jervis 2013, 112). The belief that the nuclear deal will work originated from two assumptions. The first derives from the fear that if Iran gets the bomb, the unpredictable policymakers in Tehran will threaten the United States and its allies with nuclear diplomacy. Such presumption is reasonable and requires a non-rational course of action, which is relevant to the current rulers of Iran. Nuclear diplomacy also presumes a strong incentive and indubious conviction that the target poses an intermediate threat to the attacker's national security. Both conditions currently prevail in U.S.-Iranian relations. The other assertion insists that the threat that Tehran poses to Washington is military in nature and could be deterred through multilateral agreement. The latter assertion's validity turned irrelevant to the Iranian aspirations for regional hegemony. What threatens Washington in Iran is political aggression and anti-Americanism. The supreme leader of the Shia state, Ayatollah Ali Khamenei, has a clear vision of America as an aggressor that supports the ultimate Iranian adversaries – Israel and Saudi Arabia. The American withdrawal from the Nuclear Deal and the recognition of Jerusalem created a slow but decisive shift in the regional balance of power, which favored Russia and China. If Washington launches a preemptive strike against Iran would be as useless as self-defeating. Even if the forthcoming Presidential administrations succeed in resetting the Deal, it will not work without Sino-Russian support. Therefore, the second limit of American power equalizes with the *limits of universal commitments*. The balance of political, economic, and military influence between the United States and China reflects the global distribution of power and the emerging spheres of influence. Power cannot act unilaterally in its adversary's traditional areas of predominance without risking retaliation. For example, if China invades Taiwan, the United States will not be able to defend the Taiwanese with a conventional military strategy. If America decides to intervene, it will have to strike Beijing first to negate the potential threat of Chinese retaliation. Similarly, if China ever tries to intervene in Latin or Central America, history will probably repeat, and the world will witness another Cuban missile crisis. Therefore, a more wise American policy will avoid universal commitments to external partners or even friends by creating preconditions for closer ties with allies. Strengthening alliances will assess the Chinese strategy of establishing partnerships through economic expansion. If America, however, voluntarily offers its national interests to the shrine of global commitments, Washington will, quite literally, abdicate from the essential purpose of U.S. Foreign Policy.

A more detailed assessment of the U.S.-led system of alliances in the post-Cold War era will confirm the assumption of Mearsheimer and Walt that the strategy of offshore balancing benefits U.S. Foreign Policy better than bearing responsibility for costly debacles (Mearsheimer and Walt, 2016, 71). The misjudgment of offshore balancing often refers to isolationism. To say that the United States will give up its superpower status is to equalize husbanding American strength with divorcing American influence. It is a liberal misinterpretation, which neglects the realist conclusion of Stephen Walt that alliances are not collective security agreements (Walt 1997, 152). Walt further highlights that collective security commitments require institutionalization. The effectiveness of institutionalized security, however, is highly dubious. It illuminates the fundamental misunderstanding of the institutionalist strategies that a threat to one's national security presumes collective defense.

Such a view is unhelpful and detrimental to American national interests, for it is incompatible with a fundamental principle of U.S. Foreign Policy – protecting U.S. national security. Article Five from The North Atlantic Treaty postulates that the Parties agree that an armed attack against one or more of them in Europe or North America shall be considered an attack against them (Rupp 2000, 156). For the first time in history, America invoked Article Five in response to the September 11 attacks. It was, however, a primary response to the actions of a non-state actor – Al Qaeda. How can Washington guarantee that it will keep its obligations if Ukraine joins the Alliance? The Treaty implies that the allies do not have much choice in a matter of armed force. How the leading party – America – could make the ultimate choice if neither policymakers nor Americans have the will to do so? Not only are such obligations at odds with the U.S. national interests, but they also neglect a very realistic scenario – nuclear holocaust. Will Washington and Brussels be better off if Moscow sends nuclear submarines in the Black Sea in the days preceding another Russian annexation? It will certainly drive proponents of liberal hegemony out of office and further polarize American public opinion. The West might be willing the support the Ukrainian accession to NATO, but history shows that the Clinton administration had a better assessment of the situation when integrating the Balkans into the Alliance. In the years preceding the accession of Bulgaria and Romania to NATO, Russia was a broken shadow of the Soviet Union. Moscow, at present, engages actively in world politics, although it is highly dependent on China. America will not benefit from the miscalculations that Ukraine is ready to join the Alliance. Washington should consider one argument which advances in favor of those misjudgments: only Russia knows its backyard so well that it could assess the preparedness of Ukraine to become a NATO Member State. The truth is that the Alliance does need to overstretch. What America and its allies need is a revision of NATO's global commitments. It is obvious even to Moscow that the Alliance has overloaded its mandate of action, which has failed to save the day in Afghanistan. The future Presidential administrations should encourage Euro-Atlantic solidarity but reject interventions that could expose the allies' national security to global threats. Yet, what NATO Member States and most particularly America should seek is what President Biden calls effective burden sharing (Biden 2000, 10).

A far more appropriate example of constructive cooperation is the Treaty of Mutual Cooperation and Security between Japan and The United States of America in 1951. Article Five from the agreement states that each Party recognizes that an armed attack against either Party in the territories under the administration of Japan would be dangerous to its peace and safety and declares that it would act to meet the common danger in accordance with its constitutional provisions and processes (Stranger 1965, 16). Why then the U.S.-Japanese Treaty is a model of better cooperation. It is again the strategy of commitments. An attack on Japanese soil will certainly threaten American national interests and the effectiveness of the U.S. Grand Strategy in the Asia-Pacific. However, the implications of potential American support for Tokyo are much weaker than the U.S. commitments to NATO. Another difference predetermines the extent of the American involvement in Europe and APAC. In the former, U.S. military presence in Europe guarantees collective security among the Member States of the Alliance. In the latter, the ultimate purpose of the American troops in Japan is to ensure the positive effect of Article Nine. The Constitution of Japan from 1947 states explicitly that Aspiring sincerely to an international peace based on justice and order, the Japanese people forever renounce war as a sovereign right of the nation and the threat or use of force as means of settling international disputes. To accomplish the aim of the preceding paragraph, land, sea, and air forces, as well as another war potential, will never be maintained. The right of belligerency of the state will not be recognized (Van Hoften 2002, 290). Since World War II, Japanese policymakers, Japanese Self-Defense Forces, and even the Imperial court have faced the security dilemma if they cannot defend Japan from external threats. Tokyo will instead request American support than sacrificing its vital interests in a confrontation with China and North Korea. If Japan, however, chooses to pursue a policy of unilateral involvement in the APAC, it should seek to modify Article Nine in favor of its policies. By doing so, however, the Japanese government will risk losing Washington's support, but if Tokyo is successful, Japan will regain its status as a dominant power in the region. Former Prime Minister Shinzo Abe had a reasonable strategy for resolving the dilemma. Abe implied that a possible revision of Article Nine would help Japan deter rising China. However, the misperceptions of the Japanese revival obscured political attitudes in South Korea and the United States. Irrational fears from the so-called Shinto restoration roamed Seoul, clouding rational decision-making with historical mythologies. Yet, if America and Japan had reached a consensus on Article Nine's revision, Beijing's aspirations for regional hegemony would have faced a serious setback.

A final critical assessment of the American involvement in Afghanistan raises the question should the United States transform alliance building to offshore balancing. The answer of this book is yes. I further discuss the points of transformation in the final chapter. For the purpose of this section, it is necessary to explain how coercion will benefit offshore balancing. I assume that it will be more punctual to use the word *evolvement* instead of transformation for two reasons. Apologists of Fukuyama blame Stephen Walt for offering a non-realist explanation of alliances (Moravcsik and Legro 1999, 38). Walt, however, is evident when stating that there is a structural difference between alliances and institutionalized collective defense (Walt 1997, 152). However, even liberals will agree that neither state actors nor institutions last forever. To argue that they do is to proffer a theoretical utopia. Therefore, the first reason for evolvement originates from the false presumption that the end of the U.S. military commitments will leave the American allies alone. Offshore balancing does not exclude support for allies. It rather encourages them to act independently and presumes American intervention only when U.S. national interests are at stake. What offshore balancing rejects is the presumption that the United States should seek to control the way that state actors exercise their sovereignty. For example, if Russia takes over the rest of Ukraine without threatening the Baltic States or if Moscow agrees that Minsk should further integrate into the Eurasian Union, the United States should not risk an intervention. If, however, Kremlin attempts to undermine the energy sovereignty of the European allies, America should consider imposing heavier sanctions on Russia. If international institutions are as omnipotent as their defenders argue, the former could prove the latter's assumption by influencing Russian behavior.

Another issue refers to ideology. Morgenthau argues that power expresses a psychological relation of man's control over the minds and the actions of other men (Morgenthau 1985, 14). Shared ideology often leads to successful alliances. However, the most powerful driving force to unite allies is asymmetrical dependence. It is arguable to say that the balance of power in APAC depends on democracy and human rights. Washington supports its allies and anti-Chinese actors such as Taiwan against Beijing and North Korea. However, psychological relations and perceptions among allies and partners prevail over ideology. Japan, South Korea, and Taiwan, which were irreconcilable in the past, follow the U.S. lead for a simple reason: American power. United States won World War II, reshaped the Korean Peninsula, and opposed the Chinese aspirations for regional leadership.

On the other hand, should we say that Israel and Saudi Arabia, both American allies, share a similar ideology? With the relations between Israel and Iran deteriorating, Riyadh makes a favorable gesture toward hesitant interference in the Israeli-Palestinian talks. Following the American withdrawal from Afghanistan, there are currently no options for relaunching a military campaign against the Taliban, which could tilt the balance of power in favor of China. Therefore, institutionalized alliances will not work in MENA and APAC. Europe represents a rare exclusion from this rule because NATO keeps the image of the common enemy alive.

To conclude, the third limit of American power is *alliances overstretching*. I assert that the limitations of the U.S.-led system of alliances are two: misperceptions of their nature and misperceptions of their mission. One of the most successful aspects of U.S. Foreign Policy is that, in the years after World War II, America drew others into a system of alliances and institutions that lasted for sixty years (Nye 2004, 16). However, Walt reminds us that, in a unipolar world, the unipole tends to distract a wide array of foreign policy problems due to several issues such as counterhegemonic balancing and weakened credibility (Walt 2009, 100). The post-Cold War commitments of the United States have equated alliances with international cooperation (Moravcsik 1992, 11). Yet, what is true of Walt's theory has turned out to be relevant to security cooperation after the Cold War: American national interests determined the direction of the U.S.-led system of alliances, and thus, U.S. behavior shaped world politics. The fundamental issue with U.S. Foreign Policy was not that Washington cooperated with its allies but that America enjoyed unprecedented global dominance. American primacy was the sole relevant precondition for security cooperation or institutionalized collective defense. Interdependence was of secondary importance to the nations, who praised the American leadership or criticized it, but after all, came to terms with it. Those, who opposed it, fell under the hammer of the very same liberal paradigm that promotes peace through cooperation and that identifies the U.S. national interests with indefinite hegemonic commitments.

If misperceptions of alliances prevail over perceptions of U.S. national interests, how does that affect coercion? One might argue that the logic of distinguishing defensive from offensive postures and defensive from offensive advantages applies to coercion. My concern is that the mentioned analogy is debatable. For instance, the Sino-American confrontation primarily presents a security dilemma, aside from the cultural clash between American liberal democracy and Chinese communism. Bipolar confrontation during the Cold War, quite the opposite, reflects the conflict of two irreconcilable ideological systems. Although ideology could provide a powerful motivation for using force, moral arguments have no place in politics among nations. Anarchy and selfish behavior prevent ethics from influencing great powers competition. American democracy differs from European democracy, and furthermore, opposes Asian communism and Russian Neo-Eurasianism. It is obvious, however, that national interests determine foreign policy decision-making, not ideology. For instance, relations between China and Russia range from strategic alliances to hidden Russian servility. European economic dependence on Beijing offers another example of dualistic behavior. Considering ideology and social narratives as sources of power behavior or weapons of foreign policy is deceptive. Moreover, such assumptions benefit U.S. adversaries such as China, which promotes a charming amalgam of Confucianism and the cultural legacy of the Dragon to counter the American dream.

A second problem arises from the intellectual frailty of liberal hawkism. Not only is the hegemonic temptation of shortsighted depreciation, but it also eliminates any preconditions for rational decision-making. It deviates U.S. Foreign Policy from its primary purposes and corrupts domestic security strategies in a way they cannot react to essential threats such as public polarization and the crisis of representation. Washington could simply assess alternative scenarios to the enlargement of NATO or military interventions in Taiwan to realize how detrimental hegemonic crusading is. Limits of American power do not originate from limits of coercion. In September 2001, Mearsheimer highlighted that America does not tolerate peer-competitors and that Washington should follow a strategy of offshore balancing to preclude the emergence of such competitor (Mearsheimer 2001, 46). However, the Bush doctrine endorsed a strategy of global war on terror and, regardless of its tools, purpose, impact, and relevancy to the American military presence in MENA. Misperceptions on terrorism lured policymakers to fight enemies against whom conventional military strategies and post-war regime building held less effectiveness. This is not to say that the United States lost the war on terror. Proponents of liberal hegemony simply abandoned it. Their ambitions clouded rational decision-making, and paradoxically, unipolarity became a victim of its previous successes. An outcome which Robert Jervis stated in his prediction that unipolarity might have then within it seeds if not of its own destruction, then at least of its modification (Jervis 2009, 213).

Sovereignty and principled realism

The proto-source of power, which privileges state actors over international institutions, is sovereignty. Liberal criticism often implies that realism rejects the sovereign equality of states and thus, advocates nationalism over cooperation within the international community (Ikenberry 2009, 75). Although nationalism empowers state actors, it does not represent a core aspect of realism but rather predetermines the right of great powers to shape world politics.

To begin, one should consider the theoretical gap between nationalism and realism. Kenneth Waltz points out that the sovereign state with fixed borders has proved to be the best organization for keeping peace internally and fostering the conditions for economic well-being (Waltz 2000, 51). The gap, therefore, is not simply philosophical but also political. The lack of sovereignty exposes non-state actors to objective institutional weaknesses, which prevent them from building armed forces and pursuing an independent foreign policy. With no military potential at hand, such entities do have clear perceptions of threats and do not possess the power to oppose them. To identify national interests with nationalism is to reject the right of a state actor to pursue an autonomous foreign policy. In addition, subversion of national interests to institutional entities is irrelevant to great powers competition. For instance, Europe, which has the most developed supranational architecture, cannot pursue a common foreign policy toward Russia because European institutions do not always reflect the national interests of Member States. Even now, when the threat of Russia is military in nature, European Union could not counter Moscow's influence without NATO. Ever since the dissolution of the Soviet Union, it has been futile to assert that Europe can contain Kremlin by promoting democracy and human rights. Although Russia is not the USSR, its strategic predominance in Eurasia is similar to the dominant American influence in Latin America. The European attempts to deter Moscow's influence in Belarus by promoting European values are as wise as a potential Russian strategy to export Orthodox tradition into Poland. Thus, effective containment of Russia in Europe leads to a rational necessity that Member States tend to avoid – establishing European armed forces within NATO. The vision of the European army does not contradict the concept of Europe, United in Diversity, either it would oppose NATO. The point is that the Member States, even those that strongly oppose partnership with Russia, reject the idea of delegating more sovereignty to supranational institutions, more particularly in the field of collective security.

In 1993, the United Kingdom conceived of no greater challenge than for the European Union to create an army that would duplicate NATO. London's concerns were not with another war in Europe but with the unavoidable loss of the *Rule Britannia* sovereignty. Two decades later, European leaders, who have always respected the British no, no, no, could have expected that the United Kingdom would leave the European Union. What happened after BREXIT was another logical result of what British decision-makers considered a primordial right to protect the UK's sovereignty, combined with the revival of Eurocentrism. One might argue that BREXIT is but a manifestation of British nationalism. Such arguments do not rely on rational assumptions, for they equalize national interests with nationalistic behavior and anti-globalism. The trouble is that the aforesaid equation applies today to the political attitudes of the most developed democracies and neglects one particularly essential part of national interests – security.

Was it possible for the United Kingdom to deter the rising influence of China within the European Union? London could not afford to compromise with economic and political dependence on Beijing as most EU Member States did. Two years after BREXIT, Britain, the United States, and Australia forged a mutual security pact – AUKUS – countering the increasing Chinese presence in APAC. AUKUS is a military pact which does not presume institutionalization or collective defense and within which London, Washington, and Canberra seek to build a nuclear cordon to deter Beijing. It is indeed a kiss between cousins, which reaffirms the realist assertion that nations have good reason to worry about their survival in a world where nation-states threaten each other (Mearsheimer 2011, 10).

Two years after Donald Trump won the 2016 U.S. Presidential Election, he declared himself a proud nationalist (Leidig 2019, 80). Although nationalism is a strong driving force for the foreign policy of wannabe realists, Robert Jervis specifies that President Trump's foreign policy that followed his campaign statement would be hard to square with realism and that it would provide test for many international theories (Jervis 2018, 5). In truth, President Trump's doctrine reshaped U.S. Foreign Policy in a way that it presented the realist paradigm with the ultimate test to explain the difference between nationalism and realpolitik. For the purpose of this book, I seek to peel off the infamous stamp that depicts President Trump's *principled nationalism* as realism. My criticism challenges the concept of *principled realism*, which some scholars attribute to the Trump doctrine (Chifu and Frunzeti 2019, 77). The working definition of principled realism explains it as the pursuit of realism (maximizing state power in an anarchic and competitive system) with a moral compass based on values (the principle part) (Kirkey 2018). I begin with a comparative study of both terms and assess theoretical challenges to realism.

The first test that realism faced was, paradoxically, *moralistic*. It is theoretically evident that the concept of principle realism in its very nature is an oxymoron. Ethics, principles, and moral codes might provide presidential candidates with populist legitimacy. However, they have no place in foreign policy. Principles cannot and should not replace national interests. To maximize the power of a state actor with a moral compass is an approach that combines realist assumptions with the liberal temptation of hegemony. The persuasive attempts of the Trump administration to shape a new Manifest Destiny out of Make America Great Again put the United States in a less favorable position in MENA. In his thoughtful criticism of the Trump doctrine, Muqtedar Khan deduces that President Trump's foreign policy was informed to some extent by neoconservative views about Islam and the Middle East (Khan 2018, 16). Was Washington ready to relocate its embassy to Jerusalem? Moreover, if it were, would it go forward alone against its Muslim allies by imposing a travel ban on Muslims coming to the United States? Here, the ambiguity of President Trump's moral compass overplayed U.S. national interests.

The second test for realism was *rational*. There was a non-rational contrast between President Trump's rapprochement with Russia and his efforts to withdraw from the Joint Comprehensive Plan of Action. Proponents of the Trump doctrine would argue that it defends American national interests in Asia and MENA. American rapprochement with Russia, however, created psychological preconditions for further deterioration of the Euro-Atlantic relations. Perceptions on U.S. Foreign Policy towards Russia, combined with the anti-NATO rhetoric of the Trump administration, ruptured the political nexus that existed between European and American decision-makers. It was an irrational delusion that the partial lack of shared burden within the Alliance would improve the relations between Washington and Moscow. A foreign policy that follows such a line reflected President Trump's misperceptions of Russian intentions to undermine the U.S. influence in Europe. Although Washington's claims for the shared burden were reasonable, rapprochement with Kremlin was inconsistent in that Russia encouraged right-wing movements in Europe and America. A potential withdrawal of the United States from the Alliance does not favor the U.S. national interests. The perfect evidence for that was another decision of the Trump administration to relocate U.S. troops from Germany to NATO's Eastern flank. The difference between callings for shared burden earlier when some Member States did not contribute enough and strategic military relocation to the Russian borders demonstrates a complete lack of rational decision-making. It was also a decisive discrepancy between rational understanding of American national interests and principled nationalism, which was willing to sacrifice the U.S. military presence in Europe to rapprochement with Russia. In truth, Europe owes more to the United States, which liberated Paris in 1944 and established NATO to deter the Soviet influence, than to an American president, who started a trade war with China and rapprochement with Russia without assessing the limits of U.S. national interests. Those, who warned President Trump against a potential Chinese retaliation or Russian fraud, were realists.

The final test was *structural*. A mature narrative of the Trump doctrine's supporters is that the President, in contrast to his predecessors, did not start a military conflict. Kenneth Waltz reminds us that a profound understanding of international politics requires awareness of how structures affect actions and outcomes in addition to man's innate lust for power (Waltz 1988, 617). Wars are natural and vary in frequency. Moreover, political forces that determine relations among nations act on an international level. Therefore, a realist approach to the Trump doctrine should better set up a theoretical framework which is autonomous from domestic or moral factors such as religion and domestic behavior. U.S. Foreign Policy should emerge and adapt to international anarchy if it wants to emerge victorious from politics among nations. Thus, it would be more rational and relevant to assume that the balance of power in the international system during Trump's presidency did not allow him to launch a military conflict. Principled nationalists should shed the veil of moralistic disguise which surrounds the Trump administration and lures a lot of realist scholars to support principled realism.

Donald Trump offers a rare example of an American President whose perceptions of international politics did not distinguish between self-motivation and structural fluctuations in the international system. His presidency, quite the opposite, was coeval with the decisive stage in the emergence of another pole, which finally accumulated the resources to challenge the American global dominance – China. Before the rise of China, the United States owed its survival as an independent and strong nation to the essential amalgam of democracy and realpolitik. In the aftermath of the Cold War, the symphony between the former and the latter ended with the dissolution of the Soviet Union. After September 11, polarization in American society and hegemonic temptations wasted the resources of Washington and created preconditions for overstretching. Democracy and foreign policy became faint and symbolically transformed into an idol rather than a source of inspiration for all nations. The overstretching after September 11 that two Presidential administrations considered the American foreign policy was a manifestation of the transition from a U.S.-dominated unipolar world to Sino-American bipolarity. By the time President Trump won the 2016 Presidential election, U.S. Foreign Policy had been pursuing moral principles, in the global image, Washington sought to transform the world. The resources the United States and its allies spent on regime changes and post-war building obscured their perceptions of the structure of international politics. Under such conditions, it was easier for President Trump to modify the global principles but harder to start a military conflict in the face of China's warlike policy. Principled nationalism was a valuable and effective instrument for manipulating public opinion at home and overseas, supporting the good old conservative values. The bad news is that principled nationalism, or as its proponents call it, principled realism, polarized Americans and undermined the trust of major U.S. allies in America. When Donald Trump lost the 2020 Presidential election, a crowd of angry principled nationalists tried to break into the Capitol and hang Vice-President Mike Pence. A less visible detail was that principled nationalism has become a consistent part of U.S. behavior and, combined with the hegemonic temptations of other policymakers, provoked the greatest failures of U.S. Foreign

Policy. This is particularly detrimental to U.S. national interests in Europe, APAC, and MENA, for in these regions, American influence today is at stake.

To sum up, principled realism is but a manifestation of nationalism. The concept itself does not fit common realist strategies such as offshore-balancing or containment. Moreover, it neglects perceptions and misperceptions in international politics and thus, misjudges the behavior of both American allies and adversaries. It identifies U.S. national interests simply with Make America Great Again, without elaborating further implications on U.S. Grand Strategy. Preserving the predominant position of the United States is the cornerstone of U.S. Foreign Policy. However, one should be aware that no state actor could threaten American global dominance without the support of China. Therefore, it is vital for the United States to deter the Chinese influence more, particularly in Europe and APAC. Beijing's economic and political interference in the affairs of American allies such as Germany, Japan, and Australia is the only option for China to challenge the U.S. national interests directly without risking military confrontation with Washington. Since a threat to U.S. Foreign Policy could emerge predominantly from China, the United States should struggle to prevent other negative consequences from the Trump doctrine. The bad news is that the doctrine deprived the United States of the ability to apply the oldest tool of its foreign policy, dating back to the Monroe doctrine: defending American national interests through expansion through a wisely structured grand strategy.

U.S. President James Monroe has made the first significant revolution in U.S. Foreign Policy, planting the seeds of modern American diplomacy. In his Seventh Annual Message to the U.S. Congress, the President issued a declaration that contained the expression of his doctrine. The Monroe doctrine was indeed a rule of policy growing out of the fundamental principles which the founding fathers of the United States laid down in their foreign policy (Moore 1921, 31). It has three elements: policy of non-colonization, abstention from Europe's balance-of-power system, and rejection of any European interference in America's backyard. The military upheavals in the Old World posed a challenge to U.S. Foreign Policy and overshadowed the strategic outcomes of America's geographical advantages. European powers maintained the multipolar world order through political unions and endless wars, for which they drained resources from their colonies. Peace was but a utopian dream in the minds of the European leaders who struggled for power.

In such a hostile international environment, the United States could achieve recognition of its foreign policy only through enclosing its own "backyard." It has become evident that the systematic strategy of President Monroe would make Washington a protector and to a certain extent – master of the republics of North and Central America (Pillet 1914, 133). The doctrine, however, was *not* uniformly imperialistic. Maintaining the U.S. influence in Central America was an objective process, not a product of American imperialism. Most of the former European colonies enjoyed the protection of Washington against their former metropoles. For others, however, the Monroe doctrine became a manifestation of cultural and economic imperialism. The ultimate purpose of the United States in that period was to devise a foreign policy strategy which could create a reasonable starting point for a more systematic approach to relations with Europe and the American republics. The Monroe doctrine was efficient because the challenges it faced – criticism in Europe and accusations of expansionism – were not detrimental to the U.S. national interests. Obstacles emerged when Washington's military involvements in its backyard imposed the need for the doctrine's modification.

Since, for a variety of reasons, it was more difficult for America to reshape than to defend the Monroe doctrine as long as the European powers did not interfere directly, Americans convinced Europeans not to press Washington's backyard to the point of the war. Besides its diplomatic approach, however, European empires demonstrated their military power in the colonial regions and challenged each other's to increase their prestige in the eyes of the Americans. The most drastic expression of the European power in America's backyard was the attempt of the declining Spanish empire to sustain its control over Cuba. Cultural mobilization turned out to be an obsolete tool for Spain to consolidate its colonies, and thus, the monarchy needed to restore its reputation for power. The Spanish feared that if their intervention failed, the colonial fiasco would put the United States more advantageous to control the region. At that point, President McKinley sought to deter Spanish imperialism and prevent further tensions with Europe. However, the territorial claims of Spain, combined with its policy of prestige, triggered the Monroe doctrine. Spain became a victim of what Morgenthau calls harmless foolishness – the prestige policy and shared cultural identity eventually lured the empire to believe that international politics reflect domestic affairs (Morgenthau 1985, 52).

For the majority of the European states, the Spanish-American war of 1898 has determined the place of the United States in the Great Powers family. The Monroe doctrine appears under the guise of isolationism, yet its theoretical core proves inconsistent with the powershifts of multipolarity and needs modification. America overcame the imperial ambitions of Spain and reshaped its foreign policy with the deeper intention to expand its influence worldwide. The international system at that time depended on the degree to which great powers feel threatened and on the perceptions of the latter for the rest of the world. Considerations appeared when another great power, a former European colony not in possession of monarchical tradition or Europocentric aspirations, challenged those perceptions and succeeded in its attempt to achieve moral and military victory against Spain. Henceforth, peaceful powershifts would be possible only if the United States supported the balance-of-power consensus among the other major powers. The foremost purpose of the Monroe doctrine was to demonstrate to the rest of the world a wisely structured foreign policy aimed to defend the U.S. national interests.

To apply the Monroe doctrine today would presume prevention of any preconditions, which could benefit the Chinese influence in APAC. However, neither principle realism nor proponents of liberal hegemony could negate the advantage of China to expand its influence without fearing a potential strike at the heart of its power – Beijing. With Russia dominating Eurasia and North Korea building its nuclear arsenal, the United States cannot reshape the balance of power in Asia, even if it deploys nuclear submarines in Australia. Principled realists tried to undermine Beijing's influence by starting a dialogue with North Korea, hoping that talks with Pyongyang would tilt the balance of power in favor of America. Liberals, on the other hand, offered resistance to Beijing by backing every nation which opposed China's global influence. It is of this concern that both Presidents Obama and Trump intervened in APAC on the side of Taiwan and that U.S. Foreign Policy so largely aligned with that of the United Kingdom and Australia. From the establishment of the United Kingdom – United States of American Agreement (UKUSA) in 1946, a primary objective of the Five Eyes has become to sustain the balance of power in APAC. The United States opposed any actor that sought to gain ascendancy over its adversaries and consequently threatened the West Coast and the sovereign right of America to defend its national security.

Polarity and the unipolar syndrome

The sovereign right of a state actor to exercise coercion in the anarchic system of international politics is an objective and natural expression of the constant struggle for power among nations. Realism assumes that the distribution of capabilities largely determines what the behavior of the actors in the system will be, and thus, polarity is a materialist concept, which refers to the number of great powers, not to the coalition structure among them (Buzan 2012, 125). While it is easy to imagine that polarity depends on great powers competition, the end of the Cold War presented the realist paradigm with another ultimate test: unipolarity. The most profound form of criticism derives from the assumption that post-Cold War realist explanations have become less determined, coherent, and distinctive and that the gloomy predictions of realist scholars undermine realism itself (Moravcsik and Legro 1999, 6). In the aftermath of the Cold War, however, the United States enjoyed its global predominance and, being involved in global commitments, did not define the limits of its power. The gloomiest prediction, which overshadows liberal criticism, is Kenneth Waltz's ascertainment that the number of great states in the world is so limited that two acting in concert or one state driving for hegemony could alter the balance of power (Waltz 1964, 901). With the collapse of the Soviet Union, the United States became less concerned with Asia. China, on the other side, did not hold such importance to U.S. Foreign Policy as Europe did. Furthermore, the moral aspiration of the United States subverted its foreign policy in a measure to which U.S. national interests aligned with Washington's global commitments. Yet, due to that subversion, American policymakers could not detect the detrimental effects of their hegemonic temptations. Initially, the end of the Cold War was a victory for the United States in a measure beyond which no other nation could challenge the American primacy. However, the fall of the Soviets unleashed another temptation, which affected the behavior of the United States – the unipolar syndrome.

Not only in Europe and Asia but also on a global level, U.S. Foreign Policy has identified moral aspirations with political behavior. We can trace the origins of the unipolar syndrome in Waltz's warning that overwhelming power, in international politics, repels and leads others to try to balance against it, and thus, unbalanced power constitutes a danger even if it is the American power (Waltz 1991, 670). Even where foreign policy doctrines operate without facing significant opposition, as they did during Bill Clinton's Presidency, the vital American interests have little to share with the liberal hegemony. Washington has acted decisively and unilaterally in Iraq and Afghanistan, but policymakers succumbed to the temptation of aligning national interest with moral aspirations. In terms of actions, the crusade against global terrorism predetermined American misperceptions of foreign policy by following abstract universalistic strategies. Thus, non-rational attitudes clouded U.S. Foreign Policy and deprived U.S. decision-makers of the challenges to American national interests, such as China's rise, Russian nationalism, and cyber warfare. In addition, the moralistic overstretch of U.S. Foreign Policy misjudged important lessons from the Cold War, such as the Soviet invasion of Afghanistan in 1979. Instead of adapting American politics to unipolarity, the struggle for liberal hegemony sacrificed one particular aspect of the American uniqueness: anti-imperialism. Liberal scholars will argue that American imperialism dates back to the Monroe doctrine. The Roosevelt corollary, however, refutes that claim.

It was crucial for the United States not to stagnate its foreign policy by sticking to the Monroe doctrine without calculating the risk of war between the great powers. Thus, in his annual message delivered to the Congress on December 5,

1904, President Theodore Roosevelt issued a corollary to the doctrine, warning that America would exercise power as a last resort to ensure that Western nations meet their financial obligations and to prevent further interference in the American nations' family (Meiser 2010, 20). Neoliberal scholars tend to assume that the Roosevelt corollary is an entirely new principle, which epitomizes the big stick view in foreign policy and perverts the Monroe doctrine (Ricard 2006, 17). I reject this view for two reasons. First, such perceptions of U.S. Foreign Policy misinterpret its doctrinal nature. A distinctive aspect of American politics, particularly regarding political relations with other nations, is that national interests are central to foreign policy. American decision-makers define their strategies not in terms of power but of vital interests, national security, and economic prosperity. Second, each Presidential doctrine illustrates and vindicates the use of force explicitly and rationally. A doctrine's aspects derive from natural political, economic, and cultural necessities and incarnate objective political actions such as defending U.S. allies and deterring U.S. adversaries. The Roosevelt corollary embodies three pillars: defending U.S. political and economic interests in the Western hemisphere, protecting the U.S. national security from potential aggression, justification of the American foreign policy in Latin America. It is but a corollary, which shocked the European powers, once the United States had accomplished what Europe could not: expansion without colonization. It was the nature of Roosevelt's corollary to *disguise* the use of coercion by conducting mediation between other great powers or attending intergovernmental forums such as the Algeciras Conference. However, while America globalized its foreign policy in the Western hemisphere, objective events threatened the American national interests overseas. It was the Great War which posed the first global dilemma for the United States.

Therefore, the unipolar syndrome occurs when the unipole fails to adapt or refuses to comply with the circumstances under which unipolarity operates. Robert Jervis defines three such conditions, which are applicable to the post-Cold War reality: high costs of war, great benefits of peace, and the dominance of liberal (not capitalist) values (Jervis 2009, 201). Once the unipole ceases to comply with those conditions, its predominance is bound to fail. History shows that eventually, great powers succumb to that temptation. Realism believes that the essential reasons for these processes are the selfishness of human nature and the lack of international sovereign to preside over state actors. To say that the unipole is destined to dethrone history is to repeat the USSR's utopic mistake. In 1992, U.S. Foreign Policy and unipolarity were identical, and Washington alone had the power to manipulate the balance of power. However, the retreat from that power position began in 2001, when the United

States blinked the operating conditions of unipolarity and traded them for illusionary omnipotence.

Washington's expansion in the years after September 11 illustrates the demise of unipolarity. U.S. interventions in MENA seemed to defend American national interests rather than export values. The concept of preemptive strike put the mark of success on the American troops. U.S. decision-makers failed to realize that the United States should not bear the moralistic mission to rebuild broken regimes and promote liberal democracy among societies who resist the liberal ideology. Moreover, the subsequent political, military, and cultural impact of the liberal crusades undermined the American global influence; thus, unipolarity itself could no longer benefit the United States. The unipolar syndrome has three essential symptoms.

American predominance is more than a combination of values and culture. They are indeed powerful tools, but Robert Jervis specifies that the distribution of most forms of soft power will roughly correlate with the distribution of economic and military resources values (Jervis 2009, 192). Therefore, the first symptom appears when a superpower seeks to reshape the balance of power through alternative sources of capability such as values. In the first years after the Cold War, the United States witnessed the favorable striving for liberal democracy that unfolded in the post-Soviet space. Since the 90s, the United States has supported Bulgaria, Romania, Poland, and Hungary to join NATO and the EU. The result of democracy promotion appeared to Central and Eastern Europe as a chance to change their civilizational choice. The enlargement of NATO and EU simply translocated the Berlin wall and transformed it into a post-Soviet barrier. With democracy established in the post-Soviet states, Washington's perceptions of international politics changed. U.S. Foreign Policy fell into the moralistic trap of democracy promotion, believing that the struggle for power and its history ended with the Cold War. American politics then aimed to universalize the export of values in other parts of the world, seeking to identify U.S. national interests with global democratization. Throughout the post-Cold War period, American decision-makers misinterpreted the influence of international anarchy and defined the nation's foreign policy in moralistic terms. Where America has found the opportunity to export values, as in MENA, Washington's moral crusade derived from the presumption that domestic perception of democracy could inspire other nations to convert their political culture. For instance, in the wake of the Arab Spring, when the United States sought to increase its commitments to the region, a few considered the potential ideological overstretch. Comparing the most developed democracy in the world – America, with the political culture of MENA's societies, the Obama administration failed to assess that they were inconsistent. In addition, ideological overstretch did not benefit American national interests. Instead, democracy promotion in the region predetermined the emergence of polarization in American society. It was a process similar to the one that triggered European revolutions that forced the decline of Europe two hundred years ago. To cure the symptom of ideological overstretch, the easiest path for the United States, in contrast to the European powers earlier, was not to intervene in regions where non-state actors such as the Taliban and Al-Qaeda had a particular advantage in terms of ideology or military tactics. Washington, however, sought to preserve its global dominance through smart strategies, which deprived democracy promotion of its universal validity. Even if the use of force garnished the export of values, Washington refused to recognize that regime building did not benefit U.S. national interests. America had the strength to fight and win all wars, but it could no longer reshape the balance of power through peacebuilding as it did before September 11.

Although U.S. Foreign Policy is central to world politics, American decision-makers coin their decisions not by choice – to promote democracy, to enlarge NATO, deter China and Russia, and respect their commitments. The inert legacy of unipolarity presses them to pursue a policy of values. The international environment forces Washington to seek solutions, reshape its strategies and redefine its vital interests, from which it has retreated. U.S. Foreign Policy still follows the unipolar logic of American exceptionalism as a supreme value, which jumps beyond the limits of American power because it obscured rational perceptions of international anarchy. In one sense, democracy promotion originates from the utopic vision that peace can forever replace the struggle for power among nations. In another sense, however, one should be aware that the philosophical and moral attitudes of general validity did not save European colonial powers from imminent decline. America's biggest advantage was that it achieved expansion without colonization. Ideological overstretch undermined that advantageous position of the United States for two reasons. First, power politics is a natural force that drives political relations among democracies and non-democratic nations. Therefore, even if democracy has won the Cold War, the states did not cease to struggle for power. The unprecedented domination of America thus foreclosed the future competition between the former and rising China. Second, even if we construct a moralistic vision of the international system, where democracy is good, and the rest of the regimes are evil, could we assume that the former can eradicate or at least convert the latter completely?

The Roman Empire shaped its foreign expansion policy by dividing people into citizens of the world, Romans, and uncivilized barbarians. The essential aspect of Rome's strategy was to assimilate the cultures it conquered for centuries. The unipolar syndrome emerged when the Empire identified its domination with Romanization – political incorporation through enfranchisement and institutional changes under the Roman rule (Woolf 2013, 118). Rome had the power to expand and defend ist outposts but slowly lost its perceptions of domination. Romans, who considered the Mediterranean Sea a lake, were tempted to identify Roman predominance with universal hegemony. The Roman Imperial Cult marked the final step of that unfortunate decadence. Similarly, to equalize American global dominance with liberal hegemony is to tie the U.S. national interests with the indestructible chains of an abstract Manifest Destiny, which has no place in the foreign policy of a rational actor. Although the Manifest generates strong motivation for populist leaders and their electors, it conceals power politics under the mask of liberal, conservative, or pacifist politics. Moral goes under the name of politics, while power strategies presume the use of force, and thus, history fulfills the prediction of Waltz, who warned that with benign intent, the United States has behaved, and until its power is brought into a semblance of balance, will continue to behave in ways that annoy and frighten other (Waltz 1991, 669).

Ideological overstretch leads to the second syndrome – misperceptions of war. Kenneth Waltz introduces a thoughtful comparison between Marxism and liberalism when stating that both have linked the outbreak of war or the prevalence of peace to the internal qualities of the states (Waltz 1988, 617). However, the Cold War remained cold due to bipolarity. Survival and self-preservation were central to the foreign policy of both the United States and the USSR. Domestic ideologies and European struggle for intergovernmentalism have little effect on conflict resolution and peacebuilding. It is tricky to say that the unipolar world order presumes led to hierarchy, where democracy and international institutions will shape world politics under the eye of Uncle Sam. Such a vision of international politics still enjoys considerable support among many American and European policymakers though it nourishes domestic polarization between right-wing and left-wing movements in America. Wherever Washington has intervened in support of democracy, the United States has chosen to defend its national interests through regime change and foreign policy decisions, which followed the moralistic vision of regime building. The reality that Washington refused to accept is that war and peace are manifestations of the constant struggle for power between international actors. The United States should defend its national interests regarding survival and self-preservation, not ideology. Although the Presidential administrations after the Cold War opposed each other, U.S. Foreign Policy followed three similar lines. The administration of President George W. Bush represented an amalgam of unilateralism, hawkism, and regime change. President Trump's doctrine refers to principled nationalism, which, as discussed above, embodies a paradox of modification of the liberal agenda and unilateral actions. The doctrines of Presidents Clinton and Obama offer an example of an idealistic foreign policy approach that endorses a strategy of combination between military force and the promotion of values. The most evident similarity is that survival and self-preservation are of secondary importance to the post-Cold War foreign policy doctrines.

One might argue that no state actor could challenge the United States in that period. However, Robert Jervis points out that hegemony magnifies the sense of threat: American power is great but far from unlimited (Jervis 2006, 12). Moreover, I assume that omnipotence itself does not preclude self-preservation. In 2003, the U.S.-led coalition dethroned Saddam Hussein, maintaining control over Iraq, and thus, the UN faced American omnipotence. Military obligations in the region and the lack of presumable WMD implied that Washington should bear the responsibility for the post-war building of the Iraqi regime. Policymakers, who opposed a further military presence in Iraq, insisted that national interests prevail over moral commitments. The ultimate dilemma was should Washington sacrifice more American lives and even its security to a region which opposed the very concept of liberal democracy? If the United States withdrew from Iraq and Afghanistan in 2005 or 2007, were there any subsequent risks to its national interests? These questions lead us to the point where international qualities such as ideology and domestic attitudes overshadow rational decisions and the struggle for survival. Without nuclear weapons on Iraqi soil, Baghdad was just a failed regime. However, the war on terror guided U.S. Foreign Policy for two decades at very high costs.

The final and perhaps most destructive syndrome concerns peace. Liberalism criticism challenges Waltz's theory for his "reductionist" argument that nuclear weapons can explain war-proneness in the context of polarity (Lebow 1994, 254). Similar theoretical considerations might apply to the post-Cold War reality if the Trump administration has not withdrawn from the Joint Comprehensive Plan of Action and if the President has not suspended the Intermediate Nuclear Forces Treaty with Russia. Defensive and offensive realists have consistently agreed that nuclear weapons have little utility for offensive purposes unless only one side in a conflict has them (Mearsheimer 2007, 76). The American withdrawal from both agreements is a perfect example of nuclear behavior, which could warm up even the coldest confrontation. Nuclear peace, however, is not obsolete. Kenneth Waltz reminds us that even under the nuclear stability of the Cold War, peace has become a privilege of nuclear powers (Waltz 1995, 11). Thus, nuclear peace serves the national interest of nuclear actors. Yet, liberal concerns over the deterrent power of nuclear weapons could argue that Waltz's argument does not apply to the unipolar world order.

Primarily, the unipolar syndrome makes superpowers less rational. This is not to say that America has become reckless and thoughtless enough to launch a nuclear attack on Russia. In 1994, the threat of nuclear apocalypse seemed to have passed, and the United States indulged its misperceptions of WMD proliferation. Washington stood at the beginning of the unipolar era, neglecting that the end of the Cold War did not transform international anarchy into an abstract network of international entities. When the Soviet Union collapsed, U.S. Foreign Policy lost its rational view on nuclear proliferation and delegated its trust to international organizations. Furthermore, the United States could not predict, even when transnational terrorist networks threatened to get nukes, that nuclear disarmament would not benefit American national interests. Only the power of nuclear weapons, which no international actor can deny, could allow Washington to defend its nuclear interests. In 2003, the Bush administration involved America in a preemptive war against Saddam Hussein for the same reasons, although uncertain to the President, Washington was willing to limit its nuclear arsenal in a U.S.-dominated unipolar world. Iraq threatened the balance of power in MENA, and it was a rational decision to eliminate the risk. However, it was irrational to build democracy in Iraq, although the absence of WMD turned out to be a major intelligence failure. In short, President Bush pursued a rational target for the wrong reasons. Not only did the American crusade harm the U.S. national interests in MENA were further shattered through nuclear talks with Iran and North Korea. The struggle for nuclear disarmament also has detrimental effects, for which there is a perfect example of bipolarity: the Presidency of Jimmy Carter.

President Carter's doctrine offers a rare example of a concept which outlived the Cold War and occupied a central place in American foreign policy: *oil diplomacy*. The Carter doctrine proclaims that the United States would use all measures, including military force, to deter outside aggression in the Persian Gulf (Leffler 1983, 245). It is fair to say that great powers competition reaffirms the realist assumption that the most powerful state actors are rational in their actions and their struggle for the distribution of resources. Oil diplomacy provides objective justification for U.S. Foreign Policy required to launch interventions in the Middle East and maintain control over regions of crucial importance to the petroleum industry. With the assumption that the United States and its adversaries exercise offensive coercion to acquire common resources such as oil and that the distribution of resources benefits national interests, my book joins the realist consensus that wars, coming from the planned culmination of one's foreign policy do not hold superpowers under any moral obligations. A further explanation of the Carter doctrine will prove this hypothesis.

Carter's doctrine proved decisive to the U.S. – Soviet competition and the American perceptions of bipolarity. Following the Soviet invasion in Afghanistan, any attempt by Washington to revive the concept of positive coexistence and cooperation between the superpowers was fraught with utopic idealism and irrational pacifism. Instead, a more rational and structural view of the U.S. Foreign Policy focused on oil diplomacy and confrontation with the Soviet Union provided Washington with a far more productive outcome. During his years in the White House, Jimmy Carter attempted to prevent any chance that the Cold War become hot. A structural transformation has taken shape in the tools, strategies, and philosophy of U.S. Foreign Policy, with major implications for the future of bipolarity and energy dependence. President Carter also revisited Nixon's legacy of détente. Brzezinski rejected Kissinger's assumption that the alternative to détente would be a nuclear war and presumed that the Soviet Union would be deterred regardless of the state of Soviet-American relations (Schweigler 1978, 83). Since the emergence of Brzezinski's concept, especially after he was appointed National Security Advisor of President Carter, Washington has experienced major difficulties balancing the risk of nuclear holocaust with U.S. vital interests overseas. The old generation of paradigms, such as containment, nuclear diplomacy, and Kissinger's détente, has been challenged by the Brezhnev doctrine and its ability to limit American global commitments and negate U.S. strategic advantages. The fear of mutual assured destruction dominated the American policymakers and prevented the United States from decisive actions against the Soviet interferences in the Western hemisphere. Moreover, nuclear scenarios prevailed over rational leadership and thus, blocked the rational perceptions of decision-makers. Brzezinski's détente provided President Carter with various strategic options to refocus U.S. Foreign Policy from the apocalyptic vision of nuclear holocaust to another tool of pressure over the Soviets – human rights.

Instead of providing universal support for all, Washington employed human rights as a yardstick by which America could define the limits of its support. While President Nixon signed the First Strategic Arms Limitations Treaty to minimize the possibility of nuclear escalation, Carter dreamed that SALT II would lead to nuclear disarmament. However, unlike his predecessor, President Carter's strategy underestimated the Soviet leadership. Instead of modifying his doctrine according to the American expectations, Brezhnev hampered the Carter doctrine by claiming that protecting human rights worldwide presumed observing them at home. The Soviet rhetoric affected American policymakers, who were more divided over racial segregation than their predecessors were. In the past, USSR abstained from criticizing the United States on human rights because the dissident movements in Poland and Czechoslovakia disrupted the potency of the Soviet leadership. After the Prague Spring and following the ratification of the Helsinki Accords, however, the Soviet propaganda endorsed a smarter approach: discarding some of the orthodox Stalinist shibboleths and replacing them with anti-Western narratives. Such changes, combined with constant recall about the American violation of the Helsinki Accords and racial discrimination, created a strong anti-American sentiment and shaped the belief that the United States could not supervise human rights. Kremlin's actions, combined with the Soviet-Afghan war, triggered an erosion of confidence in the durability of President Carter's doctrine.

Therefore, it is a resentment for the liberal assumptions that Waltz's reductionist argument proves valid for the unipolar system. While in the 90s, the false promise of nuclear disarmament sounded rationally and logically, it now stands untenable against the Chinese nuclear ambitions and AUKUS. What is prominent for the course, which AUKUS is to take in the post-pandemic future, is a war-prone nuclear scenario. The United States, the United Kingdom, and Australia isolated Europe from the security pact. Proponents of liberal hegemony could dig into their delusions by assuming that the Australian suspension of the French submarine deal was but intended humiliation for Europe. As it joined the Five Eyes in 1956, does Australia not have the right to uphold its national interests and self-preservation? Does the United Kingdom not have the right to maintain favored relations with the Commonwealth over Europe? Liberal institutionalists failed to understand the argument of Waltz that nuclear weapons have not altered the anarchic structure of international political system (Waltz 2000, 5). Nuclear disarmament, nuclear behavior, and nuclear diplomacy result from objective and natural conditions, which exceed the foreign policy of nuclear powers and refer to international anarchy. Each nuclear power pursues and executes its policy, and it is groundless to assume that the United States and France will respect any moral obligations such as their historical friendship in the face of rising China. The French policy of sustaining good trading relations with China predetermined Europe's economic dependence on Beijing. The United States, quite the opposite, seeks to contain the Chinese influence in APAC by enhancing cooperation with major U.S. allies such as Australia and Japan. Thus, nuclear disarmament in a nuclear age is as irrational to foreign policy as is hegemonic temptations. Policymakers who oppose nuclear strategies and encourage diplomacy in practice admit that nuclear sovereignty is a burden rather than a privilege. My concern is that the Iranian Nuclear Program and North Korea's nuclear reactor undermine the validity of such presumptions. I assume that decision-makers, who seek nuclear disarmament through the export of democracy, succumb to the temptation of applying their delusive visions to American foreign policy and international politics in general. In reality, nuclear demilitarization and export of values are opposed to the essential core of U.S. Foreign Policy and reject its primary purpose – to defend American national interests.

Endurance and misperceptions on power

The sense of survival and self-preservation are as ancient and distinctive features of human nature as are war and peace among people. From the times of the Old World through Classical Antiquity and Ancient China, humans have been fighting for their survival as beings and political animals. However, identifying endurance that originates from human nature with the endurance of state actors is methodologically and empirically misleading. To remind, Kenneth Waltz highlights that international politics are autonomous structures and can be understood only if the effects of the structure are added to the unit-level explanation of traditional realism (Waltz 1988, 616). It is only since the collapse of the Soviet Union that liberal institutionalism questioned Waltz's approach and assumed that balance of power calculations are trumped by imperatives, rising from political democratization, global trade liberalization, belief systems, international law, and institutions (Moravcsik and Legro 2001, 80). For thirty years, IR scholars have struggled in vain to establish a system of universal values by which to suppress the rational instinct of states to guarantee their survival and self-preservation through maintaining territorial integrity and autonomy (Mearsheimer 2001, 16). The strategies of regime building, domestic change, persuasion, and global institutionalization still occupy a considerable place in U.S. Foreign Policy though policymakers seek to revisit them. International entities still issue declarations, resolutions, and directives through state actors who violate them actively. In truth, it all ended on September 11, when America was under attack. Both institutional commitments and political democratization did not benefit the United States in responding to the terrorist attacks through a preemptive strike. In 2003, both international law and international institutions undermined the American right to self-defense and supported the claims of the United Nations that Operation Iraqi Freedom was illegal and broke the UN Charter (MacAskill and Borger 2004). Thus, liberal assumptions, which sought to determine the balance of power through intergovernmental institutionalization of American national interests, failed to protect American sovereignty. Even after Washington toppled Saddam Hussein and backed the Arab Spring to oppose dictatorships in MENA, liberal institutionalists believed that U.S. Foreign Policy should prioritize soft power to fight global terrorism and promote political democratization. Therefore, what happened, particularly after the emergence of ISIS, appeared as a direct consequence of the democratization and liberalization of MENA: survival and self-preservation remained central to American foreign policy, but perceptions of the balance of power degraded. Consequently, four basic misperceptions of power politics affected the U.S. ability to intervene and negate the influence of its peer competitors and more particularly, proved the assertion of

Robert Jervis that the power of our preexisting beliefs shapes the way we see new information (Jervis 2017, 31).

The first problem refers to the preservation of power. By preservation, I mean the policy of a state actor, which seeks to defend the status-quo (Snyder 1991, 20). The military conflicts after the Cold War have shifted the balance of power in favor of major American adversaries such as Russia and China. Many U.S.-led military interventions sought to sustain the status quo by preserving American power. That strategy, however, lacked rational foundations because the United States needed support for its military operations. Joseph Nye is right in his assumption that the military victory in Iraq has confirmed the new world order (Nye 2003, 60). However, it was not a viable purpose for the U.S. strategy to rebuild and repair broken governments. What makes it implausible is that in most of the conflicts, the United States did not seek to defend the status quo but to expand its influence beyond the Cold War's victory. The expansion was not a condition for American survival or self-preservation but a geopolitical caprice of a Presidential administration which could afford to pay the high costs of war and offer moral arguments in support of their war on terror. In one week, the European economy would collapse if France invaded Libya alone to defend its former colony. What was particularly detrimental to U.S. Foreign Policy was Washington's willingness to spend billions of dollars in MENA deserts and thus enter into economic dependence on rising China.

Preservation of power, however, does not presume isolationism. When regional conflicts threaten vital American interests, Washington should intervene to prevent the actor's foreign policy pre-orientation in favor of China or Russia. The point is that since the end of the Cold War, the United States has not been able to steer the ideological development of minor state actors. Washington tried to promote liberal democracy in Afghanistan, Cuba, Venezuela, and Libya, but neither of those strategies favored the status-quo's preservation. In most cases, China or Russia opposed the American influence, or worse – the domestic regime itself degenerated into a failed state. The argument of Robert Jervis provides us with a reasonable explanation of American foreign policy towards non-democratic regimes: a state may not see the extent to which its actions will upset the status quo (Jervis 2017, 53). Ideological involvement and regime change invoke two fundamental challenges that U.S. Foreign Policy will continue to face in regions that have died or simply do not work. The first challenge arises from the outright support for democracy in authoritarian regimes that promote anti-Americanism.

In most cases, conversion to democracy requires either military intervention or at least political commitments to the opposition. It is necessary to highlight that democracy-building in the post-Cold War period seldom benefits U.S. Foreign Policy. One might argue that Central and Eastern Europe could serve as an example of political democratization. The democratization of post-socialist states such as Bulgaria, Romania, North Macedonia, Croatia, and Poland, however, expresses the result of their accession to NATO. Furthermore, the great majority of those countries, which remained on the other side of the Iron Curtain, enjoyed democracy before World War II. For the United States, without whose support Central and Eastern Europe would never enter the Alliance and might have become part of the Eurasian Union, political democratization benefited the American presence in the region. As for the Arab Spring, the revolutions were an irrational risk to amplify the American military presence and expand liberal democracy. For America, it was a chance to topple authoritarian regimes and fight terrorism. Even so, it is untenable to assume that the purpose of U.S. military interventions in MENA was to maintain the status quo. The United States might have perceived its involvement as a pillar of the status quo. Still, it eventually upset it to an extent beyond which Washington tended to confuse power policy with democracy building. The second challenge refers to the scope of the American commitments. Preservation of power represents the balance between isolationism and over-engagement and, thus, precludes changes in the distribution of power itself.

When Beijing threatened Washington's interests in the South China Sea, the United States sent an aircraft carrier without planning further intervention in APAC. It was a rational perception, which indicated that America supports the sovereignty of Taiwan but also sticks to its cooperation with Japan and Australia without further plans to restore the Sino-American Mutual Defense Treaty. The annexation of Crimea in 2014, quite the opposite, marked the limits of the Western aspirations to the post-Soviet region. The defeat of Ukraine was complete, and Europeans sought to predict what the future Russian strategy would be. From Moscow's point of view, a potential accession of Kyiv to NATO could pose an immediate threat to Russian military security. The United States provided military and financial support for Ukraine as tensions with Russia escalated, and thus, Washington did what it could to prevent another Russian intervention. However, Ukraine demanded to become a Member State of the Alliance, which, to a greater extent, would reshape the balance of power in Eastern Europe. NATO has had enough history of integrating post-communist states and conducted several military operations in the post-Soviet region. Yet, it is arguable that the accession of Ukraine would put the Alliance, and more particularly the United States, in a more advantageous position than Russia.

The second misperception refers to maximizing power. It is cynical to suggest that it is the nuclear scenario, which should prevent the United States from developing its nuclear arsenal, or that nuclear disarmament is for the sake of self-preservation and survival. Considerations of why America should get more bombs and why Washington should advocate nuclear bans with the irrational promise for global peace will lead U.S. Foreign Policy to the Soviet failures. Mearsheimer points out that in the nuclear age, great powers must have a nuclear deterrent that can survive a nuclear attack against it, as well as formidable conventional forces (Mearsheimer 2001, 3). The United States and its adversaries could not achieve MAD so quickly. For instance, China pursues political and economic influence in Asia, not similar to Russian foreign policy in Eurasia. The foremost purpose of Beijing and Moscow is to shift the American influence in their backyard. However, American power, especially after AUKUS, presents a direct challenge to Beijing's national security. An eventual Chinese intervention in Taiwan will end with a complete victory for Beijing. If China maintains a permanent military presence on the island, it will directly threaten Guam, the Philippines, and the North Pacific. On the other side, NATO seems stable but weakened by temporary tensions between the allies. Western powers believe that Russia does not have the economic potential to intervene again in Eastern Europe, although a divided Ukraine might fit better Russian interests than the chaos which could emerge from another annexation. Those perceptions, however, cannot predict Russian foreign policy after Putin. The Russian President has a dualistic vision of the post-Soviet space. Putin wants to take over the former Soviet satellites, not members of either EU or NATO. For the rest of the post-Soviet space, Putin's strategy seeks to influence the decision-making process in Bulgaria, Romania, and North Macedonia through gas policy and soft power rather than conquer them.

However, Putin's grand design will not last forever. The gullible belief that the heir of Putin would not pursue a war-like approach to NATO due to the Russian economic instability is irrational for a simple reason, which Stephen Walt defines as "poisoned relations with Russia" (Walt 2018, 10). Moreover, Europe embarked upon a policy of building European armed forces, which is likely to succeed if France and Germany reach a consensus about the shape of the EU's military identity. Both states hold the primary position in Europe after BREXIT. The French attitude towards AUKUS is the strongest motivation for Europe to complete its military and political self-identity. By supporting Europe and deterring Russia, the United States might have hoped to prevent China from economically affecting European policy. However, the American expectations of a friendly Europe, which will take, at some point, the responsibility of its defense, could ruin if the European allies decide to establish EU's military forces outside NATO. The potential success of this seemingly untenable scenario could become real due to three reasons: European economic dependence on China, right-wing extremism that inspires anti-Americanism in Europe, and Russian gas policy. Therefore, the United States should reinvent the tools of nuclear diplomacy and align them with the essential priorities of American national interests. Any agreement that could prevent America from sustaining nuclear deterrent and conventional forces would be detrimental to the U.S. status of great power, which presumes the possession of sufficient military resources for conventional warfare.

Nuclear diplomacy owes its success to the devastating power of nuclear weapons. Mearsheimer gives a punctual definition of great power: a state, which possesses sufficient military assets to put up a serious fight in an all-out conventional war against the most powerful state in the world forces (Mearsheimer 2001, 3). Therefore, war and peace are tools that serve great powers' foreign policy. Successes and benefits from nuclear diplomacy are the perfect examples of the empirical robustness of Mearsheimer's definition. A logical question arises from the post-Cold War era: should nuclear diplomacy be of an offensive or defensive nature? My definition of nuclear diplomacy expresses a well-known axiom in international politics – do not confront a nuclear power unless you have nuclear weapons. Any realist scholar, who has considered the MAD scenario a plausible reality, should note that self-preservation and survival prevail over reckless behavior and nuclear holocaust.

My conclusion is that nuclear diplomacy is an offensive approach that would benefit the balance of power in the post-pandemic age. By offensive nature, I mean an approach that advocates nuclear proliferation among state actors. In a system of nuclear bipolarity, getting more nukes is the safest way to deter your adversary, or as Waltz points out, power begs to be balanced and nuclear balance means stability (Waltz 2012, 2). However, my concern is that nuclear powers should limit nuclear diplomacy to *states* only. Realism believes that states are rational actors. In the aftermath of September 11, non-state actors such as the transnational terrorist networks seek to obtain a nuclear arsenal. Although state actors hold primacy in international politics, nuclear powers should not ignore the threat of nuclear terrorism. North Korea can get the bomb and maintain control over its nuclear arsenal. The terrorists, however, could establish a nuclear Caliphate, or worse – could attack another state to achieve a considerable impact of their actions. This entire theoretical scenario could become a reality if nuclear powers try to suppress or reject the irrational nature of terrorist strategies. Graham Allison warns about Al-Qaeda, or another group, getting a nuclear weapon and explode it to destroy a target (Allison 2010, 106). Obviously, after the U.S. withdrawal from Afghanistan, Al-Qaeda could regroup again, or the Taliban regime could lead to the rise of another ISIS. What if Pakistan decides to support Kabul and the Taliban, who have maintained close ties with terrorist networks? By neglecting the threat of nuclear terrorism, state actors underestimate the ideological aspirations of radicalized extremists, who, as Allison assumes, could strike a city without making rational calculations for the outcomes of their actions.

Choosing between conventional and hybrid warfare, which is a prevalent concept in Europe, is to say that both are equally destructive. I reject this view. Minor actors might enjoy their outcomes of using soft power, but great powers are determined largely based on their relative military capability (Mearsheimer 2001, 3). The extent of Mearsheimer's assumption about U.S. Foreign Policy after the Cold War is central to understanding the Sino-American competition. Unlike the Soviet challenge, it presumes a conventional approach rather than ideological containment to a greater extent. Deterring Chinese communism is not enough, especially after the military reform of President Xi Jinping. Xi's military policy resulted in a complete institutional, organizational, and operative restructuring of the People's Liberation Army (PLA) (Sanders and Wuthnow 2017, 3). It is evident that the United States also needs a major military and intelligence reform, which will inevitably lead to an armed race with Beijing. However, any U.S. President, who attempts to proceed, will face considerable opposition. The disapproval will come from policymakers, which are natural supporters of democracy building and regime change and oppose larger military spending. The strongest resistance, however, belongs to those who moralize conflicts, blaming the realists for not distinguishing between good and bad states (Mearsheimer 2001, 13). Their disapproval expresses their optimism that the liberal world order could survive China's rise. To agree with such an optimistic view is to accept the delusion that the world is still unipolar. Unfortunately, most policymakers and electors tend to consider China a successor of the Soviet Union, a perception that is far from clear and rational.

Demonstration of power originates from fear, which Mearsheimer explains as a fundamental aspect of relations between nuclear powers (Mearsheimer 2003, 24). Mearsheimer's examples of China's military maneuvers nearby Taiwan in 1995 and Imperial Germany's submarine campaign during World War I. Misperceptions of fear refer to exaggeration of danger or unwarranted apprehensions (Jervis 1988, 699). For America, fear is a legacy from the Cold War. However, I assume that fear is still central to great powers competition. The attrition of liberal hegemony, regardless of its detrimental implications for the U.S. Foreign Policy, is a process that indicates that World War III's apprehension will dominate the post-pandemic world. For example, Chinese aspirations for regional hegemony in the APAC are the first signal that foretells the justified fears of three major U.S. allies: Japan, South Korea, and Australia.

The United States initiated an agreement for security cooperation with the Australians, although Washington preferred not to involve Tokyo or Seoul. The deployment of nuclear submarines on the Australian coast raises the possibility of military conflict between the United States and China. However, if Washington wants to be in a favorable position, it should invite Japan and South Korea to join AUKUS. The misjudgment that U.S. Foreign Policy in the APAC should promote a limited military involvement of Japan has as its contrast the justified fear that China could invade Taiwan. The U.S.-Japanese alliance offering unreliable support to Tokyo reflects the conviction that Washington has chosen to prioritize its allies in the region. As a result, when the fears of a forthcoming Sino-American clash tighten, the United States will not distinguish between allies that require full military commitments and others that demand limited engagement. Therefore, an American ally could support Washington against Beijing due to fear of survival, aside from ist relations with the United States. Another problem could arise from the nuclear ambitions of North Korea. I assume that Pyongyang is a rational state actor. Still, in case of military conflict between the United States and China, North Korea will intervene due to apprehensions of the American victory. It is therefore essential for the United States to calculate and determine all possible scenarios that could give preference to fear over rational decisions. The extent of the American political and military commitments should not rely on apprehensions unless Washington still believes that the rearmament of Japan would be detrimental to the U.S.-led system of alliances in Asia. Is Australia as important to America as Japan and South Korea? On the other hand, is it more or less significant than the latter? Fear of nuclear war with China and North Korea will answer this crucial question.

U.S. Foreign Policy in Europe, more particularly after BREXIT, is clear. European integration is central to the peaceful coexistence of the European states. However, it does not benefit America to the extent NATO does. Solidarity within the U.S.-dominated Alliance prevents far-right movements from reviving nationalism and political extremism. It is futile to assume that the EU could exist without NATO, at least in its present condition. Therefore, abstract fears of the resurgence of European nationalism are groundless. Member States such as Hungary demonstrate firm commitments to nationalistic and neo-conservative values, which European tend to consider the fundamental challenge that provokes anti-Americanism and Europhobia. Even so, it is highly arguable that populist leaders like Victor Orbán are true nationalists. Populists become nationalists in charge but fail to keep their trust when they lose elections. I assume that the financial support of Brussels or Moscow determines the real motivation of European populistic leaders, not nationalism itself.

European primary concerns are with Russia. Relations between the Big R and Uncle Sam are central to Europe's security. Another issue arises because there could be no diplomatically prevention of those apprehensions. The United States tried to envisage a decision in the face of the former Russian leader Boris

Yeltsin. With Putin in charge, to whom Russia owes its active involvement in world affairs, Kremlin transformed the Old Soviet doctrines into a Neo-Eurasian strategy, which I will discuss in the final chapter of this book. For the purpose of this section, I will stress the main apprehensions of Europe that determine European policy towards Russia – the fear of another intervention in Ukraine and the Russian gas policy. Are those fears relevant to American national interests? A strictly military approach to Russian foreign policy, with a particular focus on NATO, presumes relocation of the U.S. troops in Europe to the Eastern flank of the Alliance. A rational political approach, quite the opposite, would encourage a selective deterrence of Russia. By selective, I mean a strategy of prioritizing vital interests over reasonable compromises. This is not to say that Washington should follow a policy of rapprochement with Moscow. That policy failed when President Trump attempted to close ties with Kremlin. U.S. Foreign Policy should aim to deescalate tensions with Russia in the Black Sea and Eastern Europe and thus, dispel the fear of a military confrontation between Washington and Moscow. The hard approach is particularly popular among decision-makers, who want a clean and fast solution to the post-Cold War syndrome, and policymakers, who underestimate Kremlin's influence in the European capitals. The U.S – Russian relations, however, are far from simple.

In contrast to the Chinese, Russians are far more sensitive and prejudiced toward Americans for two reasons: the loss of the Cold War and the Neo-Eurasian doctrine that envisions relations with the United States as natural and imminent confrontation (Dugin 2015, 11). In the short-term, selective dialogue with Russia should delineate a red line to divide the Americans from the Russian zone of influence. The former will include all NATO allies, which will limit power demonstration to the Russian zone in coordination with the United States. The latter will regroup the rest of the post-Soviet states that are not the Member States of the Alliance. One might argue that the selective dialogue with Moscow is a repetition of the Cold War and could lead to unpredictable U.S. foreign policy results. However, one should not forget that the major interferences of NATO outside of its mandate lasted for twenty years and ended in decline. Even Kosovo, given the specifics of the Western Balkans, is still a region of ethnic tensions and unresolved disputes between former Yugoslavian Republics. Overall, the policy of selective deterrence will favor the United States in its efforts to accumulate more resources for the containment of China.

Demonstrating power in MENA is crucial for the strategic implications of U.S. Foreign Policy. It is indisputably that global politics, especially after September 11, was driven by fear of Islamic revivalism and Muslim fears of American hegemony and Western cultural imperialism (Khan and Haskologlu 2020, 4). It is also a great delusion to assume that the United States can restore the balance of power in MENA simply by a policy of prestige or export of democracy. The Taliban are in a position to regroup the remnants of the terrorist networks in MENA, and thus, an attack similar to September 11 would be more likely. The regime in Kabul will continue to challenge the West, as it did in the past, to the point where Washington should face the dilemma again whether to strike the terrorists. However, at that stage, demonstration of power will be ineffective. What prevents extremists from launching attacks against the Western powers is the fear of the American response. In similar, what prevents the United States from striking global terrorism again is the apprehension of another twenty years of war. However, the fears will not last forever. In the long term, the Sino-American competition is likely to divide MENA into a sphere of influence, and thus, major U.S. allies such as Israel and Saudi Arabia are more likely to join their forces against the Taliban and Iran. From that perspective, the United States should rely on rational rather than cultural or moralistic foreign policy perceptions. For MENA, the offshore-balancing approach of Mearsheimer and Walt could benefit U.S. Foreign Policy rather than exhausting military commitments to regional actors. If Washington applies offshore-balancing to its foreign policy, it should encourage its allies in MENA to take the lead and contain potential threats to U.S. national security. Suppose the United States endorses persists in the offshore approach, even if Washington involves again in a military conflict to defend its national interests. In that case, the conditions for victory will be much more favorable than those that followed the preemptive strike against Iraq. Americans cannot suppress the fear of Islamic revivalism through post-war terror. Aside from the security threats which another war will pose, considering the balance of power that exists in MENA after the fall of Kabul, the apprehension of another terrorist attack will have a significant impact on American policymakers. The rising Islamophobia during the Presidency of Donald Trump threatened the foundations of American democracy and undermined the international prestige of the United States. With Americans polarized at home, the United States could not project enough power in MENA, APAC, and Europe, which benefited Russia and China.

President Biden's approach to demonstrating of power has both offensive and defensive nature that expresses his efforts to rebuild the U.S.-led system of alliances, design new forms of cooperation between allies, and deter major U.S. adversaries such as China and Russia. In contrast to President Trump's doctrine, the Biden administration follows the balanced strategy of *America is back*, which seeks to remedy the negative impact that *America first* had on U.S. Foreign Policy. One might argue that the Trump doctrine partially benefited the United States in its quest to sustain American global dominance. Even so, a doctrine that polarizes a nation deprives even great powers of exercising power effectively when necessary. The Soviet Empire collapsed because the Soviet leaders could not keep the illusion of the United Proletariat. The realities could have been different if Joseph Stalin had been in charge of the USSR at that time, not Gorbachev. Therefore, any American President, who succeeds in consolidating the Americans, as President Ronald Reagan did, will demonstrate power in defense of the national interests. Finally, it is untenable to believe that the post-pandemic world order will preclude the demonstration of power. The rational dilemma before the United States should be to exercise power to defend its national interests or help American allies even if the outcome would gamble the U.S. vital interests.

Exercising power differs from demonstrating power in that the state actors invoke the former for the sake of their own survival and their self-preservation. Power is the best mean to survival in a dangerous world (Mearsheimer 2001, 19). For example, the primary purpose of U.S. Foreign Policy refers to American national interests and U.S. national security. From the position of great power, however, America also faces specific risks and responsibilities that derive from its status as a global actor. America has to take risks if it wants to remain a great power or withdraw from world affairs following the decline of the British Empire. One might argue that even great powers have to respect international law and the will of international organizations. However, do international organizations make foreign policy? Does international law protect American citizens from terrorist attacks and external aggression? Multilateral agreements might say so, but the right to self-defense is primordial to each state actor. What happens if a global actor exercises power to expand and faces another great power? The history of the Kennedy doctrine provides us with a perfect example.

In his essay on American politics, President Kennedy declared that his looks at U.S. Foreign Policy had detected two structural weaknesses: the rise of nationalism worldwide and the lack of decision in the U.S. leadership (Kennedy 1957, 44). The political struggle between two factions in the American political elite to define the global commitments of the United States took the form of a geopolitical debate under Kennedy's presidency. Washington wanted a confrontation with the USSR to remain a primary source of American globalism. Still, most decision-makers opposed the development of a pacifist foreign policy as long as Communist movements spread in Latin America. Mainstream Democrats favored a strong global commitment of the United States, while the Republicans endorsed a more evasive position on the American responsibilities to defend its allies directly. Much of the debate over President Kennedy's doctrine stemmed from his conviction that Washington had underestimated the capacity of the Soviets to build a huge military arsenal. The President was receptive to those divisions, and he wanted to reconcile both.

Controlling Communist revolutions and pursuing the Atlantic community occupied a central place in the Kennedy doctrine (Paterson 1989, 105). The doctrine's justification was clear: countering the Soviet policy of exporting communism, strengthening alliances in the Western hemisphere, gripping the containment, and ensuring the U.S. presence in Africa. Moreover, JFK foretold the rise of China and stressed its destructive military potential. Although the United States and Europe shared a similar security strategy, their perceptions of Communist China differed. The European global attitudes of Beijing originated from the rise of the left-wing parties in Europe and their views on U.S. Foreign Policy towards Israel. American perceptions of China stemmed from the consequences of the Sino-Soviet split and its impact on the relations between the two communist powers. President Kennedy, therefore, pursued a dichotomous strategy of nonrecognition and – at the same time – aspirations to rapprochement with Beijing. A policy he was not meant to elaborate.

In 1962, the first event to define the limits of the bipolar confrontation – the Cuban missile crisis broke out. In truth, at the moment of this writing, history offers no parallel to those thirteen days of October (Allison 2008, 256). It was able for the superpowers to demonstrate their full potential because, in contrast to the vision of the Kennedy administration, Nikita Khrushchev had elaborated the Soviet strategy earlier in terms of support for Cuba and possible scenarios. The Soviets realized that Kennedy did not seek a direct confrontation. However, Kremlin was aware that Washington could not afford to lose prestige and that the U.S. President was under enormous international and domestic political pressure. Coercion could not help much since NATO represented the supreme solidarity of the Western hemisphere. Americans and Soviets understood explicitly that a war between the United States and USSR would result in mutual assured destruction. A nuclear holocaust could lead to neither powershifts nor the distribution of resources. However, the Kennedy administration underestimated the Soviet willingness to act because the ultimate decision had not yet moved to the point where a potential retaliation could be launched. Following the deployment of the ICBMs required further American actions to prevent the Soviet Union from targeting most of the continental U.S. The swift succession of the blockade permitted both sides to endorse offensive strategies, elaborate on them, and outline several scenarios. Twelve days later, after the secret negotiations between Moscow and Washington, Khrushchev laid off his terms for the missiles' withdrawal, which he did after Kennedy agreed to displace the Jupiter deployments from Turkey. In Soviet thinking, the aftermath of the crisis and Fidel Castro's sense of betrayal were interchangeable. Without support from Kremlin, there was little to prevent Castro from going independent and pursuing his development path as a socialist leader. The prospect of Cuba being invaded by American troops scared Moscow and all Latin American countries, but it also mobilized Washington to cringe its containment strategy. President Kennedy realized that he could lose the Nation's backyard to the Communists unless Uncle Sam became a unifier, not simply the Big Brother. If other states in the region rejected U.S. Foreign Policy, the rationale for American backyard and presence would disappear. Therefore, containment and deterring the communist ideology became essentially two sides of the same coin, while the purpose of the former was no more limited to the Soviet Union, as proponents of the Truman doctrine postulated.

However, global containment presumes global commitments. The ideological unification of the U.S. backyard required a complex strategy: military or political interventions in Central and Latin America to appear nonthreatening to Kremlin. Henceforth, the Kennedy administration faced two obstacles. First, by maintaining and imposing American-friendly attitudes in its backyard, Washington would sparkle domestic conflicts in the region. Second, a potential regroup of states like Costa Rica and Uruguay against Cuba and Venezuela could easily trigger another missile crisis. The Kennedy administration designed and launched its plan for institutional and political reforms in Central America through economic integration (Dunne 2016, 437). The President also launched several initiatives for political cooperation with Latin America, declaring his intention to support the values of freedom and liberty. Economic integration was intended to appear non-hostile to the USSR. At the same time, political cooperation sought to revive the spirit of Pan-Americanism so that the nations could feel culturally and historically bound with the United States. One might argue that communist movements in Central and Latin America mobilized due to the success of the Presidential strategy. However, the Kennedy doctrine succeeded in making the region more predictable and less susceptible to conflicts.

Unlike the United States, the Soviet Union failed to expand its influence in America's backyard. In reaction to Moscow's claims to be the supreme leader or *vozhd* of the world communist society, left-wing factions in Central and Latin America considered the USSR a source of legitimacy even after the dissolution of the Communist International. By publicly supporting Kremlin, later communist dictators like Salvador Allende and Anastasio Somoza gained popularity against their counterparts and persuaded a policy of anti-Americanism. However, the Soviet financial assistance for its Central and Latin America satellites did not meet their expectations. Moreover, official support for Marxism-Leninism under the Soviet leadership was one thing; integrating those values into the local culture was another issue. Thus, socialist fiascos in the region came to naught months or years after they had come into existence. Although Cuba remained the lonely red island, Cubans could not easily convert to Marxism-Leninism. Castro initially believed that there were but two options to legitimate communism: his charisma and continuous propaganda of anti-Americanism. The former moved ahead to untie Havana from Moscow and promote nationalism, while the latter associated America with an evil expansionist empire. In future years, the offensive capabilities of the United States and the Soviet Union exceeded the political ambitions of both superpowers. For precisely why Washington did not launch a nuclear strike against Moscow, mutual assured destruction – Kremlin was not reluctant to invade Europe. The Soviets, however, found their potential to dominate Communism at an end: China extracted from the hesitant nuclear policy of Moscow legitimacy to challenge its ideological primacy. Beijing sought to distort Kremlin's leadership by establishing strategic ties with the West with its technological, military, and economic rise.

Powershifting and wishful thinking

I hope no realist scholar will assume that the Coronavirus Pandemic is merely responsible for transforming the unipolar world order. The controversy of the assumption that COVID19 has caused powershifts in the balance of power emerges from misinterpretations of the post-Cold War period. The Pandemic poses a historical challenge to U.S. Foreign Policy, but great powers' behavior and objective geopolitical realities after September 11 are more essential to understanding the post-pandemic powershifts. State actors behavior, as Mearsheimer points out, originates and shapes under the material structure of the international system (Mearsheimer 2001, 12). Therefore, great powers behavior depends on objective material conditions that predetermine powershifts. I consider those conditions *objective* because I assume that military conflicts, overstretch, economic shocks, and humanitarian catastrophes are geopolitical realities which coexist and influence the balance of power in international relations (Jervis 2009, 193). In addition, they are *material* because states that maximize relative power are concerned primarily with the distribution of material capabilities (Jensen and Elman 2014, 185). Immaterial conditions have a limited capacity to trigger powershifts and cannot alter or establish international anarchy (Jervis 2009, 192). Moreover, immaterial sources of power that inspire liberal institutionalists deceive rational decision-making and overshadow the pragmatic judgment of policymakers. The belief that an international world order based on universal values and institutional hierarchy could secure peace contradicts the dualistic character of the international system that combines selfish human nature with international anarchy.

A foreign policy that promotes moral guiding principles or abstract universal philosophy is bound to undermine the primacy of the great power which has endorsed it. It would be praiseworthy if state behavior originated from the decisions of idealistic and virtuous policymakers, who seek to maintain the balance of power through securing peace. The delusion came when unipolar optimists considered Washington immune to hegemonic failures and thus, failed to predict that the unipolar world order would be a short-live transitional phase from bipolarity to multipolarity (Layne 2012, 204). Therefore, the liberal revision of U.S. Foreign Policy, which put the mask of moralpolitik and blamed realism for its methodological insufficiency, degraded into a hegemonic temptation. In this book, I operationalize Jack Snyder's theory of overextension to illustrate the post-pandemic powershift from unipolarity to the U.S.-China contested bipolar order.

Jack Snyder elaborates on the concept of imperial overextension to explain how policymakers, who base their strategy on the myths of empire, are likely to undermine their power and security (Snyder 2013, 5). I assume that all three categories of myths introduced by Snyder provide a logical explanation for the post-pandemic powershifts. The most striking example of the American proneness to the domino theory is democracy building. One might argue that conquest precludes the export of values in terms of military operations. I consider such a claim deeply one-sided. The conquest of Iraq was central to the Bush doctrine for three reasons: retribution for September 11 and defeating the Taliban. Such analysis of the foreseeable implications of the U.S. intervention is not enough. The domino effect has another aspect, which we should approach with a realist view that envisions the hidden face of overextension – ideological overstretch. The United States put itself into a dead-end position of great power, which, instead of following the rational line of justified retribution, sought to both conquest and liberate. Are great powers destined to liberate or to rule? If one argues that America has acted rationally, what alternative was more rational for Washington – to make the Taliban pay for September 11 or build democracy? History shows that the United States has supported all kinds of regimes against major U.S. adversaries, which benefited U.S. Foreign Policy during the Cold War. Therefore, ideological overstretch strengthens the domino effect and, on a further stage, transforms it into a checkmate effect: cumulative gains turned against the great power's foreign policy.

The offensive/defensive strategy of great powers also presents us with a perfect example of what Snyder calls overextension. When U.S. policymakers interpret their actions, they always define them in American national interests. In the years after 2001, NATO has been acting as an offensive alliance. The misinterpretation of its core mission was due to Russia's geopolitical revival and the Member

States, which supported NATO's enlargement after the annexation of Crimea. However, Ukraine's aspirations for membership originate from Kyiv's policy to prevent Russia from taking over all Ukraine. In the light of Putin's foreign policy, Moscow will seek no justification for its actions. If the allies, however, are decisive enough to press Kremlin, the results of the Ukrainian or the Georgian accession to the Alliance could trigger a global military conflict. Policymakers, of course, face reelections and should stick to rhetoric that favors good relations with European allies and a decisive response to the Russian aspirations for controlling the post-Soviet space. However, suppose one assumes that it is in the U.S. national interest to support uncritically Ukraine for membership in NATO. In that case, one could conclude that America would go to war with Russia if Kyiv invokes Article Five. Washington, of course, should be aware of the Russian moves in the Black Sea and Moscow's attempts to undermine democracy through supporting populist leaders in the United States and Europe. However, the core mission of NATO presumes an integrated system of collective defense against any threat. Further enlargement and overextension, quite the opposite, could deprive the Alliance of its legitimacy and thus, undermine the mutual trust between the United States and its European allies. The result will be a security infrastructure of collective defense, in which America will have to fight a war with Russia if Moscow invades Europe.

Perceptions of threats constitute the third category of Snyder (Snyder 2013, 15). From this myth, which has been dominating U.S. Foreign Policy since September 11, overextension received legitimacy. American policymakers have been sticking to global threats such as terrorism and radicalization, regardless of Chinese economic growth and Russia's aspirations to the post-Soviet space. The Bush administration considered global terrorism and political Islam major threats to the national security of the United States but failed to prevent the primary long-term challenge: the rise of China. The American withdrawal from Afghanistan in 2021 illustrated that the aggressive foreign policy of President George W. Bush was self-defeating and the pursuit of security through expansion in MENA led to the point of a dead end. There is no need to further explore the concept of war on terror because, for none of the pillars embodied in the Bush doctrine, overextension applies more than for Iraq and Afghanistan. The U.S. perception of threats blurred when President Bush overstressed the U.S. military presence in Iraq and President Trump issued a Muslim ban. The fact that the United States is the most powerful nation still inspires American allies, but with the annexation of Crimea and the increasing Chinese appetites for Taiwan, the certainty that the American power could secure peace is debasing. The assumption that security is achievable through expansion dominates U.S. Foreign Policy and thus, concerns relations between America and its allies. National security is the primary purpose of every state's foreign policy, and it has nothing to do with interventions and global commitments. One might argue that the U.S.-dominated system of alliances benefited America after World War II and predetermined the collapse of the USSR. Even so, alliances presume security cooperation without collective defense. Equality between allies has symbolic implications, deprived of content. Walt reminds us that one of the fundamental reasons for alliances survival is hegemony (Walt 2013, 55). Therefore, if the dominant ally invokes an alliance to expand, it should be aware that its overextension could not gain legitimacy in the eyes of the rest of the allies.

The undisputed dominance of the United States was central to the U.S.-led system of alliances. With the rise of China, however, Washington cannot afford to lose allies and pursue a policy of confrontation with long-term partners only for the sake of hegemony. Moreover, overextension could undermine security cooperation within the alliances and disintegrate unity among states. For instance, when Beijing challenges America's predominance in the APAC, the United States should not exclude Japan from AUKUS. Although Washington does not tolerate peer-competitors, it should encourage peer-friends. Whatever scenario exists for mutual military action between the United States and Japan, it will signal to China that historical ties between Washington and Tokyo are strong and that both states will work together to counter any threat to regional stability.

The categories of myths that Snyder introduces in his book eventually mark the borders of U.S. overextension. In addition, I assume that there is another category, which, by following Snyder's theory, I call *cognitive delusion*. By cognitive delusion, I mean the cognitive misperceptions on powershifting. For instance, what conclusion can we draw from U.S. Foreign Policy towards Taiwan? The only strategy that seems to have realistic implications is China's annexation of the island. Will the U.S. trigger AUKUS to defend Taiwan? The Biden administration tries to demonstrate a delusive commitment without any rational foundations. Will America go to war with China for Taiwan? It was by virtue of the Sino-American Mutual Defense Treaty from 1954 that the United States could deter the Chinese aspirations for Taipei. However, President Jimmy Carter terminated the Treaty unilaterally, and therefore Washington is merely under moral or strategic obligation to support Taiwan.

Moreover, what will be the setback for the major U.S. allies in the region? In truth, a detailed consideration will show that China is in a far more advantageous position than the United States, given the nuclear aspirations of the North Korean regime. One of the great delusions that dominate U.S. Foreign Policy is that Beijing's rhetoric is a bluff, which exposes the Chinese inability to confront the United States yet. The cognitive problem here arises from a fundamental difference between Western democracies and the Asian tradition: long-term decision-making. The United States seeks to maintain the balance of power in its present condition, while China aims to reshape it without limiting its strategy in terms of time and scope. Western policymakers should expect annexation of Taiwan, but it could be in one, ten, twenty, or even thirty years. The Chinese parabellum paradigm, analyzed by Mearsheimer for truth, demonstrates the essential core of Beijing's military, but its dimensions do not correspond to the Western perceptions of Clausewitzian warfare. By neglecting the long-term strategy of Beijing, Washington could enter into China's trap and relocate a significant amount of resources in the South China Sea with the intent to secure the region. However, American decision-makers will have less freedom of action in preventing a nuclear apocalypse with more U.S. troops deployed in Taiwan and more naval forces in Taipei's territorial waters.

Although overextension is central to powershifting, Robert Jervis infers three explicit challenges to unipolarity, which I call objective material realities. The first objective reality refers to the economic impact of September 11 and the subsequent economic downturn (Jervis 2002, 38). The Global Financial Crisis of 2007 shocked democracies, which, until then, rejected China's economic growth. However, instead of remembering the lessons from the Great Depression, developed states partially recovered from the huge economic collapse. Although President Obama succeeded in negating the detrimental effects of the Crisis, another issue entered the public agenda – economic inequality. The American economy recovered, but the downturn's impact was so severe that it polarized Americans like never before. Unfortunately, U.S. policymakers abdicated from rational approaches and succumbed to escapist perceptions of the future of American global dominance. Domestic issues overshadowed foreign policy decision-making, which weakened the U.S. ability to prevent the rise of regional hegemons. President Obama eventually realized that Beijing was Washington's peer-competitor when he met President Hu Jintao and criticized him for human rights in China. The attack on Ukraine was another surprise in NATO's backyard that raised concerns about Moscow's military capabilities. European allies did not expect to witness how Russian troops occupied Eastern Ukraine under the Russian flag. The unipolar realities transformed into unipolar temptations for liberal hegemony and universal commitments. Policymakers in the United States and Europe denied the reality that the Global Financial Crisis has marked the transition to multipolar world order and endorsed the misleading presumption that promoting democracy would prevent the rise of China and Russian Neo-Eurasianism. Western political elites, however, failed to prove that the United States and Europe should bear the moral and political responsibility for democracy building. Moreover, liberal democracy became less attractive as it grew more militant. Military interventions in MENA exposed the inability of Western democracies to maintain liberal societies, and thus, the United States behaved like an empire that enjoys its privileges but is unwilling to fulfill its imperial obligations (Khan 2003, 274). A perfect example of Muqtedar Khan's portrayal is U.S. Foreign Policy in the Muslim World under the Bush administration. The post-modern turn in Washington's strategy originated from the neoconservative aspirations of democracy building. The Muslim World rejected that policy simply because Washington behaved much like former empires that had left their mark upon their Holy Lands. The United States was the world's largest economy, but the days of the Crusades were over.

There is a misleading tendency among policymakers to underestimate the consequences of environmental degradation and widespread diseases. Typical misjudgments on those challenges originate from misinterpretations of their impact. While public opinion in democracies might have envisioned nuclear war as the worst probable end of times during the Cold War, the Coronavirus Pandemic had a similar response in 2020. Thus, the misinterpreting of China's responsibility for the COVID19 outbreak provoked a strong wave of xenophobia against Asian-Americans in the United States, similar to Islamophobia after the September 11 terrorist attacks. The impact of the Pandemic can be understood in detail only if we explore its implications through the psychological perceptions of decision-makers. By exploring how COVID19 affected U.S. perceptions of China, this book rejects conspiracies that identify the origins of the virus with Beijing. My concerns are that such claims are irrational and self-defeating for every policymaker who tends to equalize Chinese foreign policy with the Coronavirus outbreak. It is methodologically preposterous to argue that China has released COVID19 to dethrone the American primacy. One might argue that Beijing could use the Pandemic to topple Washington but seizing the opportunity is not the same as fighting biological warfare. Logical assumptions in international politics rely on rational arguments and objective interactions, while conspiracies originate from abstract truths and universal moral codes. Speculations might serve as the perfect scenario for a movie, but they have no place in foreign policy and rational decision-making. What happened after Wuhan then? Why did the President of the United States call COVID19 "the China virus"? The answer of this book is wishful thinking, more particularly expressed in three aspects: behavior, correlation between desires and perceptions, and expectations (Jervis, 2017, 366–368).

Foreign policy at the level of states interludes with the political behavior of individual decision-makers. Although political rhetoric does not represent public opinion in democracies, politicians speak on behalf of their nations. President Trump's aggressive behavior was a direct consequence of his belief that China is responsible for the Coronavirus outbreak. It was helpful but irrational for the Trump administration to hold Beijing accountable for the Pandemic. It was vaguely evident that, for the sake of his political survival, the U.S. President sought to trade domestic problems for the image of the "Chinese virus." The foremost purpose of the Presidential behavior was to rally the polarized Nation against external threats. The expected outcome was a second term in the White House and political support for a trade war against China. With behavior that neglects the Pandemic and advocates conspiracies, how could a policymaker pursue a subsequent and fruitful strategy against another peer competitor? Foreign policy decision-making does not simply require electoral support and wishfulness, it also involves what is true objectively and rationally, supported by evidence or illuminated by reason (Morgentau 2006, 34). Political behavior is rhetoric that explains how political leaders defend national interests. A policymaker could infer an objective and rational judgment about the policy one should pursue from public opinion. However, wishful thinking obscures the public perceptions of political behavior, the latter becomes severely radicalized. Should a state actor then rely on its policymakers to act in a rational manner? My concern is that such behavior could throw the state into a military conflict with an unpredictable outcome.

Correlation between desires and perceptions is central to understanding President Trump's COVID behavior. From a realist point of view, wishful thinking implies a comparison between what people believe and the true state of the world (Jervis 2017, 368). Trump's wishfulness emerged from two beliefs: that a trade war with China would prevent the rise of Beijing and that the pressure on the Chinese to investigate COVID's origins would mobilize the affected allies against Xi Jinping's foreign policy. Preoccupation with anti-Chinese rhetoric and accusations against the World Health Organization became a political creed for the Trump administration. Relations between the President's beliefs and the objective geopolitical realities predetermined U.S. Foreign Policy towards China and escalated into dangerous hostility, which Barack Obama avoided during his Presidency. Aside from President Trump's personal intentions, only a small part of the American political elite believed that the unipolar world order was still sustainable. The uneasy economic dependence on China and constant tensions with European allies forced even the downright neocons to admit that the United States could not maintain its global influence, with Beijing seeking to expand its influence in the APAC. In addition, instead of considering Russia's increasing role in the international system, Washington misjudged Moscow's aspirations for Eurasian hegemony. The Trump administration failed to realize that the trade war would open Pandora's Box for another bipolar confrontation instead of preserving America's image as a global leader. A state actor, which endorses a war-like strategy, should be ready to enforce it. The President's belief that Washington could win a trade war with Beijing and eliminate the interdependence between the world's largest economies did not fit the international system's actual state: China's economic rise was irreversible unless the United States decided to attack the Chinese. Moreover, only part of the American allies supported the Trump administration in its Sino-centric foreign policy. Japan, South Korea, and Australia backed the United States for the sake of their survival, but Europe's concerns were stressed primarily on Russia. This leads us to the second discrepancy between Trump's desires and perceptions. The idea that the Coronavirus is a product of Communist China's foreign policy was an expression of what Robert Jervis calls optimistic decision-makers, who choose a policy because they think it will have some measure of success (Jervis 2017, 368). President Trump's perceptions of COVID undermined his optimism that further pressure on China would sully the face of Beijing. The Coronavirus death toll surpassed the number of American lives lost in World War II, which cooled down the ambitions of the Trump administration for an optimistic outcome from the Coronacrisis. Donald Trump and his fellow policymakers eventually failed to assess the psychological impact of COVID and thus, misjudged the difference between China's strategy of seizing that impact and the "Chinese virus" conspiracies. In short, rational decision-making of U.S. Foreign Policy became a victim of populist speculations. The belief that blaming China for the Coronavirus would weaken Beijing's position in international relations finally turned against the Presidential administration itself with the outbreak of Asian hate.

Although we cannot explain the expectations of the Trump administration, two possible assumptions could provide a plausible assessment of the Presidential attitudes. My first assumption is that expectations for political liberalization of China shaped U.S. Foreign Policy towards Beijing during the post-Cold War powershifts. American policymakers and liberal scholars considered the rise of China an opportunity for partnership between both powers and silent de-centralization of the Chinese political system. Proponents of interdependence like Joseph Nye predicted that if America treats the Chinese as enemies, Americans will guarantee an enemy for the future (Campbell 2018, 66). It was a rare consensus among realists and liberals that Sino-American relations could shift the global balance of power and challenge the unipolar world order. Policymakers, however, preferred to blame Beijing for the violation of human rights instead of pushing for internal reforms in the 1990s. The expectations that China would give up its political identity and transform into liberal democracy were an expression of American wishful thinking and the belief that the end of history had finally come with the end of the Cold War. All hopes for change died when President Xi Jinping conducted several strategic reforms that modernized the People's Liberation Army and sought to increase the Chinese military capabilities. Thus, instead of a liberalized friend, the United States got a peer competitor in the Asia-Pacific. Was it rational to believe that Beijing would quit Communism? As rational as to believe that post-Soviet Russia will become a liberal democracy. The answer of this book is that neither close relations with China nor Hong Kong riots will quench the Chinese desire to become a global leader. What proponents of liberalization failed to comprehend is the original truth that the origins of cold wars are found in the anarchic ordering of the international arena (Waltz 1988, 620). In other words, to expect that a rising power will liberalize for the sake of abstract moralistic values, whether democracy or communism, is to assume that the British Empire would have granted the freedom of its American colonies voluntarily two centuries ago. Sino-American competition originates from the natural law of international anarchy – that no central authority or institution could impose its decisions or cultural patterns on other nations. The unipolar world order was even more anarchic than the Cold War, and thus, China's rise and competition between Beijing and Washington would have a productive and fruitful effect on the balance of power.

My second assertion is that the final purpose of the Trump administration was war with China. As Graham Allison argues, the Thucydides Trap emerges from the Thucydidean syndromes of rising and ruling powers that China and the United States display in full (Allison 2017, 161). Allison's predictions explain Trump's attitudes, assuming that an economic conflict could lead to war (Allison 2017, 162). The central dilemma here is what would have happened if Washington had started the conflict. It is important to highlight that wishfulness would make a significant contribution to such a decision. President Trump's ambitions to punish China for the Pandemic and counter Beijing were derivative of the firm belief that America would win against China. I will further discuss different scenarios in the last chapter of the book. For this section's purpose, it is important to highlight that parallels with the rivalry between Britain and Germany provide a perfect example of the most probable outcome of an eventual Sino-American conflict. Victory, however, is a fragile and broad concept that depends on casualties. The United States is similar to Britain was a few decades ago. The British defeated Germany in two World Wars, but Britain was no longer a great power in the aftermath. Aside from the MAD scenario, the United States could achieve a decisive victory against Beijing, although particular complications would lead to prolonging the conflict. However, if expectations are valid, realities will differ when China loses to America regarding the death toll and post-war recovery. War with China will cost Washington its great power status. A military clash between both powers will shift the balance of power to such an extent that the world economy will fall into a deep recession while the ideological impact will countermine liberal democracy completely. It will be a global disaster, which will remind both Americans and Chinese that victory over that, so long as victory can be attained, stupid haste is preferable to clever dilatoriness. (Sun Tzu, art war, 34).

Six lessons from the pre-pandemic world

I conclude this chapter by posing an essential question: is the unipolar world order worth saving? The answer lies beyond human rights and democracy in the autonomous sphere of action – politics (Morgenthau 2006, 37). If the United States can still exercise power to control its political actions, manipulate the balance of power, and influence political relations among nations without relying on moralistic values or international institutions, liberal foreign policy can serve the U.S. national interests. If, however, America needs to promote democracy and follow the guidance of international entities to achieve the short-term and long-term purposes of its foreign policy, then Washington should come to terms with the fact that liberal policymaking will not survive in the realist world of international anarchy. Interdependence can no longer benefit the U.S. national interests, for it serves the interests of American adversaries like China and Russia. Cooperation, more particularly after the outbreak of the Pandemic, has evolved into fear and mutual distrust between great powers. Alliances have lost their robustness, and allies have blurred their perceptions of common enemies. The crisis of unipolarity came to existence shortly after its proponents declared that the last man would embrace democracy in pursuit of eternal peace. However, Waltz reminds us that peace is fragile (Waltz 1988, 620). The longer the state of peace lasts, the more destructive supervening conflicts are, regardless of their scope and intensity. The ten years of undisputed unipolarity and the subsequent war on terror provide striking proof of the realist belief that international anarchy is not alterable. I will provide six arguments that summarize why the liberal approach to U.S. Foreign Policy failed.

Altering the anarchy. International anarchy offers global actors the opportunity to maximize their military capabilities and, thus, manipulate the balance of power. The unipolar world order provided the United States with the unprecedented opportunity to choose between maintaining the post-Cold War status quo in the Western hemisphere and expanding the U.S. influence through promoting values or military interventions. Washington's struggle for liberal hegemony was a huge gain for emerging great powers, which sought to introduce alternative development patterns and deter the omnipotent American influence. Liberal policy-makers considered the realist perception of international anarchy outdated and even detrimental to U.S. Foreign Policy. The benefits of spreading ideology exceeded those limiting Washington's primacy to the Western hemisphere, which inclined policymakers to believe that the United States should pursue hegemony. Liberal scholars would probably argue that hegemonic behavior benefits American national interests and that unipolarity favors U.S. primacy. Mearsheimer counters assumptions as those with the argument that realism clashes with American values and moralistic optimism of Americans (Mearsheimer 2001, 14). Another explanation of hegemonic behavior is irrational consistency. Robert Jervis argues that when a person believes that a policy contributes to one value, he is likely to believe that it also contributes to several other values, even though there is no reason why the world should be constructed in such a neat and helpful manner (Jervis 2017, 128). My explanation combines both.

President Clinton believed that democracy would spread and the United States should intervene in any conflicts that violate human rights. Presidents like Bush and Obama believed that democracy-building could prevent terrorists from striking again and that only unipolarity was sustainable. Finally, President Trump offered a miscalculated response to China's struggle for global dominance, which exposed the vulnerabilities of the U.S. Grand Strategy in the APAC. To sum up, all Presidential administrations after the Cold War pursued a single purpose – to alter the international anarchy and to design a hierarchic world order dominated by a sole superpower. Moralistic optimism prevailed even in the last days of the U.S. military presence in Iraq and Afghanistan and merged with the belief that democracy-building has increasingly contributed to the states of MENA. Thus, irrational consistency has dominated U.S. Foreign Policy since the end of the Cold War. The primary reason for the misfortunate optimism was the collapse of the USSR. Western political leaders truly believe that the rest of the world will convert to democracy and that even the last remnants of totalitarian dictatorships will fall under the pressure of domestic reforms or external interventions. The assumption that democracy and interdependence can run the unipolar world order proved the argument of Kenneth Waltz that Marxists and liberals are much alike in their efforts to link war outbreaks and prevalence of peace to the internal qualities of the states (Waltz 1988, 617). Nevertheless, Washington endorsed a policy of values that aimed to reshape those qualities through hard, soft, or smart power. Regime changes occurred, internal rates changed, and liberal revolutions flourished, although most replaced secular dictatorships in MENA with self-declared emirates. Alternately, Western nations enjoyed peace, freedom of movement, collective defense, yet suffering from the terrorist attacks of ISIS and falling into economic dependence on China. In short, American foreign policy, seeking to maintain the unipolar world order, acted and systematically undermined the unipolarity structure itself. Although the political sensitivity to threats remained, the United States has already lost its strategic susceptibility to detect emerging peer competitors. America held enormous power it did not know and where to use it.

Exporting values. In terms of coercion, I defined three limits of American power that mark the transition from U.S.-led to Sino-American contested world order: producing global democracy, establishing global commitments, and alliances overstretching. Liberal scholars might argue that, although structural realism's concept of international anarchy has applied to the bipolar structure of the Cold War international system and has lost its relevance after the collapse of the socialist bloc. However, Waltz highlights that changes in the system structure are distinct from the changes at the unit level (Waltz 2000, 5). Liberalism tends to consider Waltz's theory insufficient to explain state behavior due to the distinction between theory of international politics and foreign policy (Nye 2021, 10). However, foreign policy and state behavior depend on the limits of power. History proves that if a state actor holds the military, economic and cultural primacy in international politics, it succumbs to the temptation of hegemony. When the hegemon reaches the limits of its strength, preservation of the status quo becomes central to its foreign policy. In addition, unipolarity does not exclude the need for structural analysis. For instance, the United States needs to exercise coercion to preserve the status quo. Hard, soft, and smart power provide different tools of U.S. Foreign Policy, but their purpose is common – to maintain American leadership. Promoting democracy and fighting terrorism is the expression of the connection between two variables – power and politics.

Power and politics, without a profound understanding of anarchy, however, cannot provide a rational image of the other states actors' behavior. Washington might have considered Russia an ally in the war on terror. Still, the annexation of Crimea proved that, in the lack of central international authority, the structure of the international system influences state behavior. The long-term strategy of Neo-Eurasian doctrine is to replace the unipolar world order with multipolar, while the Chinese grand strategy seeks to establish bipolarity. History shows, however, that profound shifts in international relations occur through wars, whether hot or cold. When the League of Nations failed to prevent World War II, a few remembered the wise decision of the U.S. Senate not to ratify the Treaty of Versailles. Therefore, to assume that spreading democracy will secure peace is to neglect the historical truth that war has been the natural state of international relations and that the structure of the international system predetermines the foreign policy of the poles. Policy of values and liberal theories cannot remedy, erase or explain the profound difference between domestic and foreign policy. Waltz's argument that the neorealist theory of international politics explains how external forces shape state behavior proves that his approach is one-sided, but combined with Morgenthau's assumption for the infinite lust of human nature, it provides a plausible explanation of state behavior, states interaction, and international outcomes. Coercion and the limits of American power that I inferred in this chapter present a robust example of how both theories could answer the liberal claims of insufficiency. The struggle for liberalization and hegemony is a simple expression of the theoretical equation discussed above. Even in most developed democracies, policymakers seek to maximize their power through politics. Whether multipolar or bipolar world, foreign policy represents the natural predisposition of human decision-makers to exercise coercion and create a structure of international politics that benefits their country's national interests. When that structure is unipolar, however, politicians who govern lose their rational perceptions of international politics and tempt to employ domestic policymaking for foreign policy decisions. The tragedy of great power politics, as Mearsheimer calls it, comes when the most powerful state actors embrace a universal truth and reject their objective limits.

Moralizing Realpolitik. Whether hard or soft, power originates from each state's sovereign right to defend its national security. Liberal scholars and policymakers, however, tend to forget that *realpolitik* contributed most to the American victory in the Cold War by strategies that contemporary liberalism would consider irrelevant or pessimistic. Paradoxically, scholars, who challenge the realist paradigm, assign emphasis on the state-society relations (Legro and Moravcsik 1999, 32). Liberal criticism would be praiseworthy if American society in 2019 were united and harmonious as it was thirty years ago, during the Cold War. The point beyond which liberal criticism loses its robustness is the striking political, economic, and ideological polarization in the United States today. Domestic politics in democracies presume and advocate pluralism. Foreign policy, however, should not reflect the moralistic views of any nation. To say that the export of democracy could dethrone dictators is an objective reality, but to assume that building broken regimes will secure peace is a false assumption. My concern is that liberal foreign policy repeated the mistakes of the USSR, which sought hegemony through military and ideological expansion. It was a misjudgment that lay in liberal optimism and its disregard for rising powers like China. In other words, the lack of rational decision-making diffracted the most essential aspect of U.S. Foreign Policy – national interests. Instead of protecting national security, Washington believed it was in the U.S. national interests to preserve the unipolar world order. The post-Cold War pursuit of peace has eventually deluded American policymakers due to their belief that promoting democracy and advocating independence would minimize conflicts and benefit the U.S. primacy. Washington failed to realize that peace is important as long as it serves national interests. One might argue that the U.S. involvement in the post-Cold War conflicts deprives my argument of its validity. The point is that military operations and the subsequent initiatives for peaceful post-war recovery have contributed less, if any, to the U.S. national interests. I hope that no realist scholar would assume that Operation Enduring Freedom has been beneficial for the United States or that economic interdependence between Washington and Beijing would prevent China from annexing Taiwan.

The false promise, then, belongs not only to international institutions. It is a product of what I defined as principled nationalism and its vision of international politics, which Stephen Walt discusses when analyzing the concept of "democratic peace." (Walt 1998, 39). Since both nationalism and liberalism failed to predict the unipolarity's collapse, realism prevailed over both. As discussed above, the ultimate test for the a realist paradigm was the Trump doctrine, which some scholars depicted as principled realism doctrine (Chifu and Frunzeti 2018, 77). In a nuclear world shattered by a widespread disease, foreign policy decision-making should rely on rational perceptions, without tempting to adopt moralistic views and without succumbing to the promise that international bodies can alter the anarchic system. Liberal scholars would argue that structural realism does not offer a sufficient basis for understanding international politics. Even so, the liberal paradigm failed to offer an alternative either. Moreover, its strategies and tools provoked a strong opposite reaction in the face of rising nationalism and Trumpism. The bad news is that the polarization in the most powerful nation at the moment of this writing – America – triggered a domino effect in all democracies. Regardless of its motivation, the moralization of foreign policy resulted in a global crisis of representation. A process that benefited China, which has been sticking to realpolitik since the end of the Cold War.

Sacralizing peace. War and peace influence foreign policy decision-making more than any other variable, shaping state behavior. Therefore, what American doctrines had to endorse after the Cold War should have relied primarily on balancing potential adversaries such as Russia and China. Alliances are the basic units of security cooperation, but in great powers competition, the essential concern is with direct attack (Jervis 1978, 170). In the years after 1992, U.S. Foreign Policy rearranged its priorities, following the idealistic vision of a long-term unipolarity, where the Prisoner's Dilemma has no place. However, values cannot prevail over foreign policy, and thus, ideological overstretch corrupted America's foreign policy perceptions of peace and war. Both variables served the U.S. national interests during the Cold War but after September 11, Washington could no longer control them. The United States, the most powerful nation on the earth, was preoccupied with international conflicts, bearing the sole responsibility for peacebuilding. In the light of China's rise, American global commitments took an even more important place in U.S. Foreign Policy when international organizations were incapable of untangling the puzzle of global terrorist networks.

Some would argue that the war on terror is to blame for the unipolar syndrome. I reject that view simply because the syndrome originates from unipolarity. U.S. policymakers believed that the American crusade in MENA would take less time than a conventional conflict. However, in shaping the perceptions of warfare, long-term predictions are as important as resource planning. The war on terror corrupted those perceptions after the U.S. interventions took the shape of a crusade. History shows that the results are catastrophic when a military operation becomes a vehicle of moralistic values. Such was the detrimental effect of the prolonged American presence in Iraq and Afghanistan.

To sum up, the unipolar syndrome prevented U.S. policy-makers from establishing a rational image of the international system. Instead of investing more efforts in deterring the rise of China and the revival of Russia, Washington preferred to spend its resources on exhausting military campaigns and post-war recovery. Under such circumstances, peace was a distant purpose, which rested on the liberal promise that cooperation would make state actors less hostile. Why has cooperation become more attractive than competition? One possible explanation refers to the rise of transnational terrorist networks. The U.S.-led system of alliances has reinvented the face of the common enemy, and thus, Washington could again lead the free world against the terrorists. Another interpretation involves the collapse of the Soviet Union and the undisputed predominance of America. Washington's allies enjoyed the privilege of support from the world's leader and neglected Walt's warning that alliances are fragile when the dominant power changes its priorities. The United States, once vigilant and highly competitive, has now become moralistic and less rational in its belief that the Chinese economic growth is a benefit. Economic interdependence between nations favored both America and its allies, but it benefited the rise of China. Some might argue that the world's largest economies will never go to war due to the global outcome of their clash. However, realism believes that states are rational actors and that their ultimate purpose is to survive. The unipolar syndrome dulled the sense of survival, which dominated U.S. Foreign Policy during the Cold War. Even if democracy-building in Afghanistan has succeeded, the United States could not have sustained unipolarity as it contained the seeds of its own destruction (Jervis 2009, 213). Thus, the most logical treatment for the unipolar syndrome is powershifting. I assume that it will be in the national interests of the United States to secure the transition from unipolarity instead of risking another war. Some have believed that after the U.S. intervention in Iraq in 2003, the unipolar world order would survive. Few then realized that it was not America that was in decline but unipolarity itself.

Sacrificing the American power. The concept of power provokes constant debates among liberal and realist scholars. The United States does not hesitate to demonstrate power when defending its national security. However, American policymakers tend to be hesitant in defining the purpose of the U.S. military involvements. National interests are still central to U.S. Foreign Policy, but after the end of the Cold War, partially for reasons of ideology, Washington often identifies and justifies its interventions with the preservation of the U.S.-led liberal order. Unipolarity allows Washington to dominate and act unilaterally but limits its foreign policy in terms of nuclear diplomacy. However, does sustainment of the unipolar world order coincide with the U.S. national interests? I assume that we can trace the answer in the years after September 11. Proponents of unipolarity assign its benefits primarily to the power the United States can exercise in the international system. The unipole's power, however, is imperial by design (Mearsheimer 2011, 30). It is untenable to assume that the world's most powerful nation will exercise power only for the sake of peace. Such on optimistic vision has profound implications for the post-Cold War order and tempted policymakers to use moralistic justifications when shaping their doctrines. The optimistic rhetoric and the brave intentions of the Presidential administrations, who advocate global commitments, should have predicted the detrimental effects of pursuing global dominance in a globalized world. One can assume that policymakers, who shape the foreign policy of the most powerful nation, will calculate the risks of imperial temptations. When a great power has no peer competitors, the use of force often inspires those in charge to pull the trigger. For the United States to exercise power in a nuclear world, in which regional conflicts flourish and rogue states seek to maximize their military capability, requires *calculated* use of power. Since state actors like North Korea are unpredictable, and terrorist networks bind the globe from MENA to Europe, the temptation to fight a war or send troops to support another nation is unbearable. Therefore, once the unipole decides to act, it faces the imminent reality of struggling for more power and finally undertaking another commitment. While the unipole can still realize the limits of its power, it should expect another opportunity for involvement due to the consequences of its actions. Moreover, because the United States has established a global system of alliances, it needs to introduce a justification for its strategy. Even if such is present, the constant demonstration of power exhaust the unipole's resources as the initial intervention leads to another. President George W. Bush believed that the United States should strike Afghanistan but failed to predict that the U.S. military presence in the region would not prevent the Taliban from returning to power twenty years later. In other words, miscalculated power lacks the cohesion and the resources it needs to deal with the threat. Thus, the unipole behaves like an empire, which seeks to use force without further necessity to do so. The American interventions in Iraq and Afghanistan could have served as revenge for September 11 and could have left a warning message to all U.S. adversaries if it had not been for the insatiable struggle to export democracy in MENA. In 2021, the United States still enjoys its international prestige, partially because Donald Trump lost the Presidential election. However, we cannot say the same for the unipolar world order. Nor can we believe that the majority of the American people support unconditionally the U.S. global leadership.

Shifting the structure. Before the Pandemic outbreak, the Trump administration pursued a foreign policy that could lead to a military conflict between the United States and China. Neither of both powers was willing to start a war. Nevertheless, Sino-American relations deteriorated to an extent, which corresponds perfectly to Graham Allison's theory of the Thucydides trap. Why did U.S. policymakers fail to foresee the rise of China? I assume that the answer lies in neoliberal revisionism, which has dominated U.S. Foreign Policy since the collapse of the Soviet Union. The optimistic and inspirational enthusiasm of liberal institutionalism, combined with the post-Hegelian vision of the unipolar world order, rejected the most important lesson from the Cold War – that predicting the moves of adversaries requires a structural analysis of international politics. In other words, U.S. Foreign Policy has abandoned the legacy of structural realism that stressed the need for a profound and rational assessment of the international system and its structure, without which one cannot understand the foreign policy of state actors (Waltz 2000, 7). Liberal institutionalists purport to introduce an explanation of systemic outcomes of interstate interactions and argue that liberalism offers a distinctive conception of power in world politics (Moravcsik 1997, 523). My criticism of the neoliberal theory is not absolute, and this book does not reject the liberal assumptions of Francis Fukuyama, Joseph Nye, and Andrew Moravcsik. However, interstate cooperation and economic interdependence are not the only driving forces influencing state behavior. Therefore, I assume that the liberal paradigm offers a plausible explanation of the systematic outcomes through exploring political relations among nations but fails to predict the structural implications for world politics. It simply provides an elegant and precise understanding of how state actors interact and behave in the unipolar world order, how the unipole can use power (hard, soft, or smart), and how growing interdependence among states reduces the risks of conflicts.

Although most liberal scholars do not reject the legacy of realism explicitly, their assumptions rebuke the realist vision of international politics and thus, deprive U.S. Foreign Policy of its rational perceptions of great powers competition. If the foremost purpose of American foreign policy after the Cold War were to prevent another superpower's rise, it would be even more difficult for China to challenge the U.S. primacy. When Beijing finally threw the cloak off, liberal institutionalism faced its ultimate failure when Washington tried to pressure the

Chinese Communist Party on human rights. Waltz's prophecy that China would become a great power was finally fulfilled when Chinese President Xi Jinping took office. In an even shorter time, the United States refused to tolerate the Chinese as peer-competitor, although Washington has been treating Beijing as such since the Sino-American disputes in the South China Sea. Another failed prediction is that the willingness of states to expend resources in pursuit of foreign policy goal as a strict function of existing capabilities seems unrealistic (Moravcsik 1997, 524). The capacity of each state actor depends on a combination of material realities such as military strength, territory, or the stability of its government. The rise of China is a product of a long-standing strategy that seeks to maximize those aspects. Realist scholars like Mearsheimer warned that China would attempt to pursue a regional hegemony in the APAC as the United States did in Latin America (Mearsheimer 2006, 170). With nuclear weapons in its arsenal, Beijing has already established an outpost for that strategy – Taiwan. Since the small island is no match for China, the Thucydides trap of Allison seems more realistic than ever.

I will conclude this chapter with my final assumption: it is not the United States that declines, but liberal hegemony. The reason, which I consider most important for that, is the evolving post-pandemic structure of world politics. To say that the Pandemic alone is responsible for the end of unipolarity is to overestimate its impact. The Pandemic is rather the final stage of structural transition, which will reshape the balance of power in international relations as the collapse of the Soviet Union did in 1992. Since the United States and China cannot fight a war without risking MAD, their foreign policy is likely to pursue an approach similar to containment unless Washington decides to attack first. However, a war with Beijing could provoke other nuclear powers like Russia and eventually lead the world to the brink of a nuclear apocalypse. In contrast, there is little chance that China will strike the United States because, in 2021, Washington still surpasses the Chinese military capabilities. The development of either fighting war with Beijing for Taiwan or long-term containment of China will be central to U.S. Foreign Policy. Thus, with the end of unipolarity, state actors will return to the old school conventional realities, in which hard power predetermines politics among nations and in which the balance of power reflects the national interests of great powers. If the United States wants to survive the transition, it should abandon the pursuit of liberal hegemony and reshape its foreign policy by reviving the American *realpolitik*. Only if Washington focuses its primary concerns on maximizing the U.S. military potential will the United States be able to deter China, which has not ratified even a single agreement on arms control. The lessons from the Soviet fall teach us that even a superpower with a significant offensive advantage can lose the competition if the struggle for hegemony prevails over rational decision-making. A superpower with a balanced strategy that seeks both offensive and defensive advantages, quite the opposite, could overcome the threat of its adversary without fighting a war. The rise of China will certainly produce negative effects on the U.S. influence in the APAC and thus, will tilt the cooperation under the security dilemma to confrontation. Although Washington and Beijing are rational actors and aim to survive, they do not share a common vision of the world as Roosevelt and Stalin did after World War II. Liberal theoreticians could argue that comparisons between USSR and China are inconsistent. Even so, that does not change the fact that Moscow in 1952 and Beijing in 2022 behave as great powers. We should highlight that the liberal approach to the understanding of China advocates the deterrent force of the economic interdependence between Washington and Beijing. Great powers, however, especially the rising ones, tend to behave aggressively and seize the ultimate opportunity to deal with their peer competitors as soon as possible. Liberal democracies make no exclusion. National security is central to foreign policy because state actors fear each other. If China takes over Taiwan and gains a direct outpost to threaten the West Coast, what would the United States' rational response be? If Washington topples the regime in Pyongyang and unites the Korean Peninsula, what would China's logical step be? Liberal optimism melted when Russia invaded Ukraine in 2014 and annexed Crimea without seeking international approval or support for its actions. For liberal policymakers, war with China might damage the U.S. economy to an extent, which will throw the world into another global recession. The realist paradigm jumps beyond those calculations and seeks to explain that mutual distrust and antagonistic tension between Uncle Sam and The Dragon will not ease simply because both powers could lose money while fighting over Taiwan. Neither the Hong Kong protests will touch the Communist Party's concept of One-China. It is precisely the strength of realism to predict politics among nations and interpret the future structure of international politics. Finally, liberal scholars tend to exaggerate the ideological confrontation between great powers. To explain the Sino-American competition only with the clash between communism and liberal democracy is a limited approach, which cannot predict the long-term evolution of the Chinese foreign policy. Instead of searching for the the reasons for great powers behavior inside state ideology, realism introduces a more pragmatic approach, which explores the external sources of foreign policy. The dissolution of the socialist bloc and the obvious prepotency of Reagan's America doomed the Soviets, not the Perestroika. Therefore, if China reforms, the short-term aspects of its foreign policy might change, but the Chinese dream of tributary leadership will dominate Beijing's vision of the international system. Thus, we return to the profound assumption of realism that a great power's foreign policy, which seeks to alter the international anarchy and pursue global hegemony, is more likely to sacrifice its national interests and fail (Morgenthau 1949, 110). History offers no better example for my argument than the glorious rise and decline of Rome.

Chapter Three
China: The Silent Cultivator

In this chapter, I analyze China's Grand Strategy. In contrast to most writings on this topic, I employ an approach that does not follow the straightforward doctrinal analysis applicable to U.S. Foreign Policy. I have chosen to utilize a research design that explores the essential aspects of China's Grand Strategy instead of analyzing the doctrines of the Chinese leaders. I assume that, unlike American politics, which pursues strategic outcomes in the short-term, Beijing has a clear, long-term vision for the place of China in international politics. My assumption originates from the profound difference between liberal democracies and states with original cultivated traditions like China. Liberal democracies like the United States follow a policy that combines short-term goals with the long-standing dream of global leadership. Political systems like China also tend to pursue a great power policy but are more likely to endorse a long-term leadership strategy. Here, I want to stress the structural difference between Chinese Communism and other totalitarian forms of government, deprived of what I call *pragmatic leadership*. I will further discuss why this book considers Beijing an exception from the generally adopted vision of political autocracies. Another considerable gap that divides the nature of U.S. Foreign Policy from the Chinese is the individualistic load of the American Presidential doctrines. Although America pursues a great power foreign policy, its strategies vary from one President to another. China, quite the opposite, subdues the doctrines of its leaders to an ideological line, which aims to ensure the continuity of a millennial imperial tradition. One might argue that the Chinese Revolution changed the regime in Beijing and erased China's ancient struggle for longevity. Although ideology plays an important role in politics, it is inferior to power competition and security. To say that Communist China does not share the ideological framework of its predecessor is reasonable. But to assume that Communism has made Beijing less rational and less concerned for its survival is to conclude that Post-Soviet Russia does not pursue an imperialistic vision, similar to that of the Russian Empire. Finally, I argue that one should not confuse domestic politics in Beijing with Chinese *realpolitik*. In this book, I distinguish between the realist paradigm of the Chinese grand strategy and the political order which rules contemporary China. Chinese realism is a rational reflection of great power behavior that embodies the aspects I analyze below. Therefore, before discussing the aspects of China's Grand Design, we should first dismantle two mythologies about China.

The most popular myth refers to the arguable assumption that Confucianism runs contemporary China (Mearsheimer 2006, 190). All great powers in history have established their *parabellum paradigm*, through which they have expanded until reaching the limits of their power. However, I assume that the ancient tradition of China has left a tangible trail in Beijing's policy on a domestic level. The Confucian paradigm shapes the perceptions of Chinese people on the other nations (Zhimin 2005, 37). Chinese exceptionalism is much older than the American Manifest Destiny, though it is as inspirational as the latter. Confucianism, amid the revolutionary concept of Communism, empowers China to create a distinctive vision of its place in the eyes of its people. In other words, although deprived of its essential peaceful nature, the philosophy of Confucius easily legitimates the concept of "Great China" that seeks to bring harmonious coexistence between nations. Though Mearsheimer and Johnson are right in concluding that Beijing's *realpolitik* involves the existence of the parabellum paradigm, my assumption is that instead of searching the roots of Chinese foreign policy in Confucianism, we should rather consider the ancient tradition of China a source of national and political pride. In addition, Confucianism serves as the Great Wall against the ideological influence that could potentially harm the prestige of Beijing's policymakers. Yet, Confucius was a strong proponent of the Mandate of Haven and advocated major reforms in Imperial China to restore the asymmetrical relations of obedience between the Emperor and his subjects (Tu 1996, 10).

Another myth that enjoys considerable support among Western scholars depicts China as an orthodox Communist state, bound to lose the great powers competition as the USSR did. I consider such a view of China deeply misleading and irrelevant. President Deng Xiaoping, widely regarded as the Social Reformer, introduced a number of political and economic reforms, which advocated a composite approach to political participation and competition (Zhou 1993, 64). One might argue that the success of Xiaoping's reforms is dubious, but such arguments lack validity in the face of rising China. I assume that orthodox Communism and strict centralization are the temptations, which Beijing faces, although the Chinese political regime has kept its commitments to the legacy of Deng Xiaoping. However, saying that China is much like, the Soviet Union is a profound theoretical and practical misjudgment. The Bolsheviks drew inspiration from the French Revolution, and after the fall of Tsarist Russia, Lenin constructed the ideological amalgam of Marxism-Leninism by combining the Marxist view of the economy with his notable writing "What is to be done." (Lenin 1935). The concept of Mao Zedong differs from Lenin's, more particularly in that it stresses more the materialistic dialectics (Holubnychy 1964, 3). The writings of Lenin influenced Mao, which is obvious from the cited sources in Mao's books. However, the content analysis of Holubnychy indicates that Mao seemed to be especially fond of quoting Taoist, Mohist, and even neo-Confucian writings in contrast to Lenin, who despised the Christian Orthodox culture and the Eurasian writings of Trubetskoy and Savitsky (see tab. 1). To sum up, although the Chinese revolution overthrew the political order in Beijing, Mao Zedong's selective approach to materialistic dialectics incorporates some traditional ideas in the political formula of Communist China.

Table 1: Holubnychy's content analysis of Mao's four major works.

References	Percentage of references in Mao's writings
Confucianism	22%
Taoism and Mohism	12%
Chinese folklore	13%
Chinese poetry	7%
Marx and Engels	4%
Lenin	18%
Stalin	24%
Total:	100%

I assume that the Grand Design of China consists of six pillars. Each pillar corresponds to a distinct Chinese perception of world politics. My approach is limited in two ways. First, this book does not purport to introduce a theory of Chinese politics. Therefore, my analysis does not examine the doctrinal concepts of the Chinese leaders. To review and discuss the political ideas of China's elite, from Mao to Xi Jinping, will require another book. Second, my research design does not seek to provide cultural parallels between Ancient and Communist China. I assume that a historical overview of Chinese philosophers like Confucius could contribute to understanding Chinese political culture. However, this book is about international relations and great powers competition, not Asian or American studies. I have found it reasonable to include the military treatises attributed to tacticians such as Sun Tzu and Sun Bin because I considered those writings even more important to China's Grand Design than Confucius did. I have also excluded religious writings, which are vaguely relevant for this research. Finally, most of the original Chinese texts I used are of English or Russian translation, which, I believe, will not deprive this chapter of its empirical validity.

Mao's dialectics

Western scholars exaggerate the gap between Beijing's foreign policy under Mao and the interventionist approach of his successors. When Francis Fukuyama faced considerable criticism after September 11, he introduced a clarification about his theory, claiming that *The end of the history and the Last Man* reflects the master-slave dialectics of human history (Fukuyama 2006, 10). However, the writings of Mao Zedong offered another dialectical approach, and thus, I assume they are central to the understanding of Chinese Foreign Policy for three reasons. First, Mao's works reflect the Chinese post-revolutionary perceptions of foreign policy. Communism utilizes the Hegelian dialectics to restrain the radical load of revolutions and establish an ultimate purpose of history. The selective approach of Mao, however, differs from that of Lenin and his successors. Second, Mao's philosophical treatises are the source of inspiration for the Chinese Communist Party, and thus, his dialectic vision provides a plausible starting point for the operationalization of Beijing's post-revolutionary foreign policy. Finally, in contrast to the Western dialectical approach, presently dominated by Fukuyama's neoliberalism, Mao's dialectics left a sensible trail in Chinese politics.

Mao's dialectics differ from Fukuyama's in the former's perceptions of the structure of international politics and the future of great powers. For the Fukuyama-dominated Western approach to dialectics, the end of history presumes the domination of one great power – the United States – and one final form of government – liberal democracy. Mao's dialectics advocate the rise of China as a communist power but reject global hegemony. Moreover, the nature of Mao's dialectics implies that the great power status of China would not be determined by whether Beijing was a hegemon or not. Maoism defines a larger and far-reaching political horizon that envisions Chinese history as a series of rises and declines with the ultimate purpose to secure its rightful place in the international system and prevent another century of humiliation. For Fukuyama, that purpose expresses the struggle of the liberal democracies to end history and justify their universal legitimacy. Mao's dialectics does not seek to justify the general validity of Communism. Instead, it aims to subject and adapt its ideology to the Chinese national interests – a purpose that still dominates the political concepts of the Chinese Communist Party. This book suggests that Mao Zedong has set a two-level concept that revises the philosophical implications on policy-making and operationalizes the continuity with the pre-revolutionary Chinese tradition. I begin with an examination of four theoretical dimensions that serve as arguments for my assumption.

The first dimension is *isolationism*. In *On Contradiction*, Mao argues that contradictory things are at the same time complementary and that all opposite elements are like this: because of certain conditions, they are on the one hand opposed to each other, and on the other hand, they are interconnected, interpenetrating, and interpermeating (Zedong 1987, 10). Therefore, contradictions cease to exist when the conditions for their existence lose premises. Applied to politics, the concept of contradictions presumes that Chinese Foreign

Policy has sensible foundations. Therefore, Chinese perceptions of international politics have structural and complex nature. The theoretical axiom, which Mao uses to describe the essential connection between contradictive and complementary elements, predetermines the distinctive vision of Chinese foreign policy, which perceives the structure of international politics as interdependent and interchangeable. However, one should not confuse the Chinese concept of interdependence with the liberal theory introduced by Joseph Nye and Robert Keohane. In his writings, Mao provides a number of examples, referring to the economy, agriculture, and knowledge (Zedong 1987, 11). The Chinese comprehension of interdependence lies within its corresponding notion of *harmony*. However, Beijing's view on harmony presumes a two-level pattern of foreign policy, which combines the establishment of tributary dependence between China and other state actors with upholding the national interests. One might argue that the Communist ideology, which has been dominating the political life in China since the War of Liberation, had pursued hegemony as the Soviet Union did until its collapse. I reject that view. Paradoxically, the logic of Mao's Grand Design did not seek to expand Beijing's influence beyond the borders of Mainland China. The efforts of the Chinese Communist Party to regulate and maintain balanced relations with the USSR are a perfect example of Mao's ambiguous criticism of the Soviets. The Marxist rejection of politics and the Leninist interpretation of the class struggle served as a starting point for Maoism, although their reflections dominated the domestic politics of Mao. In other words, the transition from Imperial to Communist society was central to Maoism precisely because the theoretical core of Mao's writings differed between domestic politics and foreign, or as called later – imperialist policy. The Maoist axiom of contradiction sought to transform Chinese society and build a strong patriotic sentiment on the ruins of the Qing dynasty. However, Mao's interpretation of Marxism-Leninism affected the Chinese perceptions of foreign policy, reaffirming the realist core assumption that states, regardless of their ideology, are rational actors.

The second dimension refers to Mao's *vision* of international politics. Some would argue that Mao was vaguely familiar with the Western concepts of international relations, and thus, it is untenable to argue that he has designed a thoughtful paradigm of foreign policy. This book joins the academic debate by asserting that the Chinese theory of international relations is an empirical oxymoron for a simple reason: it is methodologically irrelevant to make a comparison between Chinese intellectual tradition and theoretical paradigms of international relations, dominated by Western scholars (Qin 2007, 320). Instead, the foreign policy tradition of post-revolutionary China emerged under Mao's "three worlds theory" (An 2013, 40). In his writings, Mao conducted a structural analysis of the international system, dividing the world into three: imperialistic nuclear powers (the United States and the Soviet Union), states inferior to the superpowers (Japan, Britain and the rest of Europe), and state actors that do not pursue an imperialistic foreign policy (former colonies in Africa and Asian countries) (An 2013, 45). The Chinese leader employs an approach that incorporates two variables central to Marxism: asymmetrical economic dependence between classes and rejection of colonialism. Mao's dissection of the international system positions the USSR alongside the United States and the rest of the capitalist world. Therefore, the assumption that both China and the Soviet Union pursued an expansionist policy adds empirical validity. For China, the most powerful nations during the Cold War were equal to the dark imperialistic forces, which Marx and Lenin rebuked in their writings. China's Communist Party considered Americans and Soviets no better than the Japanese, who attempted to colonize APAC during World War II or the British Empire with its endless overseas protectorates. Thus, Mao's three worlds theory predetermined Chinese isolationism, which dominated Beijing's foreign policy before the rapprochement with the United States.

Anti-imperialism is a central variable of Maoism. One might argue that the rise of China itself is an expression of imperialist temptations, similar to the historical emergence of great European powers and the United States. The assumption that Beijing seeks regional hegemony in the APAC and, in the long-term future, global leadership is empirically valid, and I do not intend to reject it. However, I assume that one should neglect the profound historical difference that exists between the Chinese strategy and Western imperialism. For the Chinese, the rise of their country is granted by nature (Xuetong 2001, 35). It is a long-term process that started with the Sino-American rapprochement during the Cold War, when the United States recognized the Chinese claims over Tibet and thus, reaffirmed the emerging policy of One-China. What is so different between Western imperialism and the rise of China?

Kissinger reminds us that, in contrast to Europe and Eurasia, China was the center of its own hierarchical and theoretical concept of order (Kissinger 2014, 10). In other words, the Chinese Grand Strategy is not pacifistic, but it opposes the Western pattern of imperialism. The reason lies not only in Maoism, it stemmed from the Ancient Chinese tradition that had dominated the political culture of Beijing for thousands of years. Some would argue that, theoretically, imperialism is an indivisible concept, and it is irrelevant to define original types of imperialist behavior. Even so, international relations scholars cannot deny that the concept of the political order in Ancient China differs from that of Ancient Greece, Rome, and Imperium Christianium. Mearsheimer is right in his claim about China, acting not always according to the dictates of Confucianism (Mearsheimer 2006, 160). If only it were Confucius alone. The Chinese concept of political order is not a simple product of Confucian philosophy. One should not neglect the essential contributions of military theoreticians like Sun Tzu, whose military treatise inoculates the Chinese military spirit. Beijing has a long history of fighting The Art of War against its neighbors, but Beijing's record of pursuing colonies is clear. Xuetong, in contrast to Mearsheimer, identifies the power status of China with the concepts of "Peaceful Rise" and "Peaceful Development." (Xuetong 2001, 13). Xuetong's claim would have revealed the future of international politics if it had not been the theory of Graham Allison with its clear emphasis on the inevitable clash between the United States and China. Allison, similar to Mearsheimer, is clear when stating that predominant powers do not tolerate peer competitors and that the rising tensions between both could lead to a military conflict. Thus, we should trace the roots of Sino-American competition in the realist explanations of war. Since the United States does not tolerate the rise of China and since Beijing rejects Western imperialism, then the probable outcome is likely to justify the concerns of Allison. However, the ultimate choice belongs to the dominant superpower. When the United States overtook the British Empire as the world's leader, Britain easily came to terms with bipolarity. History, however, seldom repeats itself. The rise of China will not be peaceful if the American policy of non-tolerance escalates into a nuclear crisis. In truth, Beijing considers Taiwan part of mainland China. It is, however, debatable if a military operation in support of Taipei is a rational cost for the American national interests. For China, reunification with Taiwan would be as essential as the British handover of Hong Kong. For America, it would be rather military aggression and open expression of Chinese imperialism. For the rest of the world, it would be a war between great powers, which seek to reshape the post-pandemic structure of international politics. The ultimate explanation, again, lies in the realist paradigm of Hans Morgenthau, who concludes that superpowers begin to deal with each other as traditional great powers, have certain interests (Cesa 2009, 181).

The third facet of Maoism, which inspires the foreign policy of contemporary China, is *continuity*. Mao assumes that each contradiction in itself is particular and concrete and that among all, one is necessarily the principal contradiction, whose existence and development influence or determine the others (Zedong 1987, 30). I call this aspect *continuity* due to its opposition to the Western vision of effective results at the costs of short-term vision. In contrast to Western perceptions and Soviet utopias, the Maoist paradigm advocates a long-term self-preservation strategy. Chinese foreign policy after the War of Liberation corresponds to the rational behavior of state actors and resembles the strategy of emerging great power. Mao's foreign policy did not pursue global leadership or utopic hegemony like the Soviet Union. Instead, Zedong's rational philosophy embodies four essential priorities: limited détente with the United States and the Soviet Union, changing the status quo in Eastern and South-Eastern Asia, securing the Chinese political and ideological independence from the USSR (Yahuda 1968, 97). A more detailed look at Mao's priorities would show that it set the preconditions for a long-term, spatially determined grand design, seeking to increase the Chinese influence and defend Beijing's national interests. It is but a realist philosophy, which promotes rational decision-making. What differentiates the Maoist concept from the Western is the central importance of spatiality. For instance, the Presidential doctrines from the Cold War era prioritized the American national interests and advocated the use of force wherever is necessary and rational. Spatiality allowed China to isolate itself from world affairs and establish a longevous framework of its foreign policy without intervening in the relations between the United States and the Soviet Union. Beijing cheated both Washington and Moscow with the universal message of Mao Zedong, which, under the guise of ideology, established a foreign policy line of pragmatic isolationism. Although Chinese foreign policy at present days is not isolationist, it still incorporates the facet of spatiality. Contemporary China does not seek military confrontation with the United States but rather tempts Washington to attack first, playing under the guise of another ideology – revisited Communism or socialism with Chinese characteristics. The foremost purpose of Beijing's Grand Design is to change the status quo in Asia, claiming Taiwan and the South China Sea. If Western rational thought has established a short-term view of foreign policy, the Chinese paradigm has jumped beyond the American perceptions of great powers competition. If the future of liberal hegemony is highly challengeable, it is by no means correct to praise the rising Dragon. Liberal democracies desire power here and now and, thus, possess the resources to achieve it. To a further extent, China pursues a great power policy, and the longevous nature of its concept predetermines its success. However, longevity is advantageous only when their state agents are in a position of enough power to emerge as great powers. The effects of spatiality can also be detrimental to Chinese foreign policy if Beijing takes off the mask of ideology before the post-pandemic structure of international politics finally overlaps. My assumption is that if China aims to complete the transition to bipolarity, Chinese decision-makers should abstain from open military interventions in the APAC. An eventual war with Washington is the only scenario that could reverse the future predominance of China.

Combined, the three facets of Maoism constitute the theoretical core of Chinese foreign policy after the War of Liberation. In truth, the primary purpose of Mao's philosophical writings was to establish his political authority and ensure the continuity of the collapsed Empire to the People's Republic of China. The Cultural Revolution, The Great Leap Forward, and the rest of Mao's political campaigns fulfilled his vision of strong and independent China. Much has been written on the differences that divide Chinese Communism from that of the USSR. Instead, I have found it reasonable to analyze the Maoist perceptions of U.S. Foreign Policy. I begin with a short review of the Nixon doctrine that is essential to understanding the Sino-American rapprochement.

Unlike most Presidential administrations, Nixon represents a perfect example of strategic teamwork between the President and his Secretary of State, Henry Kissinger. The efforts of Richard Nixon to strengthen the United States expressed the three lines of his doctrine. The first concerned limited adversary relationship through reconciling the demands of residual strategic bipolarity with those presented by the new conditions of politico-economic multipolarity (Litwak 1986, 80). While the preceding administrations sought to increase the U.S. influence and contain the USSR by weaving bipolar confrontation as a cornerstone of their doctrines, Kissinger chose to reshape the strategic perceptions of U.S. Foreign Policy. Overstressing bipolarity and confrontation with Moscow meant the imminent risk of mutual assured destruction. With the USSR dominating the socialistic bloc, Washington was dogged to deter the Soviet nuclear threat and Communism. Henceforth, Nixon and Kissinger designed a policy of rapprochement with China to undermine Kremlin's ideological primacy. They worked to establish stable and constructive Sino-American relations and motivate Beijing to act independently from Moscow. Recognizing the People's Republic of China also meant making it friendly to the United States so that the Soviet orthodox Communists could no longer consider themselves the voice of the Proletariat. American officials, however, were aware that unless the Sino-Soviet border conflict was kept under control, it could evolve into limited nuclear warfare. Therefore, President Nixon endorsed a dual strategy: to continue talks with Chairman Mao Zedong and make certain that Moscow's efforts to threaten the Chinese national interests would remain futile.

Second, the Nixon doctrine revises U.S. perceptions of warfare and defines the limits of politico-military retrenchment (Litwak 1986, 117). Historians and political scientists tend to exaggerate the impact of the Vietnam War on U.S. Foreign Policy. However, the Vietnam experience undercut the robust position of America in the eyes of its allies for two reasons. First, in terms of military strategies, U.S. decision-makers reached a consensus on the limits of conventional warfare and its inefficiency against unconventional tactics. Washington could no longer support a feasible image of its military policy if it had to act unilaterally or coordinate with its allies. The consequence was that the Vietnam War would deprive future U.S. interventions of political meaning because Washington could not easily justify its prolonged involvement in the region. The political and military weight shifted away from America to the USSR. Second, the Vietnam experience drained significant economic resources from the United States. Nixon and Kissinger realized that the future essence of U.S. Foreign Policy should reflect the national interests of the United States. Instead, the Nation's foreign policy has become an amalgam of universal commitments and containment those years of bipolar confrontation had generated. If the Nixon administration was to reshape its foreign policy, the President should start by revisiting relations with the allies and balancing the strategy of containment. For these reasons, the Nixon doctrine elaborated the basic criterion of American commitment and selective engagement. Moreover, Nixon and Kissinger calculated that diplomatic talks and bilateral dialogues with U.S. adversaries would favor U.S. Foreign Policy better than demonstrating power. Thus, the United States adopted a *détente* strategy aimed to release tensions with the Soviet Union. It was a flexible approach with the dual intent to remedy the Vietnam experience and to improve relations with China. In attempting to heal the wounds from the War, Washington forgot that the United States should inevitably develop its strategy of unconventional warfare. The Nixon administration calculated the risks of another intervention in the Asia-Pacific but misjudged the evolving nature of war.

The final line refers to détente: a strategy serving to create a favorable Great Power atmosphere in which the Nixon doctrine could be applied to permit an orderly devolution of American power to incipient regional powers. In a bipolar world, however, détente was a risky strategy. In his attempts to incorporate it into U.S. Foreign Policy, President Nixon realized that détente would probably change the dynamic of U.S.-Soviet relations and that it could deflect in challengeable directions. Apart from the fact that the Brezhnev doctrine advocated collective defense and justified Soviet military interference in the socialist camp, the Nixon administration was rigid in its decision to follow détente. However, Nixon's choice of strategy was not to patronize the Brezhnev doctrine. The Presidential administration was highly sensitive to undertaking further commitments in Europe that could favor Soviet diplomacy. The European Community opposed the U.S. actions in South East Asia, and thus, President Nixon understood the concerns that the European allies had about the future of NATO in terms of arms limitation and U.S.-Soviet talks. Years later, Henry Kissinger foretold the destructive scenario of nuclear warfare that could come to reality if the allies invoked Article Five from the Washington Treaty. In short, the Nixon doctrine was the only rational form U.S. Foreign Policy could take at that time. The United States could not guarantee that it would initiate what Kissinger called "a blood-thirsty strategy" and retaliate against a potential nuclear attack on the Western Hemisphere. Washington, however, did not lose the trust of its allies for a simple reason: lack of a better alternative. The European Community worried about the rise of the pro-Soviet movements in its Member States, apart from the negative effects that the *Eurosclerosis* period had produced. There was enough diffidence about the course European integration should take and not enough consent on economic regulations. The European nations did not trust each other, and their common distrust turned against the Americans. The way to ease Euro-Atlantic tensions was through détente and dialogue with the Soviets. President Nixon realized that the best way to shunt the European mistrust was to repurpose NATO. In 1969, during his address to the Commemorative Session of the Alliance, Nixon urged that the allies stress their mutual benefits from the collective defense and create a social dimension of NATO. A successful move consolidated the allies for another 20 years.

Throughout most of his term, President Nixon sought to reshape U.S. Foreign Policy and boost rapprochement with China in response to the Brezhnev doctrine. However, improving Sino-American relations was only one aspect of the Nixon doctrine that introduced a more relevant approach to foreign policy decision-making. More important was the compliance of the Nixon administration with two major foreign policy revisions: rethinking the U.S. global commitments and endorsing the strategy of détente. Before Nixon, the United States maintained that China was much like the Soviet Union and benefited from not recognizing the regime in Beijing. Kissinger, however, realized that Chinese Communism did not follow the anti-Stalinism of Khrushchev and thus, considered Maoism an independent ideological entity that differed from the post-Stalinist interpretations of Marxism-Leninism. In further defense of their doctrine, the Chinese even denounced Soviet Communism, claiming that the USSR preached socialist imperialism, thereby depicting the latter as a corrupted and declining ideology. There was no agreement between Beijing and Moscow about whether a Stalinist cult for the leader should provide the political formula of Communism and about whether the Soviet Union would hold the ideological primacy in the socialist bloc. Most of Mao's rhetoric had been spent on whether Moscow was a broken shadow of true Communism or a victim of its imperialist ambitions.

Even though there were many criticisms and discords about the U.S.-China rapprochement, two major presumptions have hardened the position of the Nixon administration: the unpredictable behavior of Brezhnev and the Sino-Soviet split. In effect, President Nixon's strategy of utilizing rapprochement with Beijing to split the Communist camp was successful. In another sense, the Nixon doctrine has been lost. For what was the aftermath of the rapprochement, the Sino-American cooperation did not benefit U.S. Foreign Policy in long-terms; it rather undercut the future of the American global leadership. Washington wanted China to become a buffer against the ideological and political expansion of the USSR because Nixon believed that Beijing's foreign policy would push off and contain the Soviet ambitions. Moscow sought to marginalize the

People's Republic so that it could be subsidiary to Kremlin. Both America and the Soviet Union underestimated the Chinese ambitions and thus, legitimized Beijing's aspirations for future leadership. It was but a historical and ideological compromise that shaped the dimensions of the centuries-old Chinese strategy of long-term domination. Despite the nukes, China was for match to the military potential of the superpowers. However, the *modus vivendi* of Beijing relied largely on economic expansion, combined with what the United States called pragmatic dictatorship. China accepted the American lead to counter the ideological ambitions of the USSR, but only as long as it benefited the core of the Chinese spatial strategy – pursuing a policy of global leadership through weakening the Soviet Union and the United States.

Why was Mao's foreign policy successful? Although the vast majority of Western scholars have consistently depicted the Maoist paradigm through the lenses of the Cultural Revolution, their approach seemed to be one-sided and misleading. Maoism drew inspiration from original Chinese philosophies such as Taoism and Mohism and thus, constructed a theoretical system of dialectics, which partially mirrored orthodox Soviet Communism (Holubnychy 1964, 25). In other words, Mao employed the research design of Marxism and Lenin's writings, transforming them through the prism of his philosophical creed, combined with the charismatic inheritance of the traditional Chinese culture. The personal political experience of Mao provided him with the political formula of the People's Republic. The Chinese Empire was no more, and the monarchy collapsed. However, the Mandate of Heaven did not die. For Mao, the Emperor was a product of the feudal Chinese society and the subsequent process of centralization that marked the reign of the Qin dynasty (Zhou 2016, 262). The position of *Chairman* revived the concept of Chinese leadership and, per se, restored the centralized political authority that perished with the fall of the Qing Empire. Therefore, Beijing emerged as prominent regional power primarily due to the centralization of post-revolutionary China. The Chairman, like the Emperor, was in possession of infinite power. However, Mao succeeded where the Imperial institution had consistently failed throughout its millennial history: he established a political system of hierarchical authority without involving the country in endless domestic conflicts. When China entered the Korean War, Mao sided with the Soviets for ideological reasons, but his rational concern was not to allow American troops on the Chinese borders. The modern schools of international relations would have agreed that the Chinese realpolitik had stemmed its legitimacy from the Maoist concept of foreign policy if it had not been for the ideological prejudices of the Soviets. However, this book finds it reasonable to ask another question – what would have happened if the Chinese Revolution had not been successful? Can we assume that the original Chinese tradition could have melted in the writings of Lenin and Stalin? The answers are unambiguous due to the then predominance of the USSR in Asia. Centralized China was in a far better position to stand for its political and ideological independence with the nuclear powers. It was a strategy of balancing between the most powerful nations who survived World War II. The transition to Communism, thus, was the necessary step China had to undertake for its survival after the Empire lost its legitimacy with Emperor Puyi reigning in Manchuria. Mao was the principal agent of that change, and his vision of the Chinese political order laid the foundations of New China. Although his dialectics were theoretically related to the Soviet tradition and although his campaigns are subject to ideological debates, Zedong's vision of materialistic dialectics offered a revisited political formula, a new Mandate of Heaven that refined the Soviet *Vozhdizm* and introduced a long-term foreign policy strategy to oppose the influence of both United States and the USSR.

The power of cultivation

Every scholar who is familiar with the differences between Lenin's works and Mao's writings would approve that the theoretical approaches of both authors differ from each other. This does not exclude their goal to justify the political formula of Communism, as it is true that Mao and Lenin, and Stalin considered themselves faithful followers of Marx. Lenin borrowed Marxism and the revolutionary concept of the French to elaborate the political philosophy of Marxism-Leninism. Stalin, although tempted to revive the Orthodox Church as a source of legitimacy, did not give up its Cult of Personality. Even after the de-Stalinization, his successors revisited the Eurasian paradigm to justify the political charisma of the Soviet leadership. The Soviet foreign policy, however, did not evolve into a Grand Design and thus, never achieved the extent of plausibility Beijing has succeeded in maintaining. Like the superpower it was, the USSR pursued a hegemonic policy and seldom displayed any signs of reforms. The Chinese foreign policy, quite the opposite, being more flexible and less tempted to promote universal values, was much more realistic in its purposes. The successors of Mao, and more particularly Chairman Deng Xiaoping, dealt with another set of issues, namely, one that allowed Communist China to outlive the Cold War – social reforms. One might argue that for the time of his rule Mao opposed Xiaoping's future vision of China and that Xixian's reformation was not a peaceful transition to modern China. Even so, a few would reject the profound contributions of Deng and the successful implications of his foreign policy towards the Carter administration. Therefore, if Mao laid the foundation of Communist China and its post-revolutionary involvement in international politics, Deng Xiaoping cultivated the Chinese power to coin Beijing's Grand Strategy and avoid Soviet mistakes.

It is important to highlight that partly due to the lack of enough studies on the Chinese concept of power and that because the existing resources originate from the pre-revolutionary history of China, Beijing's foreign policy is subject to theoretical misunderstandings and one-sided assessments. To summarize, we can infer two points of view, which offer valid arguments in support of their assumptions and seek to introduce a plausible explanation of the contemporary Chinese paradigm. One is the assertion of Mearsheimer, who argues that despite its Confucian claims, China's rise will be aggressive and likely to seek regional hegemony in the APAC (Mearsheimer 2006, 170). The other belongs to Yan Xuetong, who claims that Chine will rise peacefully, following the essential Confucian paradigm of benevolence and social harmony (Xuetong 2013, 100). My assumption is that Xuetong's will be valid as long as Beijing follows the policy of *silent cultivator*, while Mearsheimer's predictions will fulfill if America decides to declare war on China. Mearsheimer is right in his assumption that China has elaborated a parabellum paradigm similar to Western perceptions of warfare. However, the Chinese paradigm differs from the latter for a simple reason: it seeks to reverse the American power against the United States instead of attacking first. It is a defensive rather than offensive pattern of warfare, which benefits the Chinese strategy of establishing tributary relations with American allies (Kissinger 2012, 50). To remind, superpowers dominate the structure of international politics and seek to preserve the status quo and tilt the balance of power constantly in their favor. Therefore, I assume that it is more reasonable to ask would the dominant superpower tolerate a peer competitor for global leadership. If Graham Allison is right about the imminent Sino-American clash and its relevance to the geopolitical rivalries between Athens and Sparta, we could easily conclude that Washington will have the final word. If China invades Taiwan, that will not be a peaceful rise but rather a rational move to self-preservation and survival as Washington did when the USSR sent its ships to Cuba in 1962. The Soviet missiles could easily target the United States as the American destroyers in Taiwan waters could hit mainland China. In a nuclear age, where international anarchy predetermines political relations among nations, the vital concern of state actors is their survival. Thus, it is more rational first to assess if Taiwan is the cost both the United States and China are willing to pay to enter into a military confrontation.

I have elaborated the concept of *silent cultivator* to dissect Chinese foreign policy in a manner that is vaguely discussed among scholars. Most of the works, which explore Beijing's strategies, imply that China is a typical Communist power seeking to fulfill the Soviet dream. After discussing the differences between the Soviets and China, I find it reasonable to indicate the weaknesses of such theoretical assumptions. Chinese leaders like Hu Jintao and Xi Jinping came to be devoted proponents of China's rise, but it is untenable to assume that their doctrines blindly worship the legacy of Mao or even the social reforms of Deng Xiaoping. Contrary to the Chinese leaders from the Cold War era, Xi Jinping has the mission to hold the leadership of a rising power, which faces the predominance of another superpower. The world is going bipolar, and thus, China has the opportunity to correct the mistakes of the Soviet Union and emerge as a great power on an equal footing with America. Chinese Communism is an expression of Beijing's domestic political regime, but its foreign policy is much similar to what Western scholars would call *realpolitik* (Christensen 1996, 50). The Soviet foreign policy, quite the opposite, advocated ideological expansion, export of Communism, and unification of the World Proletariat. Even after Stalin dissolved the Communist International, Moscow's "realpolitik" represented a paradox of Communist universalism and uncontrolled squandering of hard power. I continue by introducing my concept, which, I believe, explains further the rise of China after the end of the Cold War.

Robert Jervis stresses the importance of cognitive issues in foreign policy decision-making (Jervis 2017, 205). Therefore, if one seeks to understand the rational behavior of state actors and their foreign policy, the former should start with the examination of cognitive perceptions. Despite their ideological differences, Policymakers always seek to maximize security and ensure the survival of their nations for the sake of their self-preservation. Communism is the political formula of the ruling party in China, but I assert that to limit the analysis of Chinese foreign policy to the Communist ideology is to assume that U.S. Foreign Policy does not mirror the legacy of Britain. The dominant position, which the Chinese Communist Party occupies, allows it to shape Chinese people's political and ideological perceptions. However, a few would neglect that the original tradition of China has also influenced Beijing's policymakers (Xuetong 2008, 140). When I use the term cultivation, I mean the whole branch of traditional perceptions that affect the decision-making process in Beijing on the political, military, economic, and cultural levels. This is not a definition but rather a description of what we should discuss before assessing Chinese realpolitik. I begin with an examination of the Chinese philosophical perceptions of the universe and then continue to its corresponding behavioral attitudes. This book does not deal with theology and religion, and thus, I will limit my review to those aspects of Chinese culture that concern the purposes of my research.

The first and the most profound aspect of cultivation refers to *universalism*. The idea of the "world" in Ancient China embodies three concepts: Tian-Di (Heaven-Earth), Yu-Zhou (Universe), and Shi-Jie (world) (Fa 2014, 4). The interaction between the people and the Universe they inhabited is central to the Chinese comprehension of the world, and thus, it shaped the attitudes of the most powerful groups in Chinese society through the schools of Taoism and Confucianism. The complex nature of the Chinese worldview predetermines its opposition to Western theology, which derived the conclusion about human nature from the Original Sin. Confucianism assumes that although all human beings are born with the ability to be good, each person should cultivate the virtues and overcome the self in order to control the future events and to achieve benevolence (Sternberg and Yang 1997, 101). Another important segment of Confucianism is its typologization of human nature. Confucius believed in the high importance of knowledge and thus, defined four groups of humans: born with knowledge, acquiring knowledge through study and training, turning to benevolence after deviating from the path, and finally, ordinary humans with no motivation to cultivate (Lau 2000). Therefore, the Confucian paradigm advocates the achievement of knowledge and motivates its followers to pursue actions that are justified and right. The principles and the virtues, introduced by Confucius embody a moral code, which seeks the origins of evil in the absence of good (Creel 1931, 30). Taoism moves beyond the theoretical border of Confucianism and identifies the objective reality with the eternal change (Xiaogan 1998, 20). It is a philosophy, which presumes the Universal order exists in a fragile balance and periodically transforms. Taoism does not deal with absolute truths, whether good or evil and thus, excludes the moral cleavage that Western philosophy draws between both. Moreover, the very concept of *Tao* – the right way upon which the Universe moves, presumes a contradiction similar to that Mao analyzed in his dialectics: The Something and The Nothing Produce each other (Kaltenmark 1969, 100). Thus, since the Universe changes constantly, one should follow the right way to adapt through adjusting his way to the Tao, or, as Chuang Tzu discusses, "One the man of far-reaching vision knows how to make divide things into one." Taoism advocates for its followers to achieve full knowledge of their character and the surrounding environment in order to pursue the Tao through adapting their lives to the changing Universe. Although the Taoist paradigm establishes moral standards for humble behavior, it does not advocate following an orthodox and generally valid path outside of Tao. Can we assume that Confucianism and Taoism have influenced Chinese foreign policy after the Cold War? The answer of this book is yes. Thus, I assume that the first aspect of cultivation is *Chinese Universalism*. I offer several proofs in support of my assumption. First off, Confucianism and Taoism are the ideological walls that bar Western influence and liberal democracy from spreading in China. Communism has a central place for maintaining and justifying the political authority of the Chinese Communist Party, but original traditions and their derivatives, such as Neo-Confucianism, are also distinct for the Chinese people. Confucianism and Taoism, although they have no place in the Constitution, are still a source of national and traditional pride and cultural self-identification within the APAC region. In other words, China's strategic culture incorporates the Tao, which domestic politics seek to cultivate and adapt as Deng Xiaoping did. Second, the theoretical core of both philosophies provides us with a further understanding of Chinese foreign policy. For instance, Confucianism encourages the self-motivation and cultivation of knowledge, which is essential for effective decision-making. The more knowledge policymakers acquire for the security environment, the stronger their protection is against the nation's adversaries. Investments in cybersecurity and emerging technologies provide a perfect example of the cultivation of cognitions. Third, the universal view of Taoism mirrors the notable Chinese skills of geopolitical accommodation, intercultural adaptation, and military adjustment. One can find the models of adaptation in the social reforms of Deng Xiaoping, the military reforms of Xi Jinping, or the diplomatic approach of Hu Jintao. It is the far-reaching vision of those leaders that transformed China from a post-revolutionary state to an emerging great power.

The second aspect of cultivation is *creativity*. Neoclassical realists argue that relative material power establishes the basic parameters of a country's foreign policy (Rose 1998, 140). Although realism prioritizes hard power and, more particularly, the military capabilities of state actors, realist scholars do not reject the validity of soft power. Wang's explanation of Chinese foreign policy involves the concept of public diplomacy, which involves advertising the Chinese achievements and boosting the Beijing's image overseas (Wang 2008, 260). Therefore, the soft rise of China, as Wang describes it, presumes that Beijing should demonstrate a willingness to bear the global responsibility of great power. However, the success of Chinese diplomacy relies also on another variable that amplifies the projection of soft power – creativity. The Western understanding of soft power lies in attraction (Nye 1990, 160). The Chinese tradition considers attractiveness and ideology secondary to foreign policy and excludes the export of values in its grand strategy. Instead, the spirit of Chinese politics expresses an unconventional approach that favors conflict resolution and social harmony (Staats 2009, 47). Harmony, however, does not preclude leadership. The flexible creativeness of China predetermines the far-reaching strategy of Beijing and seeks leadership through exercising soft power under the guise of public diplomacy and hard power, wherever Chinese national interests are at stake. The harmonious approach does not aim to alter the international anarchy or export Communism similar to the USSR. Social harmony promotes *multipolar globalization*, which refers to the personal political choice of each nation to follow its original path of creativity in the sense of political development and cultural creed. This is not to say that the pursuit of creativity goes by soft power only. The parabellum paradigm of China, which I will further discuss in this chapter, presumes the use of military force. However, in contrast to the Western approach, Chinese hard power is inferior to public diplomacy. One might argue that those correlations are valid only to the extent to which Beijing does not possess the military capabilities of the United States. Even so, history shows that the cultivation of creativity has raised China to the place of the world's second-largest economy and thus, achieved the assumption of Taoism and the axioms of Mao's dialectics. The Chinese economy cannot develop without the American, and the U.S. economy cannot grow without the Chinese. Both powers "produce" each other politics and coexist in a tight economic interdependence, which sustains the balance of power in international relations. A military conflict between Washington and Beijing, regardless of its origins, would lead to a global recession and large-scale destruction. Thus, the rise of China might not be as peaceful as the Chinese scholars assume, or as violent as American policymakers predict. It will be *creative*. It combines what Joseph Nye calls soft power with the parabellum paradigm, introduced by Johnson and Mearsheimer (Johnson 1998, 20). The power of creativity and cultivation, however, will prevent China from starting wars unless another state actor threatens its national interests. For the United States, the annexation of Taiwan is equal to a war of aggression, but for China, it will prevent the deployment of American troops in Beijing's backyard. The creative decision, therefore, does not presume a military conflict. China could easily wait for the American decline and launch an attack on Taiwanese soil when the United States is no more in a position to retaliate. Whether it would be after ten or fifty years, Beijing will get the opportunity to invade Taipei when the balance of power in APAC no longer benefits America. If, however, China abandons its creative approach and faces the United States in the near future, it will repeat the mistake of Imperial Japan. A plausible outpost for creative cultivation is the weakening of the alliances between the United States and its allies in the region. Yet, the foremost purpose of China should be to secure its territorial integrity in the face of domestic riots and COVID.

The third facet of China's silent cultivation concerns the *imperative* nature of Chinese domestic power. It derives from the school of *legalism* and its implication for Beijing's foreign policy behavior. As I discussed above, Chinese philosophy rejects the absolute validity of the good-bad moral cleavage. Both values mirror the Chinese perceptions of human nature, but if Confucian morality seeks to defeat the evil through self-cultivation, Legalism suggests that people are powerless to overcome evil (Cheung 2007, 87). In similar to Morgenthau's pessimism about the positive attitudes of the human sense, the Legalist school advocates strict discipline and corresponding punishments for those who violate the law. The easiest way to assess Legalism and its impact on Chinese culture is to analyze the domestic politics of Communist China. However, this book does not deal with internal sources of foreign policy since the latter begins where the former ends (Kissinger 1966, 503). It is important to highlight that although Confucianism and Taoism are central to the Chinese cultural inheritance, Legalism is another major school that shaped the intellectual history of China. An analysis, which excludes the imperative philosophy of the Chinese legalists and prioritizes the peaceful character of Confucianism, would fail to explain why Beijing's foreign policy behavior pursues a policy of great power. Legalism, in other words, advocates strong leadership, centralized decision-making, and strict hierarchy.

Moreover, it stresses the uniqueness of Chinese society and its distinctiveness from other cultures. This book assumes that if Confucius has inspired the Chinese vision of the Universe and if Taoism has formed the far-reaching vision of Chinese leadership, Legalism shaped the Chinese comprehension of human nature and still influences Beijing's foreign policy. Philosophers will criticize me for the comparison I will make, but the best way to describe those theoretical correlations is through drawing a parallel between Western concepts and ancient beliefs in China. If liberalism and socialism praise human nature with an unenviable optimist, realists tend to follow the classic example of Morgenthau, who stresses the lustful desire for power. In addition, Waltz elaborates the arguments of classical realism by arguing that the source of all conflicts lies in the structure of international politics (Waltz 1998, 620). The Chinese concept of power incorporates the peaceful attitudes of Confucianism and the spatial approach of Taoism but prefers to be more pessimistic about people and their decisions. The contemporary foreign policy of China endorses cultivation, creativeness, and social harmony but also implies that Beijing does not seek to promote its influence by limiting it to popular culture, Chinese TV series, or other expressions of soft power. The behind-the-curtains approach of China includes the establishment of what Henry Kissinger calls "tributary relations," which is similar to the dependence that Washington shares with Beijing. Once designed, the tributary network of the Chinese grand strategy benefits Beijing's policymakers even better than the potential deployment of the People's Liberation Army overseas. Thus, we can justify the assumption of Kuang-Hui Yeh that Confucian relationalism operates with Chinese interpersonal interactions (Yeh 2010, 80). However, Feng Zhang is also correct when implying that Chinese inclusive relationalism is already informing a large part of Chinese foreign policy (Zhang 2015, 20). My assumption is that although China pursues a policy largely influenced by the Confucian philosophy, Legalism also provides Chinese policymakers with a source of inspiration. The future of Chinese foreign policy, eventually, could evolve into a debate among proponents of a Confucian-style peaceful paradigm and defenders of a more offensive, Legalist-inspired strategy. I assert that China should stick to the first approach and combine its creative rise with long-term strategic planning imbued by Taoism. Legalism, quite the opposite, could serve as a domestic source of policymaking, but if Beijing moves to design a legalist doctrine of hegemonic behavior, it could easily fall into the trap of the Soviet Union. In his works, Mearsheimer poses the question of whether China can rise peacefully. Although I do not pretend to have a universal response, one should remember the lesson of history no emerging great power has risen peacefully unless its predecessor has allowed it. The more United States is inclined to start a war, the more legalist and aggressive Beijing's foreign policy will be. On the contrary, the more Confucian Chinese politics is, the more liberal and hegemonic American foreign policy. The ultimate question is can China and the United States escape both Thucydides and Han Feizi's trap.

The silent cultivation of China embodies another part of its philosophy – *patience*. I explain the Chinese concept of patience through the notion of *gongfu*. The word *gongfu* refers to the combined notion of time and energy devoted to a certain task and the human determination involved in completing it (Shih 1990, 53). Shih infers three variables that determine the successful completion of one's mission: patience (referred as to time), industry (referred to as energy), and perseverance (referred to as determination) (Shih 1990, 60). I assume that similar perceptions could provide a reasonable explanation of Beijing's Grand Strategy. Here, I offer a more detailed view of Chinese foreign policy by inferring three unique aspects of China's Grand Design.

The first aspect explains the Chinese actions in time. China did not rise instantly. It did not become a great power after a global conflict, and neither did it seek to expand outside the APAC. It returns to become a great power again. History shows that the faster a great power rises, the quicker its decline is. Beijing's foreign policy, regardless of the historical period it operates, did not struggle for military or cultural hegemony. Mao Zedong was born under the Emperor's reign, but his ascent did not change the millennial desire of China to be a great power. This leads us back to Chinese philosophy and its worldview. Political leadership in China is but a headship of the Chinese nation, which occupies the center of the Universe. For the Chinese leader, whether it will be a Chief, Emperor, or Chairman, national leadership prevails over the temptation of global hegemony. Mearsheimer is right when arguing that the Chinese policy towards its neighbors has not been peaceful through the centuries, but it has not been a policy of expansion similar to the Russian military campaigns in the Far East. China, quite the opposite, has acted in a more defensive manner when external enemies have threatened its neighbors. This is not to say that Beijing has not started a military conflict. However, Chinese politics have been predominantly *Sino-centric*, and thus, China has prioritized domestic order and political authority over the conquest of other countries. I assume that it is not a matter of *moralpolitik* but of *pragmatic leadership*. We can speak of patience on both macro and micro levels. Chinese leaders after the Cold War have been critical of capitalism and democracy, but they never attempted an open confrontation with the United States. Some might attack me that the rise of China is an objective powershift, like the ones I explained in the previous chapter. However, why do liberal democracies fail to exploit the powershift and prevent China's rise? Can we say that those objective conditions resulted from the consistent efforts of the United States and Europe to make China a technological and economic giant? China contributed only peripherally to World War I and World War II without sending a single soldier overseas. What if China is not the furious Dragon but an old Sage who supervises the great powers and who was worthy for the words of Napoleon: "China is a sleeping giant. Let her sleep, for when she wakes, she will shake the world" (Kerr 2013, 10). If so, the sleeping Sage can wait for another five decades unless another nation decides to challenge it first.

Industry, in terms of energy, sheds light on the attractive shadow of China. Communism in China does not rebuke the modern manifestation of class struggle. However, the economic paradigm of Beijing follows the legacy of Deng Xiaoping, achieving an impressive balance between political stability and economic growth. The success of China reflects two essential components of its model: integrating elements of liberal economic policy by opening it to foreign investments and permitting the ruling party to sustain its grip on government (Zhao 2010, 419). The labor cost is what lured the wealthiest American corporations to relocate their facilities to China. Despite the attempts of President Trump to prevent the export of capital to Beijing, it turned out that a few investors would offer their financial outcomes as a sacrifice to the Neocons. Western economic theories stress the nature of the financial outcomes and the complicity of long-term purposes. The Chinese approach, on the contrary, focuses its predictions on the ability one should have to achieve outstanding results. If the pre-election motto of Donald Trump was "Buy American, Hire American" (BAHA), China has already offered a more magnanimous deal: "Buy American, Hire Chinese" (BAHC). Instead of spending its resources to produce and export goods, Beijing has cultivated the inflow of investments and the labor market in favor of the state. After applying the policy of BAHC and mobilizing its resources to deter the American predominance, China succeeded in globalizing its currency. The Chinese Yuan joined the family of the main reserve currencies, which boosted the Chinese economic growth. In pursuing the establishment of the digital yuan, Beijing posed a direct challenge to the dollar dominance, though exposing the world economy to the risk of another recession. However, I assume that a digital competition of currencies will be less detrimental to the balance of power than fighting a war.

Finally comes perseverance. The rise of China is not a unique and undeniable achievement of a single leader. Although regarded as a great revolutionary and founding father of the People's Republic, Mao Zedong serves as a source of ideological inspiration for the Chinese people, yet, his legacy evolved under Deng Xiaoping and his successors. I find it important to emphasize the personal charisma of Chinese leadership and its implications for perseverance. The position of *Chairman*, or as evident from its official translation – *President*, is an expression of the centralized and undisputed primacy of the Chinese leader. Section Two of the Chinese Constitution explicitly defines the office of the President of the People's Republic (Zhang 2021, 10). However, the office of the President possesses a deeper implication that refers to the development of one's personal and political skills. Confucianism stresses the importance of personal behavior and presumes that one should strengthen his character through refining it in practice (Wah 2010, 281). Confucius also argues that in political leadership, the government is ruled by the leader's personal and moral values such as discipline, flexible behavior, self-restraint, and *perseverance* (Robertson 2000, 260). I believe that the latter is central to the Chinese leadership for two reasons. Most Chinese leaders have a long history of preparation for state offices and an outstanding record in intercultural mediation. Their political and ideological perseverance shapes the foreign policy of China and impersonates Beijing in the face of its adversaries. Second, although the leaders change, their policy remains subject to the future of China. Whether it will be a devotion to Communism or Confucian romanticism, Chinese leadership advocates for leaders with individual charisma and rational personal character to lead the Chinese nation and endure its national interests.

Sinocetrism: Tributary Diplomacy vs. Military Paternalism

Much has been written about Chinese *realpolitik* and its methodological relevance to Western paradigms. If we employ a standard approach of theoretical analysis, we should be able to dissect the realist paradigm of China outside of the popular political mythologies about the similarities between Soviet foreign policy and the strategy of Beijing. I assume that the Chinese realpolitik represents a successful approach to emerging great power for a simple reason: its origins. Most IR scholars seek to explain Beijing's paradigm by assessing the balance of power in APAC or explaining Chinese foreign policy towards the United

States. Although I consider both approaches useful and rational, I have chosen another starting point for my explanation, which refers to the roots of Beijing's Grand Strategy. This book argues that the success of Chinese realpolitik does not only reflect its parabellum paradigm or cultivation. My assertion is that the rise of China is decisive and irreversible due to its substantive design. In other words, instead of duplicating and recreating American realpolitik and U.S. behavior, China has elaborated a distinctive approach that seeks to reshape international politics. I will provide three examples in support of my claim.

The Eurasian paradigm, which is central to Russian foreign policy, follows the American approach but differs in terms of strategic perceptions and ideological implications (Ivanov 2021, 58). Russian culture and its military constitute the cornerstone of Moscow's aspirations for regional hegemony in Eurasia. Although the Russian strategy has revisited the old Soviet doctrines, it did not abandon the dream of restoring the USSR through the unification of Eurasia. Alexander Dugin highlights that United Eurasia will be a glorious Empire, although different from the Soviet Union in terms of ideology and economic system (Dugin 2014, 20). The majority of European scholars have elaborated a specific term to describe the Russian Strategy: *hybrid warfare*. Although there is a growing body of literature about asymmetric conflicts, and although definitions vary, most theoreticians have consistently agreed that Russian foreign policy utilizes sequentially hard and soft power to achieve its goals under the guise of Orthodox Christianity or monarchist nostalgia. I assume that the most detailed and systematic explanation belongs to Strukov. Strukov's theory defines Moscow's approach as a manipulative strategy, which supplies a combination of hard and soft power tools, on one level, on another, traverses the binary dynamic of power positive/negative, external/internal, and vertical/horizontal, and instead operates as a multi-directional, ambiguous and often contradictory, polyvalent, and parasitic system of influence (Strukov 2016, 35). In short, Russian foreign policy combines soft and hard power in a pattern, similar to Joseph Nye's concept of smart power (Nye 2009, 8). The definition of Strukov indicates the similarities between Russian and American smart power regarding the policy of manipulation, although his explanation is a little different from Nye's top-down approach. Russia, which seeks to unite Eurasian economically and culturally and take advantage of the region for its global claims, applies the soft power of Russian Orthodoxy and Eurasian culture, combined with military interventions. Although the scope of the Kremlin's smart power is limited due to the reduced capabilities of post-Soviet Russia and because of the declining Russian economy, Moscow's interferences in Ukraine and the Balkans still challenge the American influence in Eastern Europe.

European Union is the most advanced example of *suis generis* community, which inspires liberal institutionalists with its political architecture. Yet, there is no academic or even political consensus about European foreign policy, especially after BREXIT. Europe's foreign relations mirror the vision of France and Germany for a multipolar world, the Old Continent finally emerges as a great power. Moravcsik even calls Europe "the quiet superpower," claiming that it has risen rather than declined and that it has pursued a military and active foreign policy (Moravcsik 2009, 410). Even so, the quiet superpower will not be so silent once it truly unites, which is likely to happen after the United Kingdom left the EU. In assessing the European power status, Moravcsik eventually confirms my assumption that Europe has endorsed a foreign policy similar to the American. This is not to say that I consider the European community politically and institutionally equal to the United States as a state actor. Soft power is central to European foreign policy, and it will remain so until Paris and Berlin agree on creating European armed forces. The variables introduced by Moravcsik illustrate that Europe, despite its limited military capabilities, enjoys the privilege to influence the defense agenda of NATO. Political and social values, trade, finance, transatlantic convergence, and investments imply the Ancient Greek tactics of promoting the Hellenistic culture that even penetrated the hard attitudes of the Roman Empire. The need for smart power is obvious for Europe, and more particularly, for those Member States which follow the step-by-step approach of the European founding fathers (Dîrdală 2013, 125). However, if the European Union seeks to become a global actor equal to the United States, it will inevitably follow the American example of increasing its military budget.

Chinese realpolitik rejects the Western approach to international relations. For China, resources such as military power and culture are secondary to the Sino-centric nature of its foreign policy. Mearsheimer assumes that Beijing follows Uncle Sam's footsteps and thus, infers three global aspects of Chinese realpolitik (Mearsheimer 2006, 165). The first aspect is the Chinese strategy of maximizing the gap between Beijing and its neighbors with the foremost purpose of establishing regional hegemony. I assume that China has partially fulfilled Mearsheimer's prediction. The PLA, especially after the military reforms of Xi Jinping, is in possession of the most advanced weapon systems, while the Chinese nuclear arsenal has rapidly grown up. Beijing's military technologies have already surpassed the Russian, and even though Moscow enjoys global nuclear primacy with more than six thousand warheads in its stockpile, Chinese cyber capabilities could easily prevent a MAD scenario. Japan has always been superior to China throughout its millennial history. With Article Nine of the Japanese Constitution, however, Tokyo can repel a Chinese intervention only if it takes place on Japanese soil. India, which also occupies a central place in Mearsheimer's explanation, possesses impressive military manpower, and its aspirations for Tibet provide a reasonable argument for Indian hostility towards Beijing's domestic politics. Here, I will refer to the Chinese-Indian conflict from 1962, which originated from India's support for the Tibetan national uprising (Garver 2006, 90). The Chinese victory in the Sino-Indian War predetermined India's revanchist approach to Beijing. China, however, has a notable record of using the Tibetan autonomous region as a buffer against its southern neighbor. Another advantage, which benefits China, is the Chinese-Pakistani Economic Corridor that provides Beijing and Islamabad with the opportunity to establish a further regional framework for security cooperation in the Indian backyard after the American withdrawal from Afghanistan.

This leads us to the second assumption of Mearsheimer, who predicts that it is highly unlikely for China to attack another Asian country due to its huge territory and striking economic growth (Mearsheimer 2006, 170). Mearsheimer leaves less place to consider an eventual Chinese intervention in Taiwan. President Xi Jinping merely declared the importance of Taipei, which appears to outgrow the Presidency of Joe Biden. My assertion is that Beijing, in the next to say, fifty years, will annex Taiwan to reaffirm its regional claims in the APAC. The mechanism of Chinese foreign policy, as discussed above, does not involve the *blitzkrieg* logic of Western military art. So far, the United States has neglected the inevitable accession of Taiwan. Beijing, at present days, does not have the military capabilities to oppose a U.S. retaliation, and thus, the Chinese administration is aware of the complication that Beijing would face when sending troops to the island. However, the process of reunification is inevitable for two reasons. First, China could easily castigate Taiwan economically. Beijing and Taipei are bound in a mutual economic dependence, which is a considerable precondition that Chinese policymakers will not risk starting a war without calculating the costs. More generally, China could attempt to impose an economic blockade on Taiwan instead of risking a direct confrontation with the United States. The Chinese sanctions will affect Taiwan's economy and eventually create favorable chances for military intervention. Second, it is arguable that the United States will defend Taiwan in case of a Chinese attack on the island. With President Biden in the White House, Washington is likely to offer help, but the final decision will depend on many factors such as costs of war, post-conflict recovery, probability of limited nuclear retaliation, and the likelihood of Russian intervention. With Europe being economically dependent on China and the Korean Peninsula, threatened by Pyongyang's nukes, the United States and Australia will face the ultimate choice to launch an attack on Chinese soil.

Chinese realpolitik involves another strategic purpose that Mearsheimer interprets through exploring the neighborhood policy of China (Mearsheimer 2006,

175). My conclusion is that the Chinese foreign policy approach divides its near-space into three regions. The first region covers the Sea of Japan and the Korean Peninsula. Japan and South Korea do not possess the military capabilities of China but enjoy American support. Here, I join Mearsheimer in his assumption that Beijing will try to keep Seoul and Tokyo's military weakened. The tensions between South Korea and Japan eventually favored the Chinese strategy since Seoul and Washington still resist the reform of the Japanese Constitution. The second region covers Tibet and Nepal and refers to India's cultural aspirations for the former. The Chinese strategy here is dichotomous. Beijing maintains good and favorable relations with Pakistan and can use Nepal as a buffer to deter the increasing Indian influence in Tibet. If China is successful, India will have to balance between containing Pakistan and conducting military exercises on the Chinese borders. The final advantage of China concerns Russia. This is not to say that Moscow would blindly follow Beijing in its confrontation with the United States. The logic of the Sino-Russian partnership originates from the common adversary – America. I assume that Russia is more likely to endorse the role of conflict provoker between Washington and Beijing, which, under the current circumstances, is a far misfortune scenario for the international system. From the position of the mediator, Moscow will be on a favorable move to deepen its relations with China while deterring the American global influence. Yet, Russian policymakers will strongly oppose American troops operating in Moscow's backyard as the Chinese will in case Washington tries to topple the regime in Pyongyang.

The three global aspects of Chinese realpolitik discussed above constitute the cornerstone of Beijing's grand design. It is worth highlighting that in contrast to the mainstream IR perceptions of China's rise, there is a growing discussion about China's behavior and its implications. Hwang and Cho, for instance, argue that the realist perspective maximizes the gap between the superior West as the Self and the Other (Cho and Hwang 2020, 177). Their explanation rejects the Western-centered approach of IR theoreticians as one-sided. I find this remark reasonable, methodologically, and empirically. The state of nature, which is a central concept of realism, does apply to all people but not in a similar way. The understanding of democracy, which is a sacred value to Western societies, provides us with a perfect example of the profound difference that exists between West and East regarding the state of nature. If we trace the roots of liberal democracy back to John Locke, we will summarize the iconic comprehension of Western liberalism that "the form of the government is a perfect democracy: or else may put the power of making laws into the hands of the few selected men, and their heirs or successors" (Locke 2003, 100). In other words, Locke believed that democracy would take people out of the state of nature and create the perfect form of government. I stress the theory of Locke because, in contrast to

Hobbs and Burke, Locke's theory introduces the concept of the social contract, which regulates the relations between people and the state. I believe the social contract is the most distinctive achievement of Western liberal thought and that it dominates the political life in the United States. I doubt, however, that scholars would identify the ideas of Locke as applicable to Eastern societies, and more particularly – to China. Even if they do, they should not neglect the historical truth, which Kissinger reminds us by saying that the Chinese concept of political order differs from the Western one (Kissinger 2014, 100). When Western paradigms fail to explain Chinese foreign policy, they often consider Kissinger's reminder outdated. In contrast to the mainstream understanding of the Western Self, as Hwang and Cho define it, the Asian "Other" World envisions a political order, which consists of three pillars.

The first pillar is *patron-client communitarianism* (Neher 1994, 949). The Chinese concept of society stresses the individual as part of the group, per se, of the nation. Leadership is central in people's attitudes, and Western scholars attribute that to Communism. Indeed, Chinese Socialism cultivates respect for the Supreme Leader of China. However, the importance of political authority and its central place to people's attitudes in China is not a distinct feature of Communism. In the eyes of the Chinese people, it is a perception of what China should be – a state destined to be a great power and led by a strong leader, regardless of his title. In his *Black Book of Communism*, Jean Margolin calls Mao Zedong "Red Emperor," stigmatizing the oppressions that followed the War of Liberation. For the Chinese, however, Mao was but a political incarnation of the Supreme Patron, the Chairman, or the lost Emperor, who the People's Republic needed to survive after the fall of the Empire. Democracy has never been an alternative for the Chinese people.

The facet of *personalism* constitutes the second pillar of the Chinese political order. Personalism stresses leadership over laws (Neher 1994, 965). For Western democracies, no political leader is above the laws. Chinese perceptions regard the Leader and his charisma as the source of Law. Political charisma has much to do with cultivation in terms of pluralism and Asian-style democracy. In short, Chinese politics invest in individual leaders, not in political parties. President Xi Jinping, who seeks further reforms to expand the term of the Chinese Presidency, enjoys the same charismatic vision and huge support of the Chinese people. Like Mao and Deng Xiaoping, Xi symbolizes the Chinese political order in the eyes of the people and all of Asia. The President of the People's Republic is the leader to whom other Asian countries refer when they shape their foreign policy towards China. Authority and a strong state are the next pillars of the Asian political orders. In contrast to Western democracies, Asian political systems advocate clear institutional hierarchy and dominant state authority

(Neher, 1994, 970). The Mandate of Heaven, which ruled in Ancient China, is a proto-source of Chinese political authority. Communism advocates the Personality Cult and totalitarian state, but after Mao's death and, more particularly, after Deng Xiaoping's reforms, the political authority in China gave more place to the principle of *meritocracy*. Daniel Bell defines meritocracy as the equality of opportunity in education and government, with positions of leadership distributed to the most virtuous and qualified members of the community (Bell 2016, 10). The strong state doctrine, on the other hand, does not limit to leadership. It implies regular and significant interventions of the government in the Chinese economy, combined with reforms to ensure a cheap labor market and state capitalism.

The third pillar of the Chinese political order is the *one-party state*. Political parties in the United States emerged from the Protest communities, who inhabited the former British colonies and laid the foundations of the American political system. In Europe, democracy was born with the French Revolution, which triggered a domino effect of rebellions against absolute monarchy. In China, political parties never emerged. After the death of Empress Dowager Cixi, who modernized the Empire and ensured the continuity of the Imperial institution, the country fell under the influence of the West. The Republic of China, established in 1912, was but a period of a constant struggle between warlords, who sought to control the country while the Emperor "ruled" in the Forbidden City. When Communism took over in Beijing, it became the political formula of the People's Republic, and the one-party state succeeded the institution of monarchy. It is important to highlight that the concept of social harmony, rebuked by most Western scholars due to its literal interpretation, presumes hierarchy and strict dependence instead of *peace*. The centralized party rule turned out to be quite effective and unifying for the Chinese people, and the Western idea of eternal peace and individual freedoms gave way to collective wisdom and political cultivation. Party competition, quite the opposite, is vaguely familiar to the Chinese society and thus, failed to provide democracy as an alternative to China's monarchy.

Another misconception of Western theories presumes the superiority of the Western over its Others (Cho and Hwang 2020, 180). Western-centrism suggests that a single path leads to civilization and history, and that is the one represented by the West. History offers no better proof of the inconsistency of Western-centrism than the fall of the colonial Empires. The rise of China horrifies the proponents of liberal hegemony precisely because Western powers did not expect Beijing to emerge as great power so soon. A few, among which Kissinger, Morgenthau, and Waltz, warned about the detrimental effects of universalism, assuming that the struggle for power and the evolving structure of international politics will sooner or later tilt the balance of power in favor of another state actor. Western-centrism, in fact, is the most evident proof of the realist assumption that all conflicts and reconfigurations in polarity emerge from the anarchic nature of the international system. Competition between great powers is a process, which does not depend on variables such as values and culture, or at least, the limited examination of those factors will not provide us with a plausible explanation of the international system. For instance, when analyzing the end of unipolarity, Ikenberry assumes that there is no grand ideological alternative to liberal international order and that China does not have a model that the rest of the world finds appealing (Ikkenberry 2018, 23). The claim that future global powers do not have a universal model to suggest is a popular aspect of Western-centrism. Does the world really need a superhero to protect it? Universalism might favor conflict resolution and global peacebuilding, but it cannot alter international anarchy. If a state actor is in possession of the resources to become a great power, its foreign policy is likely to pursue a policy of values. However, if that policy becomes central to the state's behavior and even more important than survival and self-preservation, other states are likely to acquire a polar status and challenge the primacy of the dominant power. The rise and the fall of the European empires present a thoughtful criticism of Ikenberry's assumption. European colonialism, which promoted Europe's values under the guise of religious and messianic universalism, collapsed when Europe considered itself the center of the world. World War I and World War II reflected the European struggle for universal predominance but resulted in a global catastrophe. When Churchill finally gave up on his idea to revive the British Empire, Roosevelt and Stalin found themselves the new masters of the world, but none of them prioritized universal values over rational decision-making. The primary concern of the United States was with Japan, still fighting in the Far East, while the obsession of Stalin to achieve nuclear parity with Washington dominated the Soviet policy. The arms race has prevented the superpowers from destroying each other and preserved their rational behavior. Promotion of democracy or socialism was part of their foreign policy, but it occupied a secondary place to national security. When the USSR collapsed and bipolarity transformed into what President G. H. W. Bush called the "New World Order," Washington decided to build a *Pax Americana* based on culture and values instead of focusing on emerging great power like China. If the United States had sought to prevent the rise of potential peer competitors, Beijing would have hardly challenged the American primacy. However, in the world's history, there is no *if*. The claim that the predominance of a great power lies in an ideological alternative or universal model might be valid for the Soviet theoreticians, who envisioned the perfect socialist society as the global pattern of development for all nations. However, it does not explain why the unipolar world is in decline and why, despite its inability to offer an ideological alternative, China is on the rise. My answer is simple – that is precisely because of Chinese realpolitik and due to the unwillingness of Beijing to provide a universal path of development.

What are the implications of Western-centrism on Chinese realpolitik? Before discussing each, I will provide a few arguments in favor of the assumption of the non-intervention approach of Beijing. Chinese realpolitik is *pragmatic*. Beijing does not seek to export Communism or to encourage red revolutions in Europe, the United States, and their allies. I assume that the strategy of China does not exclude Mearsheimer's assumption about Beijing heading towards regional hegemony in APAC. However, the Chinese concept of hegemony is not cultural or universal, it is imperative. China pursued a great power policy, but in contrast to the United States, the Chinese Grand Strategy is not straightforward. Beijing's realpolitik combines the establishment of *tributary diplomacy* with future *military paternalism*. My assumption is that the former is the first generation of Chinese foreign policy tools that provide China with the opportunity to project influence without sending troops overseas. By tributary, I mean relations of trade and economic dependence. It is an approach that draws inspiration from the concept of Imperial China's tributary system and that shapes the foundations of modern Chinese diplomacy (Fairbank 1942, 150). One might argue that tributary relations do not benefit Chinese foreign policy if they evolve into interdependence. I assert that quite the opposite, by establishing a network of interdependencies, China limits the freedom of action that the United States and its allies enjoyed in the 1990s. Besides, my claim is that tributary diplomacy is a long-term strategy since we can trace its origins to Ancient China, in the writings of Lao Tzu, who considers contradictions producing each other. Mao also cited Tzu later in his writings, as I discussed when analyzing his dialectic approach. With the social reforms of Deng Xiaoping, tributary diplomacy became central to Chinese foreign policy and served as both tools of fosterage and castigation.

Military paternalism is the second generation of Beijing's foreign policy tools, which China is likely to adopt once and if it achieves military parity with the United States. I assume that such a scenario is highly probable in the next fifty years unless Washington strikes Beijing. If, however, China emerges are a global military actor, there are two plausible scenarios for the future of its realpolitik. The one will fulfill Mearsheimer's prediction if China behaves as a hegemon, imposing its global dominance, as the United States did after September 11. In that case, my prediction is that Beijing will repeat the mistake of the American policymakers, who endorsed global commitments at the high cost of overstretching. Under the second scenario, Beijing could employ a Chinese-style offshore-balancing by husbanding Chinese power and preserving its global impact. The problem arises from the lack of Chinese allies to support Beijing in its global quest. In contrast to the United States, which enjoys a decades-old system of alliances, China will have to use its tributary diplomacy to gain some allies among the states which oppose America. An alternative strategy would involve a weakening of the relations between Washington and its allies, although such campaigns will require a significant revision of tributary diplomacy. If Beijing, however, succeeds in combining the latter with limited military interventions of defensive nature, China's rise will boost to the extent of reaching the American global influence.

My conclusion is that Western-centrism actually favors the rise of China with its cleavage between the Self and the Others. Unfortunately, Western-centric approaches also trigger a strong sentiment of Sinophobia as the global response to Beijing's aspirations for global influence. While analyzing and explaining how Sinophobia affects the realistic assessment of Chinese foreign policy, we should stress the traditional neglect of Asian scholars in the IR theory. It is difficult to read more about the theories of Xuetong, Tingyang, Yan, or the ancient military treatises in contemporary IR studies. Although the theoretical approaches of the aforementioned authors introduce conclusions that do not correspond to the mainstream consensus, their validity is rational. The first example refers to Xuetong, who operationalizes the Chinese concept of *power* and concludes that the exercise of power relies on a combination of soft and hard power by morality and virtue (Xuetong 2013, 65). An objective observation will show a similarity between Xuetong's definition and Nye's theory of smart power. Both definitions stress soft power and insist on exercising hard power only as a last resort of action. Both concepts seek to provide great powers with a reasonable and rational strategy to maintain the balance of power. Finally, both Xuetong and Nye admit the necessity of using all available instruments of hard and soft power to achieve one's foremost purposes. Is Xuetong's concept less relevant than Nye's is? Is it less applicable to the contemporary geopolitical realities? The obvious inference is that Xuetong's smart power is *not* a Western-centric theory and thus, the IR approach, which operates with Western-centered case studies, will not be able to test it. I believe that Xuetong and Nye will reach a consensus on what hard power is, but it is highly unlikely for them to agree on the nature of Chinese soft power. Mearsheimer reaches an important point when stating that Americans dislike realism. It is precisely because of Mearsheimer's assumption about American values of optimism and moralism, being hostile to realism, that Chinese realpolitik is popular but poorly interpreted in Western IR studies.

Another misconception of Chinese realpolitik is the misjudgment of China's view of international politics. Qin asserts that connections between China and the other nations presume mutual and inclusive interaction to solve the global problems through harmonizing and reconciling disputed positions (Qin 2011,

240). A realist scholar would assume that morality has no place and foreign policy and that cooperation could not replace hard power. In truth, realism passed the tests of the Cold War and Trump's presidency. However, Qin's theory provides us with the ultimate explanation for why China abstains from large-scale military interventions. Not to say that Qin's definition jumps beyond the black-white vision of Western realists and reveals an even more effective way for a state to defend its national interests – by outplaying and manipulating its adversaries at the table of negotiations. The conventional assessment of Chinese military capabilities will show that Beijing still cannot afford to maintain a global military presence like the United States. Qin's assumption uncovers that Beijing does not want to deploy its troops overseas unless China's national interests are at stake. Some would argue that Taiwan is an exclusion from Qin's assessment. Such a claim would be valid if China did not consider Taiwan part of its sovereign territory. I hope realist and liberal scholars will not reject the fundamental truth, introduced by the Peace of Westphalia, that territorial integrity is central to sovereignty. Again, we face the undeniable legacy of the post-Cold War U.S. administration, which underestimated the potential of China and its willingness to reunite with Taipei. If President Clinton had renewed the Sino-American Mutual Defense Treaty, it would have been harder for President Xi Jinping to claim Taiwan. With Washington respecting the One-China policy, however, Beijing tricked its superior adversary by posing a direct challenge to the island.

The analyzed misconceptions expose another weakness, which most of the existing studies failed to predict – China's abstinence from entering into multilateral agreements, including those devoted to economic, environmental, nonproliferation, and regional security issues (Christensen 1996, 38). Despite the subsequent efforts of the United States and Russia to involve Beijing in Arms Control Treaties or to establish a system of regional security cooperation, Chinese policymakers are highly suspicious and hostile towards the ratification of potential agreements. In other words, one of the emerging great powers does not share the nuclear vision of its dominant adversary. With Washington and Moscow fulfilling their arms control obligations, Beijing's projects are not subject to any sanctions, especially with China being a permanent member of the UN Security Council. Chinese nuclear diplomacy will evolve independently unless Russia proposes a form of security cooperation that Beijing is highly unlikely to accept. The delusion that a nuclear power that does not share the same vision with the rest of the nuclear family will abstain from developing its nuclear arsenal is misleading. It will eventually lead to a new arms race, similar to the one of the Cold War age. The Chinese security doctrine would not tolerate arms control at the cost of its national security, or at least it does not surpass the nuclear arsenal of the United States. To assume that China will enter into a security agreement to keep good relations with its Russian partners is to assert that Xi Jinping would cut the nuclear arsenal of Beijing to respect his comradeship with Vladimir Putin.

Guang provides another explanation of Chinese realpolitik, originating from the assumption that China's foreign policy embodies hard-edged realist ideals and ideals about state power and geopolitics, clothed in the grab of nationalism (Guang 2005, 498). The definition of Guang combines interests and beliefs in the Western-style of realpolitik and thus, implies that China behaves as Westphalian-type great power. The starting point for Guang's assumptions is China's struggle for territorial integrity and its power politics. The contribution of Guang's theory is that it predicts and reaffirms the Chinese claims over Taiwan. When decision-makers in Beijing have reached to consensus about Taiwan being an indivisible part of Mainland China, Western scholars were right to assume that Chinese foreign policy is an expression of what Guang calls nationalism. However, nationalism does not limit to the struggle for territorial integrity and to the pursuit of indisputable sovereignty. Thus, it is one-sided and misleading to assume that Chinese nationalism is definitive only in terms of the strong anti-Western sentiment that dominates Beijing's foreign policy. If so, we would limit our explanation only to domestic politics, which leaves an empirical gap for further inquiry – is Guang's theory of Chinese nationalism applicable to foreign policy? When Kissinger states that foreign policy begins where domestic political ends, he means that one should not confuse domestic perceptions with a policy of values. Nationalism in China affects the decisions of the Chinese Communist Party regarding Taiwan, the Hong Kong protests, and Indian aspirations to Tibet. However, I assume that nationalism could not serve as a driving force of China's grand strategy for a simple reason: the original Chinese tradition that shapes Beijing's grand design is older and stronger than the nationalist temptations of the Chinese leaders. In other words, Chinese nationalism is like leadership. Whether it will be Xi Jinping, Hu Jintao, or Deng Xiaoping, the position of President or Chairman personifies not the typical view of the Western nationalist leaders or white supremacists but a long-standing tradition that did not die with the fall of the Chinese Empire. The policy of meritocracy, cultivation, and creativity is only part of the examples that inspired Beijing's grand design. Nationalism occupies a secondary place in Chinese politics, but Western sentiment and China's historical ambitions do not have the political and ideological potential to mobilize the political order in modern China. If nationalism is central to Chinese foreign policy, why does Beijing not preach a policy similar to that of white supremacists who initiated the Capitol Insurgency? Some would argue that the Xinjiang conflict could serve as proof of Chinese nationalism. Even so, tensions with the Uyghurs are of religious character and do not hold reciprocity to the Asian hatred which followed the outbreak of the Coronavirus Pandemic. Therefore, nationalism in China is a strong motivator but an unwise ally of the Chinese leaders, as American nationalism was not for white supremacists. The other popular assumption, which envisions confrontation between China and the United States as the cornerstone of Chinese foreign policy, could serve as an explanation for any conflict. Political relations among nations are in constant competition, and only rational decision-makers can elaborate a reasonable strategy to coexist within the international anarchy. Each state is bound to seek power, as are its leaders. However, the Sino-American confrontation by itself cannot explain why Beijing does not seek an open confrontation with the United States. Neither can it provide a reasonable explanation of the conspiracies that Beijing has released the Coronavirus to topple the Western global predominance. Last but not least, the assumption about anti-Americanism, being a driving force of Chinese foreign policy will face significant difficulties to illustrate why Confucianism and its successors had shaped China's grand design long before the United States emerged as a great power.

I have found it reasonable to conclude this section by offering a critical review of Yong Deng's theory, which purports to explain the Chinese conceptions of national interests. Deng argues that Chinese realists subscribe to the state-centric notion, albeit often less explicitly than their Western counterparts (Deng 1998, 311). I do not reject Deng's approach to Chinese politics but rather find it insufficient to explain the contemporary foreign policy of Beijing. For Deng, Chinese realpolitik views the world as an arena of interaction and merciless competition between state actors. Here, I join the author in a statement due to the obvious trends in the Sino-American competition and because of Beijing's attitudes towards Washington. Another argument of Deng refers to the potential liberalization of China, but my concern is that with Xi's doctrine dominating Chinese politics, liberal values will not gain ground in the People's Republic. Chinese policymakers do not believe in either Gorbachev's "new thinking" or Putin's Neo-Eurasian doctrine. For China, the international system is a byword of a state actor struggling for power, and my assumption is that even Western liberalism cannot affect those perceptions. The prediction of Deng that the younger generation of leaders and scholars with a more liberal worldview would have a growing influence in defining Chinese national interests is also a subject of empirical controversy (Deng 1998, 328). It is a common methodological misconception for liberals to consider other paradigms convertible to liberalism. In contrast to Deng, Feng Zhang introduces a more thoughtful approach, by assessing Xi Jinping's doctrine on two levels (Zhang 2012, 320). I consider Zhang's explanation more relevant for two reasons. First, it elaborates an original understanding of Chinese foreign policy, instead of employing the mainstream IR theories.

Second, Zhang stresses the importance of Xi's personal vision, which I believe is central to Beijing's foreign relations. Deng presumes that without attention to domestic politics and without a theory about the formation of national interests, Chinese realists cannot provide a critical analysis of their foreign policy (Deng 1998, 320). Zhang's two-level approach, however, proves that an independent treatment of domestic and foreign policy provides a better explanation of Chinese foreign policy. The domestic level refers to what Xi Jinping calls the Mission of CCP, while the external embodies the mission of establishing a community with a shared future for humanity (Zhang 2012, 333). In other words, Xi's concept of a global community that involves shared interests, mutual political trust, and cultural inclusiveness offers an alternative to the Western liberal order. In contrast to the liberal approach, however, the Sinocentric design of China does not promote universalism or export of values. Whether the Chinese concept of a shared future is attractive is yet to be seen. The ambitious purpose of Xi Jinping to build a stronger, wealthier, and prosperous China is an expression of what realists call national interests and has less to do with the liberal ideal of creating an intergovernmental authority. If Deng's prediction for liberalism gaining ground in China were to be fulfilled, it would be impossible for the Chinese policymakers to deter the influence of their American counterparts. Although Xi's doctrine seeks a weak and sealed America, it is immune to the liberal temptation of remodeling the international anarchy. Instead, China exploits the lack of global authority to advance its national interests and pursue a policy of prestige through establishing regional and economic partnerships with both allies and adversaries of the United States. I assume that the logic of Xi Jinping's doctrine applies to realism and opposes liberalism because of its inconsistency with Chinese socialism. Chinese foreign policy, however, anticipates both liberal and realist paradigms. Instead of duplicating the Western approach to international politics, Beijing has coined an original strategy, which many analysts define as realism with Chinese characteristics.

Marxism and liberalization

Scholars, who deal with Chinese foreign policy, tend to overstress the importance of the social market economy and often consider Chinese socialism secondary to the understanding of Beijing's foreign policy. In this section, I will try to remedy this approach by providing a more profound comprehension of the Chinese political order. To avoid criticism about my approach being one-sided and biased, I have chosen to use Western theories as a starting point. European scholars typically cite Napoleon, who depicts Beijing as the *sleeping giant*. American IR scholars are quite fond of depicting Beijing as the unmerciful Dragon who rises to shatter the international world order. The empirical deficiency of both approaches lies in their Western-centric comprehension of Asia. Slaying the Dragon is among the most popular concept of Western cultural, religious, and political attitudes. In Asian culture, however, Dragons are a source of wisdom, power, and longevity. The narrative of the Chinese Dragon burning the Western world and its culture is far from realist and rational.

In his prophetic article about Sino-American tensions during the Vietnamese war, Hans Morgenthau strongly opposed war with China, claiming that it is futile to think that one can contain the Chinese predominance in Asia by militarily defending Vietnam or Thailand (Morgenthau 1968, 31). I assume that the same logic applies to Taiwan. If military leaders are more pragmatic in terms of fighting, American policymakers face reelections, and it is highly likely for them to maintain the premeditated image of corrupted and expansionist China in the eyes of their voters. So likely, that it could lead to another wave of Asian hatred or the "Chinese virus." Morgenthau presents us with a perfect illustration of the Western attitude towards the Dragon, citing Goethe: "At first step, you are free, at the second you are a slave." (Von Goethe 2014, 25). It is an intellectual debility, claims the founding father of political realism, to treat all Communisms equally subservient to China (Morgenthau 1965, 156). My assumption is that Beijing survived the Cold War and the unipolar world order merely because of the very same intellectual debility that penetrated the West after the USSR collapsed. My concern is that the present-day proponents of that ignorance pursue a policy of direct confrontation with China, struggling to sacrifice millions of American and Chinese lives under the guise of the liberal crusade against Communism. One might argue that Chinese Communism under Mao differs from Xi's doctrine. Morgenthau, however, is clear when stating that Beijing's *traditional* national interests determine the basic direction of Chinese policies and that Communism adds a dynamic dimension to the means, by which those policies are to be achieved (Morgenthau 1965, 157). How can we discharge Morgenthau's arguments at present days, especially after Xi Jinping achieved a historic vote of confidence that aligns him with Mao and Deng Xiaoping? Or should we assume that the United States, as a predominant Sea nation, has rejected the legacy of Britain? Should we ignore the French sentiment towards Napoleon? Finally, should we neglect the reverse effects of colonialism that gathered thousands of refugees on the borders of their former metropolis? Ideology has always been a convenient cover for nostalgic policymakers. Yet, if a state actor abandons the pragmatic decision-making, which boosts the driving forces of foreign policy, it will share Mearsheimer's tragedy of great power politics.

Another lesson from Morgenthau's legacy is his structural criticism of U.S. Foreign Policy towards China. Liberal scholars, and even a few realists, might tempt to object that some of Morgenthau's assumptions are problematic due to their outdated context. However, his prediction that if China adds to its military capabilities the achievement of emerging technologies, it will become the most powerful nation on the earth passed the ultimate test of history (Morgentau 1962, 46). The majority of scholars would trace the roots of China's rise in the social reforms of Deng Xiaoping. A few, however, will highlight that Communism in China has proved to be resistant to the post-Cold War powershifts due to a lack of coherence with the Soviets. Beijing has never been dependent on Soviet support, and once the Communist Party realized that it could not rely on Moscow during the Cold War, China abandoned the Soviet-centric family of the communist nations. The Nixon administration underestimated Beijing's far-reaching strategy of becoming a great power and advocated a strong and decisive China to deter Moscow's influence. What the President failed to predict is that, despite its Communist formula, Beijing would elaborate a subsequent, ethnocentric approach to both USSR and United States and, thus, would later take advantage of the Soviet collapse to rise.

A popular false prediction that blurred the Western sight of Chinese Communists concerns the ideological primacy of revolutionary class fights (Robinson and Shambaugh 1995, 590). Although Marxism-Leninism served as a source of inspiration for Mao, the origins of Chinese Communism do not reflect the revolutionary class struggle in Leninist Russia. The political concepts of Mao and his successors evolved under the pressure of the Cold War and eventually did not embrace the reformation approach of Gorbachev, who, in his attempt to duplicate the Chinese model, put an end to the Soviet empire. Gorbachev's failure to pursue and complete the *Perestroika* is the most considerable proof that one should not easily identify the Chinese Communism with the Soviet ideology. I begin with a few less familiar aspects of Chinese culture, some of which outlived the bipolar world order and still legitimized the socialist aspects of Chinese foreign policy. My claim is that without the bellow-discussed facets, Chinese Communism will lose its plausibility and could easily follow the fate of its Soviet predecessor.

Chinese art and popular culture are the first original facet of Sinocentric communism. If we assess the cultural patterns of the Soviet-inspired *socialist realism* imposed in the public life of the socialist bloc after World War II, we can easily notice the huge impact of its revisionist nature. This is to say that Russian and Eastern European artists often made the Soviet culture look ugly. The spark of Communism inspired them to envision the future of the socialist society, but the lack of tradition deprived their productivity of maintaining permanent cultural influence over the masses. Chinese art, on the other hand, survived the War of Liberation. Mao harmonized the pre-revolutionary history of China and even allowed the last Emperor Puyi to conduct a public study on the Qing dynasty, shortly after pardoning him. The political regime in Beijing strongly opposed any revival of Confucian nostalgia, but Chinese leaders like Zhou Enlai and Deng Xiaoping cared more about China's appearance to the world and less about the Western attitudes towards China. The total devastation of Christian Orthodox culture in Russia and its controversial revival under Stalin did not serve the Soviets to strengthen the political authority of Communists. The sole person whose vision was central and dominated the cognitive attitudes of the Soviets, even after his death, was Stalin. Despite the attempts of his successors to the Cult of Personality, the Communist party could find no other way to sustain the picture of the Soviet glory without preaching the popular tales for "comrade Stalin." Whether Mao was different from Stalin in his domestic policy is not a topic of this book. However, Mao's rational foresight about China shaping like a superpower for the next generations advocated a more flexible approach to the Chinese Imperial legacy (Zhou and Tuma 1996, 760). Communism was central to his political vision and provided an ultimate legitimacy for Chinese art. The truth behind Mao's struggle for political authority was his pragmatism, which envisioned a combined transition to Communism. China avoided the Soviet weaknesses of cultural denial and contemptuous French attitudes towards the "Ancient Regime," paving the way for shaping political leaders with a clear vision of the future. One might argue that traditional Chinese culture and its philosophical derivatives do not enjoy the political support of contemporary China. Even so, it is arguable if the motivational power of Communism is stronger than the original power of cultivation. I assume that the process of promoting original Chinese art is irreversible for two reasons. First, regardless of Beijing's leadership, popular culture is beneficial for China's movie industry and soft power. Considering the striking polarization and the fierce debates, which dominated Western culture, China is lucky to pass the ruling party's policy in its soft power under the guise of Chinese traditions. Second, a couple of bans, imposed on popular movie genres or Western-inspired productions will not damage the Chinese cultural patterns unless Beijing's policymakers swift to the temptation of its Soviet predecessors. I assume that this is highly unlikely due to the pragmatic style of Xi Jinping's leadership. The driving forces behind Xi's doctrine might not tolerate particular narratives which dominate the contemporary Western culture. Even so, Chinese repudiation of those narratives originates from their cultural effects. It is merely a soft power *versus* soft power policy. Chinese art and popular culture will continue to make China more attractive and appealing since they imply a cultural shift to Chinese romanticism (Lovejoy 1933, 2).

The second characteristic, which supports the viable profile of Chinese Communism, is the *class struggle*. Although the notable Marxist concept was central to Maoism, the post-Maoist Chinese leaders shifted from class struggle to economic development (Peidong and Tang 2018, 5). Xi Jinping has a long history of citing Marx and Engels during his speeches and thus, he has not abandoned the class analysis of the society. When assessing Marx and Engels, however, we should not neglect the objective characteristics of the society they have created their writings. Boer summarizes Xi's premises on Marxism as follows: scientific, instead of utopic vision; absence of imposing the ruling-party theory through oppression and exploitation; theory of practice, and a guide of action (Boer 2021, 280). Of all Chinese leaders, Xi's approach differs in his insights about contemporary Chinese society. First and foremost, the Chinese President poses a fundamental question that no preceding leader touched – why does China need the future generation to read Marx. However, Xi's focus on Marxism concerns only domestic politics and thus, provides a grand design for the development of China's society. It is the political formula that China needs to emancipate from the universal claims of the Western ideologies. Xi's approach to Marxism and its place in people's life is *dynamic*. In contrast to the Soviet approach, which stresses the class struggle and the revolutionary engagement of the masses, Xi's philosophy does not advocate radical changes or inevitable revolutions. The Chinese leader builds his vision in the light of the Marxist tradition, refining it from the remnants of Lenin's shortsighted comprehension of the future. If the Soviet leaders summarized their arguments theoretically, Xi Jinping provided a different strategy for adapting the Marxist ideology to the needs of the Chinese people, and more particularly, to what he earlier called "The Chinese Dream." A path that differs from that of the Western civilization and that does not presume to convert China into a liberal democracy. The most important emphasis refers to the independence of the Chinese people. It is a reflection of China's "century of humiliation," which also occupies a central place in Xi's political rhetoric (Bader 2016, 15). In other words, Xi's interpretation of Marxism aims to consolidate the Chinese nation under the slogan of strong, prosperous, and independent China. The class struggle, as such, is not present in most of the Chairman's speeches, which does not diminish its significance. However, Xi Jinping's doctrine interprets the class struggle as more or less like part of every Chinese life. The Marxist revival under Xi, in fact, concerns the struggle for national independence and the rejection of what realist scholars call liberal hegemony. To analyze if Marxism could provide such independence will require another book. If we assume that the writings of Marx and his class analysis can provide Chinese people with motivation to preserve their original tradition, President Xi could become the first world leader to apply Marxism in practice.

This leads us to the foreign policy dimension of Chinese socialism, which Friedberg analyzes in his study on Chinese realpolitik. Friedberg is one of the few scholars who introduce the thoughtful claim that China is not so much "rising" as it is returning to the position of regional preeminence it once held (Friedberg 2011, 20). In similar to Allison's approach and most of the realist assumptions, Friedberg's study seeks to explain Chinese foreign policy with the desire of the CCP to secure Chinese regional hegemony in the APAC and to promote authoritarianism. However, the conclusion of the author that the current rulers of China seek preponderance due to the specific character of the political system they preside is arguable (Friedberg 2011, 21). I find it reasonable to remind one fundamental question, which Mearsheimer poses in his study on China's rise: are the Chinese less nationalistic than we are? (Mearsheimer 2006, 160). Friedberg, in other words, was successful in defining the not-so-rising policy of China but failed to explain its behavior. When using Cold War narratives that the adversary's ideology is evil, one should neglect the reminder of Morgenthau that politics is an autonomous sphere of morals (Morgenthau 2006, 35). China's aspirations for regional leadership are not an expression of Beijing's ideology, at least because Chinese policymakers do not seek an ideological justification for their foreign policy. In contrast to the American Presidents, who are bound to convince their voters and the Congress that it is in the interest of the United States to maintain the global liberal order, Chinese politicians do not pursue a *moral* hegemony.

Friedberg's assertion poses an essential question for this section: are the American policymakers less inclined to seek dominance and control than their Chinese counterparts are? Christopher Layne offers a logical answer: the challenger wants to change the rules embodied in the existing international order – rules written, of course, by the once-dominant but now declining Great Power that created it (Layne 2011, 110). Domination and control do not follow an ideology. The American global predominance relies on the U.S. military, economic and soft power, achieved not without subsequent involvement in international conflicts. Great powers competition is not a game of good and evil. European empires failed to maintain the multipolar world order due to their unquenchable thirst for colonization and resources. Shortly after the outbreak of World War I, Europe became a battlefield of the once most civilized nations, who failed to predict the long-term consequences of their actions. The defeat of the Soviet Union did not prevent Washington from repeating the Soviet mistakes in Afghanistan. To assume that liberal democracy is immune to the temptations of human nature is to affirm the idealist dream of perpetual peace. Some scholars will object that Friedberg's argument of democratized China, being more peaceful and less prone to conflicts, is the confirmation we need to accept the predefined nature of good democracy and bad socialism.

The liberalization of China is an old Western dream, dating back to the Opium Wars. Paradoxically, the Qing dynasty was much more likely to liberalize and modernize for the sake of its survival. It was a sacrifice, which subjected China to the Western powers and deprived it of the symbols of its national pride. Liberalization, eventually, was one of the most significant preconditions for the fall of the monarchy. When U.S. President William McKinley launched its open-door policy to China, farming was the starting point for the economic reforms in the Empire. With Japan in its backyard and Russia seeking to expand outside Eurasia, Imperial China voluntarily embraced the policy of economic liberalization to prevent its collapse. The Westernization of the Empire secured its failure to reunite the divided Chinese nation. In 2021, China faced the same dilemma when being challenged to liberalize and democratize. Friedberg argues that a democratic China will be more peaceful, but what would happen if the Communist regime collapses and the military takes over? Are there any certain preconditions that the Chinese people will prefer liberal democracy to communism? Finally, what kind of democracy would fit best to a nation, who is a successor of a millennial centralized political tradition and who is the second-largest world economy? My concern is that the potential liberalization of China could worsen the political climate in Beijing and lead to another century of humiliation, which, quite the opposite, will make the nation ever more unpredictable.

China's democratization is a political oxymoron due to another important reason. Beijing has already elaborated a traditional mechanism for political change, which I mentioned earlier in this chapter: *meritocracy*. Daniel Bell legitimizes the concept of political meritocracy by introducing a definition that combines the Confucian tradition of harmony with forms of political participation such as sortation, consultation, deliberation, or elections at the lower levels of the government (Bell 2010, 92). Marxism, of course, constitutes an important part of Beijing's political culture, but meritocracy is what empowers Chinese policymakers to undertake political reforms and cultivate future leaders. Friedberg's assumption would be praiseworthy if it provided us with an explanation of another variable: leadership. Current trends in leadership in both China and United States offer proof that regardless of the political regime, quality leaders are but a reflection of state actors' behavior. For China, the U.S. President impersonates U.S. Foreign Policy and the powers of Congress are but a part of the American Constitution. Chinese leaders are well familiar with the American political system but in their eyes, the President runs the state. For America, the Chinese President embodies a constitutional paradox of the ruling party's Chairman and Head of State. In similar to their Chinese counterparts, American policymakers have an eye for China's political system, but tend to exaggerate the ideological appraisement of domestic politics over foreign relations. This misconception is extremely popular among liberal scholars, who contend the messianic claim that the world's most powerful nation should primarily focus on promoting values. Realism, quite the opposite, believes in the primacy of pragmatic leadership, or as Morgenthau summarizes it: all nations will continue to be guided in their decision to intervene and their choice of means of intervention by what they regard as their respective national interests (Morgenthau 1966, 430). To sum up, it is untenable to limit a great power's foreign policy to abstract moralistic strategies that could obscure the outcomes of pragmatic leadership. The idea that America is bound to oppose communism and to deter it philosophically and morally has been dominating the Cold War and after the collapse of the USSR, evolved into liberal hegemony. This is not to say that America had a deficiency of leadership. U.S. leaders have a strong sense of political survival, but they are less pragmatic than their Chinese opponents. Beijing, on another side, often experiences the detrimental effects of what Friedberg calls "hypersensitivity" to separatism (Friedberg 2011, 20). Chinese policymakers are more pragmatic in terms of foreign policy but less flexible when they deal with unforeseen conflicts. The United States, as the world's most developed democracy, wants to achieve its purposes here and now. China, being the world's most advanced meritocracy, seeks to prolong the horizon of its aspirations for longevous leadership. If the Chinese, however, have a clear image and objective judgment of the American power, Washington runs to undervalue its adversary, depicting it as a typical Communist dictatorship with the nationalistic claims to rule the world. If only it were that simple to calculate the Chinese behavior. If only the Chinese strategic culture could be reduced to Confucius, Sun Tzu, or Mao. It is a misbelief as naïve as the Gaugamelian adventure of Darius against Alexander.

Strategic culture and the realist paradigm

In the years after the Cold War, Chinese military strategies have experienced a rapid evolution. When Chinese President Hu Jintao declared that his country would not seek global hegemony, a few leaders doubted his words. With Xi Jinping at the head of China, however, Western suspicion of the Chinese intentions triggered a wave of warlike attitudes about Beijing's military doctrines. While most of the assumptions misinterpret the theoretical pillars of China's strategic culture, Johnson observes that, in terms of military culture and use of force for political purposes, Beijing makes no exclusion from what the West calls *parabellum* or realpolitik "worldviews" (Johnson 1998, 25). This book joins the realist consensus about Chinese strategic culture by offering a complex definition of its nature. I begin with a short review of Shiping Tang's analysis of Chinese realism.

Realism provides materialist and rational explanations of states behavior and thus, I believe that it could best serve as a theoretical approach to the understanding of China's grand strategy. Tang introduces thoughtful research on the transition from offensive to defensive realpolitik in the context of Chinese foreign policy. Tang's claim is that Mao's offensive approach that dominated Chinese politics after the War of Liberation transformed into a policy of defensive nature under the leadership of Deng Xiaoping (Tang 2008, 154). My assumption is that Beijing's foreign policy under Xi Jinping is subject to a similar powershift, which will cause another modification of the Chinese grand design. To assess the potential implications of that change, I will first compare Mao and Deng's approaches to that of Xi. Tang summarizes Mao's foreign policy without differentiating offensive realism based on ideological calculations from realist approaches, based on power calculations (Tang 2008, 156). Mao's doctrine, thus, combines the offensive logic of supporting socialist revolutions and military conflicts with the firm belief that all obstacles to the rise of China derive from the aggressive foreign policy of the other state actors. For instance, Mao did not make a difference between the United States and the Soviet Union, claiming that they were both expansionist powers. His vision of the international system considered the bipolar structure of international politics a product of the superpowers competition. A more pragmatic assessment of Mao's perceptions will even lead us to the conclusion that Chinese realpolitik in that period was a predecessor of the later established realist approaches. Xi Jinping, in opposition to Mao, seems to demonstrate less, if any, affection for the export of Communism. In his speeches, the incumbent President of China does not imply that Beijing seeks to convert its neighbor to socialism with Chinese characteristics. Neither has he encouraged Western allies to do so. Xi, however, is more pragmatic than Mao when approaching the balance of power. Aside from the historical context, Xi does not seek a necessary and inevitable confrontation with the United States. His foreign policy is likely to blame America for trying to prevent China's rise but that is an objective outcome of the Sino-American competition and a logical reaction on behalf of the dominant superpower. Therefore, in contrast to Mao, Xi's concept of international politics is far more refined and dynamic. If Mao perceived Washington and Moscow as the ruthless expansionist power that sought to rule the world and enslave China, Xi envisions the United States as China's strongest adversary and Russia as Beijing's natural partner. The second assumption of Tang refers to Deng's defensive realism. The author explains it, again, as a complex strategy that combines four pillars: the rejection of the revolutionary rhetoric, recognizing the Cold War security dilemma, demonstrating self-restraint, and promoting security through cooperation (Tang 2008, 158). Does the same logic apply to the foreign policy of Xi Jinping? I assume only partially. Xi's Marxist rhetoric, as discussed above, seeks to promote unity and safety for the Chinese people in the face of the responsibilities which rising China will have to take when assuming the position of great power. The War of Liberation, being an integral part of Chinese history, still occupies a central place in the political rhetoric of all policymakers, but it serves more as an ideological outpost than as an inspiration for China. To assume that Beijing exports Communism and provokes revolutionary movements in Asia is to neglect the legacy of Deng Xiaoping. Socialism with Chinese characteristics is an original approach that secures the political development of China alone. It is inapplicable to other political systems, even in Asian-style democracies, which differ from their liberal friends. Bell assumes that meritocracy could remedy some of the democracy's deficiencies but the Chinese pattern of political cultivation does not seek universal validity under the slogan of abstract moralistic values. Xi Jinping's China favors economic and political cooperation, although it is hostile to multilateralism and security agreements for two reasons. First, Beijing's foreign policy does not follow the logic of defensive realism that cooperation under the security dilemma relates tightly to the Prisoner's dilemma (Jervis 1978, 170). For China, to be a prisoner of its adversaries' reactions is a strategical non-sense. President Xi strongly opposes the integration of China in any arms control agreements, without hesitating to challenge the behavior of both the United States and Russia. Second, China today is less likely to self-restrain and allow other state actors to constrain it. The reason is a lack of trust. Promoting self-restraint after the Cold War became a common tool of the Western powers to prevent the rise of potential peer competitors. The threat of isolation and the slogan of humiliation, however, cannot apply to China. Being the world's second-largest economy and leading creditor, Beijing is less likely to succumb to the Western pressure for political reforms and liberalization. The Sino-American economic cooperation, which drives the world economy, is essential for both powers, but for China, it does not presume security partnership. The Chinese membership in an international organization, on the other side, has a foremost purpose – to dominate them. The United States emerged as a superpower after establishing the World Bank and the International Monetary Fund as tools of the American economic predominance. Beijing is less likely to offer an alternative to those institutions but more likely to govern them in the future. Regional forums such as ASEAN and the Shanghai formats of cooperation present a perfect example of how China established the outpost for its further economic expansion. Finally, there is a hidden aspect of the Chinese defensive approach, which could expose the Western influence in the APAC to further challenges: the export of military technologies (Tow 1983, 51). For China, trading weapons is even more beneficial than engaging in arms control agreements. American allies in the region have a bad historical record with China, but except for Australia, they are more likely to accept a fair trade deal with Beijing. The reason is the lack of support on behalf of the United States. American foreign policy in the APAC is a victim of a historical temptation that caused the collapse of many alliances – declining credibility and changing perceptions of threat (Walt 1997, 160). If America had invited Japan to join AUKUS or if, at least, had encouraged the Japanese defense revival, Tokyo would have been less worried about Pyongyang's nuclear program. However, what is the restraining force behind the trigger of Kim Jong-un? Does Washington hold power to prevent North Korea from launching a preemptive strike on Japan in case China moves towards the annexation of Taiwan? The answer to this question is more and more likely to be seen. My final assumption is that Xi Jinping's China follows the strategic culture of what Western scholars would call "defensive realism." However, I prefer to use the term *protective realism*. It is defensive in terms of non-intervention but less cooperative than the Western approach. Its Asian-style nature is a result of a transition, similar to that Tang describes in his research. The transformation is not as overall as Deng's, and yet, it is less cooperative than Chinese foreign policy in the 1970s.

One cannot assess the strategic culture of China without a plausible definition. Scobell explains the Chinese grand strategy, explaining it as the fundamental and enduring assumptions about the role of war in human affairs and the efficacy of applying force, held by political and military elites in the country (Scobel 2002, 56). The definition, inspired by the writings of Jack Snyder and Shu Guang Zhang, combines the Western perceptions of warlike behavior with the Chinese military tradition. In other words, Beijing's strategic culture mirrors the disposition of a state actor to fight based on variables such as history and self-image. Scobell is a proponent of the mixed theory that Confucianism and Realpolitik shape the Chinese grand strategy and thus, defense is central to its tactics. Defense, however, does not necessarily presume pacifism. When a state actor faces a considerable threat to its national security, defense becomes secondary to self-preservation and survival. I believe that China makes no exclusion. Although Beijing does not seek a direct confrontation with the United States, partially due to the American military preponderance, Confucianism would advocate pacifistic behavior in case of external threat. Confucius believed that the social order is threatened when people fail to act according to their prescribed roles. If China envisions the structure of international politics as a global order, where Beijing should take its rightful place after the century of humiliation, policymakers are unlikely to compromise with any threat to the Chinese national security. Confucianism stresses the importance of peace and harmony, although not at any cost. Hegemonic behavior is another topic that emerges from the complex nature of Chinese foreign policy. Scobell presumes that Beijing does not pursue a hegemonic behavior due to the benevolent rule of its leaders (Scobel 2002, 101). Some scholars would object that all rising powers endorse a hegemonic behavior. I assume that when and if China surpasses the United States, Beijing will face the same temptation Washington faced after the collapse of the USSR. Whether Chinese policymakers will repeat Moscow and Washington's mistakes remains to be seen. My assumption is, however, that the Chinese grand strategy does not seek to build *Pax Sinica*, similar to Pax Americana and Pax Britannica, but is rather concerned primarily with its political revival. My argument is that, in opposition to the United States and the European powers, China has a millennial history of ascents and declines and thus, it has outgrown the strategic culture of its adversaries. History shows no better examples than Rome and the British Empire. Both powers ruled the world in different historical periods, but they all pursued a hegemonic behavior, sharing the same purpose – to preserve the status quo. With the Soviet Union collapsed, America enjoyed unprecedented omnipotent domination, which liberal scholars identified with the end of history. For China, however, history does not end with the Empire. The materialistic approach of realism, combined with the philosophical legacy of Confucius, presumes a permanent circle of sustaining the domestic political order and foreign policy that advocates strong and independent China. Classical realism explicitly rejects philosophy and morals as sources of foreign policy, and Chinese realpolitik goes even further, rationalizing and employing Confucianism for the purposes of foreign policy. China will rise and decline again and its ultimate goal is not to maintain or change the status quo but to keep surviving and preserve its original culture. Finally, Scobell stresses the first use principle of China that rejects the Western strategy of preemptive strike (Scobel 2002, 60). In truth, China has a good record with a number of interventions in Vietnam and border conflicts with India. The nature of those conflicts, however, does not owe the offensive preferences to China. The right of self-defensive is essential for all state actors and serves as the primary tool for the defense of national security. One might argue that the logic of self-defense does not apply to Taiwan. A few, however, would object that when the United States invaded the Hawaiian Kingdom, its aspirations to secure the American influence in the APAC logically aligned with the accession of Hawaii. For China, the annexation of Taiwan will be merely a similar act of dilation under the guise of reunification.

In a further stage, we not should neglect another assertion, which has been gaining support since Xi Jinping assumed the Chinese leadership. The claim that American theories of international relations are popular among Chinese policy analysts, many of whom are U.S. graduates, mirrors Washington's soft power that dates back from the interwar period when lots of European scholars immigrated to the United States to pursue their careers (Nathan and Scobel 2012, 32). Most of the American IR's founding fathers are European immigrants of the first or second generation. To say that the American trail in Chinese academia is robust due to its background is to state a fact, whose implications, however, are far from clear. First, in contrast to the Europeans, the Chinese have a greater sense of cultural belonging. European culture is unique with its patterns and history, but the same is even more relevant to China, where collectivism prevails over individual preferences. The impact of the Chinese tradition, combined with the domestic politics of the Communist Party, has established a profound attitude of cultural affiliation that cannot be stubbed by the American melting pot. Offensive realism is influential among the Chinese scholars, though it does not make their theories less Sino-centric. Second, most of the Chinese political officials, and more particularly, the highest rankings, are graduates of Chinese Alma Maters. Xi Jinping, for example, obtained his academic degrees from Tsinghua University. Although some political officials or their affiliates consider American IR theories a source of inspiration, Beijing has established many academic institutions such as the Central Party School of the Chinese Communist Party or groups like the Communist Youth League, which cultivate and shape the future leaders in the spirit of the Chinese traditions. The Westernization of the Chinese academic elite, and its subsequent liberalization, is an old dream of the United States and Europe, similar to the former Soviet strategy of converting Eastern Europe to Marxism through integrating the Marxist ideology into education. In China, however, the academic tools of soft power are highly unlikely to succeed due to the domestic resistance they face. Furthermore, China sticks to its selected approach to cultivation, which advocates academic interaction but filters its ideological impact. For instance, realism is the most popular Western IR theory in China, but one should distinguish between American *realpolitik* and Chinese *realpolitik* that reflects Kissinger's conclusion about the uncomprehensive nature of China's grand strategy.

In the previous chapter, I concluded that Waltz's theory of international politics, when combined with Morgenthau's assumption of the infinite lust of human nature, provides a plausible explanation of state behavior, states interaction, and international outcomes. Other branches of the realist paradigm, such as offensive, defensive realism, and neoclassical realism, provide further theoretical interpretations of international relations that elaborate on the foundations laid by Waltz and Morgenthau. I will thus give a few examples.

Morgenthau considered China the most powerful nation in mainland Asia and a prominent great power (Morgenthau 1968, 23). Aside from its historical emphasis on Communism, Morgenthau's theory about China predicted that Beijing would emerge as Washington's future peer competitor in the APAC. Another important lesson from classical realism refers to the liberal tool of isolating adversaries and exercising pressure through soft power. Morgenthau debunks that approach due to its inconsistency. The father of realism reminds us that even the most powerful nation on the earth cannot isolate an adversary that holds a permanent seat at the UN Security Council. Furthermore, contemporary China has cultural and political predominance in Asia, as well as global economic influence, which favors Beijing in its relations with most of the American allies. Morgenthau is a strong opponent of using hard power against China, and more particularly, of peripheral military containment for the reason that Beijing is immune to traditional American advantages. Therefore, one should not confuse the political challenge China poses to the United States with the military threats from Beijing's expansion in the APAC. By giving his preferences to temporary nuclear containment, Morgenthau admits that if America decides to pursue such policy, Washington should find itself in a war with Beijing (Morgenthau 1968, 30). Morgenthau's assessments of China's behavior, even taken aside from the historical context of the Cold War, sound reasonable and relevant to the post-pandemic security architecture. China is still immune to the predominant power of the United States due to Beijing's preponderance in Asia. Moreover, China and America are locked in a dead-end economic interdependence that presumes aggressive behavior on both sides. Isolating China is not a plausible option since Beijing holds most of Washington's allies in the grip of its tributary diplomacy. Allison's prediction about a war over Taiwan is highly likely in case Beijing decides to invade the island. However, a military conflict between both powers could easily trigger the deadlock of a nuclear scenario. Thus, Morgenthau succeeded in predicting the nature of the Sino-American competition but failed to interpret the Chinese behavior. His assumption that the Chinese grand strategy differs from the Soviet and that the United States will not isolate China in the short term expose the mistakes of the Presidential administrations, who invested decades of trust in Beijing's development. The assertion that the limitless lust for power is the driving force behind states behavior also depicts China's rise as an objective powershift, in which one state actor emerges as a great power. Chinese policymakers are more pragmatic than their Western counterparts but not less inclined to struggle for power than the latter. However, Morgenthau's theory does not give us a complete explanation of Beijing's behavior and furthermore – of the foreign policy, China pursues.

This leads us to the neorealist perceptions of China's place in international politics. Defensive realism is more likely to prioritize the implications of Chinese foreign policy for international security. Kenneth Waltz, to whom realism owes its most refined flavor, predicts the future partnership that dominates the Sino-Russian relations. I would not use the word "alliance" intentionally to agree with Waltz. Beijing and Moscow share a common struggle to oppose the American global predominance. Both powers have differed in their policy of values since the time of the Cold War. However, Waltz assumes that Russia favors China's grand strategy in a simple step: even in the absence of an alliance, the national interests of Moscow cannot easily accommodate the destruction of China, if that were to mean that American power would be poised on the Russian borders (Waltz 1988, 889). I assume that no realist scholar today will reject Waltz's prediction, but a few would contest its relevance to the friendly relations between Beijing and Moscow. Like its predecessor, Russia is a rational actor with the clear intent to consolidate the nations in Eurasia under the political flag of Kremlin. The image of American troops marching near the Russian borders is a long-played scenario from the Cold War and the years after Crimea's Annexation. To face the U.S. military presence on its Asian border, however, is an unbearable burden even for the Big R. In the year the Soviet Union fell apart, Waltz foretold that China would become a great economic power by the end of the XX century and would emerge as a global actor in case Beijing maintains an effective government. In other words, structural realist traces the roots of Beijing's success in its economic strategy, combined with the Chinese political formula of the one-party state. When analyzing the post-Cold War absence of the balance of power, Waltz stresses NATO's lack of vision, which alienates Russia from the Alliances and thus, favors the deepening of the Sino-American partnership (Waltz 2000, 55). It is a warning that many Presidential administrations failed to understand while the United States was preoccupied with the war on terror. The realist view about NATO's future mirrors another decisive step of President Biden's administration – to support Ukraine for membership in the Alliance. A policy, which Waltz would consider misleading and non-rational. In a further step, Waltz provides explanations of China's grand strategy in APAC, asserting that by modernizing its army, China will rapidly gain in-power projection capability (Waltz 1993, 68). Washington, quite the opposite, will face considerable difficulties due to the reduction of its forces and domestic problems such as political polarization and the huge economic gap between rich and poor. Liberal scholars, and even a few proponents of realism, tend to dislike Waltz's structural approach due to their optimistic perspective about the future of the global liberal order. For the United States, however, structural realism provides the most plausible explanation for the post-Cold War international system. Kenneth Waltz was the only realist scholar, who had the audacity to challenge the conventional American logic of nuclear deterrence by suggesting an alternative strategy of nuclear proliferation, which would benefit Washington best in deterring Beijing. If the U.S.

policymakers had endorsed Waltz's prescriptions, contemporary Japan would have emerged as a military power and tactical buffer to rising China.

Defensive realists like Stephen Walt have elaborated the approach of offshore balancing that advocates taming American power through avoiding a direct power competition with China in the APAC (Walt 2007, 13). Walt's concept, however, would inevitably face the United States with the ultimate choice of whether to rearm Japan. Taming the American power in a region that exposes America's West coast to security threats could be even more precarious than democracy-building in MENA. Offensive realism identifies China's behavior with the Monroe doctrine from the early years of U.S. Foreign Policy (Mearsheimer 2014, 25). Mearsheimer envisions the Sino-American competition as an objective power transition to a contested clash between the existing hegemon – the United States, and rising China. For offensive realists, Beijing's foreign policy aligns with hegemonic behavior and Chinese nationalism. Mearsheimer assumes that containment of China is a plausible possibility only if America fashions a balancing anti-Chinese coalition and if offshore balancing benefits the U.S. national interests in the APAC (Mearsheimer 2014, 30). Offensive realism rejects preventive war due to China's nuclear deterrent but advocates rollback, in which Washington would seek to dethrone regimes friendly to Beijing. In truth, realism believes that, regardless of their political culture, all state actors are rational but truly inclined to struggle for power. Offensive realism offers realistic scenarios about the future relations between Washington and Beijing and suggests that containment would be the ultimate strategy for the United States to prevent China's rise. Mearsheimer, however, poses two essential questions, which, I believe, provide a test for all realist assumptions on the Chinese strategy culture (Mearsheimer 2006, 160). Although those problems are still discussed by academia, my assumption is that Kissinger's concept of the world order has long provided the answers. I have found it reasonable to summarize and discuss Mearsheimer's questions as a conclusion of this chapter.

Why should we expect China to act differently from Washington?

The United States has a long historical record of successfully containing its peer competitors in Asia. Kissinger's explanation of China's foreign policy provides a partial justification for Mearsheimer's assumption that Beijing will follow the steps of Uncle Sam (Mearsheimer 2014, 20). Kissinger believes that China pursues two long-term objectives: displacing the United States as preeminent power in the western Pacific and consolidating Asia into an exclusionary bloc

(Kissinger 2012, 45). Tensions between Washington and Beijing over Taiwan are not new, but in 2021, for the first time, China claimed the island, ignoring the American warnings and seeking to reshape the balance of power in the region. Even if we accept Xuetong's interpretation of China rising peacefully, the very rise of a new superpower presumes, if not primarily military, then at least cultural and economic expansion. The United States, on the other side, will face the inevitable alternative to draw a red line beyond which Washington should act in support of its allies in the APAC.

I also believe that Mearsheimer is correct in his assumption about America likely behaving toward China much the way it behaved toward the Soviet Union during the Cold War (Mearsheimer 2014, 30). Most American policymakers consider China another version of the Soviet Union, while some even compare Xi Jinping to Stalin. Although I find such convergence deeply misleading, this book does not reject that U.S. Foreign Policy towards Beijing employs the same tools it applied to Moscow during the Cold War. However, it is debatable if Beijing will endorse an American-like approach to push the United States out of Asia. China's grand strategy might set Asia as an outpost of Beijing's great power policy but it is unlikely that the Chinese policymakers will militarily duplicate the Monroe doctrine due to the *Chine*-ness of their political culture. My assumption is that Kissinger provides the most rational argument: military imperialism is not the Chinese style (Kissinger 2005). Both realist and liberal scholars tempt to limit their explanations of Chinese foreign policy to variables such as nationalism, realpolitik, and communism. Although Kissinger admits that China seeks to displace the United States as the preeminent power in the Western Pacific, he implies that, in opposition to the Clausewitzian approach to warfare that stresses the preparation of war, Sun Tzu's art of war focuses on the psychological weakening of the enemy. I here remind my assumption that Xuetong's theory of China's peaceful rise will be valid as long as Beijing follows the policy of silent cultivator, while Mearsheimer's predictions will fulfill if America decides to go to war with China. Some scholars misinterpret the Chinese art of war, identifying the manipulation of ideas and attitudes as *sharp power*, which pierces, penetrates, or perforates the political and informational environment in the targeted countries (Walker and Ludwig 2021, 1). Propaganda, information warfare, and conspiracies might be consistent with the Russian approach of hybrid warfare, but they are inferior to the millennial military tradition of China. Besides, Joseph Nye clarifies that sharp power, although hostile by its nature, mirrors the voluntary attraction of soft power (Nye 2021, 202). Another popular statement identifies China's foreign policy with the *parabellum strategic culture*, and thus, Beijing's behavior exhibits a preference for offensive use of force, mediated by a keen sensitivity to relative capabilities (Johnson 1998, 20). Although Johnson's theory of *cultural realism* presents valid proofs for the Sinocentric nature of the Chinese foreign policy, Kissinger reminds us that explanations, which limit Beijing's behavior to Western imperialism, are not appropriate in dealing with a country that has managed four thousand years of interrupted self-government (Kissinger 2005, 2). Why do I prefer Kissinger? Kissinger's explanation of the Chinese behavior goes beyond the common understanding of the most Western-centric concepts for a simple reason: Kissinger had the opportunity to follow closely the rise of Communist China from the foundation of the People's Republic to the present day. Kissinger does not reject that Beijing seeks to increase its influence in Asia he rather criticizes the unilateral hard approach that American policy-makers tend to use when dealing with China.

Feng introduces another proof of how misinterpretations of the Chinese strategic culture affect American perceptions of Beijing's foreign policy. In his criticism of Johnson's theory, Feng stresses the importance of the linguistic discrepancies that are present in the contemporary writings on China (Feng 2007, 3). In truth, a comma or even a full stop can change the whole meaning of a sentence. Feng also indicates another weakness, which bars Western-centric theories from providing a full explanation of China's policy behavior – the exclusion of the modern Chinese leaders from the complete analysis of Beijing's grand strategy. Scholars tempt to neglect the footprints of Mao Zedong, Zhou Enlai, and Deng Xiaoping by emphasizing only Xi Jinping's doctrine, claiming that Mao's communist legacy does not provide empirical sources of analytical knowledge. However, to assess China through isolating the Communist period from its imperial tradition is misleading for two reasons. First, one cannot explain how China behaves only through assessing the external sources of Chinese foreign policy. Beijing's foreign relations are primarily directed to defend the Chinese national interests and the resistance of certain states to China's tributary diplomacy deeply affects Chinese behavior. However, even if the domestic political order does not reflect the foreign policy behavior, the beliefs of China's leaders matter. China is not a liberal democracy and its political system draws centralized legitimacy from the Communist Party and the actions of its Chairman. Second, most Western scholars typically use Western translations of the Chinese classics that, more or less, transform the connotation of the latter. Feng offers an example of misinterpretations, which provide us with misleading comprehension of essential terms such as *use, through the means of, or depending on* (Feng 2007, 5). It is precise because of that reason, I have found it useful to avoid direct borrowings from the Chinese classics and to quote more Asian scholars, who, despite having fewer citations than their Western colleagues, have introduced a better explanation of the Chinese political philosophy.

My conclusion is that China will not attack the United States or its allies in Asia unless first provoked by Washington. I use the word provoked, not attacked for a simple reason: a preemptive strike against China will certainly force Beijing to retaliate. My central argument refers to the less extent of certainty for U.S. offensive actions in the Chinese periphery. Ironically, Morgenthau logically predicted that periphery military operations would not work against China (Morgenthau 1965, 160). I believe his observations are still relevant to the balance of power in Asia and more particularly, to the American defense strategy in the region. There is, moreover, insufficient attention to regions, which are more likely to cooperate militarily with China in the future. The first point of confrontation involves India and Pakistan. India and China have a long historical record of geopolitical rivalry. For Washington, India is the involuntary ally who could provide direct access to mainland China. It is highly unlikely that the Indian policymakers will advocate the establishment of U.S. military bases on India's territory. With Afghanistan under the control of the Taliban and Pakistan enhancing its security cooperation with China, India will soon find itself trapped between Islamabad and the increasing Chinese influence in Myanmar and Bangladesh. The second point concerns Taiwan. Here, Beijing is in a less favorable position due to the unpredictable reactions of North Korea. The hopes for dialogue between Washington and Pyongyang died with the refusal of Kim Jong-un to give up its nuclear ambitions. With two American allies on its borders – Japan and South Korea – Pyongyang is likely to support Beijing in case of American provocation.

Some would argue that the Chinese aspirations for Taiwan are an expression of militarism and that President Xi Jinping will inevitably move towards the annexation of the island. My concern is that Taiwan, as Kissinger clarifies, is an exception due to its close historical and cultural ties with China (Kissinger 2005). Historically, the United States has supported the One-China policy since President Carter suspended the Sino-American Mutual Defense Treaty unilaterally. Carter's predecessor, Richard Nixon also tended to sacrifice the island in favor of the American rapprochement with China. Could President Biden gives the international community firm guarantees that tensions with China will not escalate to a dangerous level if the United States provides military support for Taiwan? In other words, supporting Taiwan will mean a violation of the One-China policy, America committed to respecting during the Presidencies of Richard Nixon, Jimmy Carter, and most recently – that George W. Bush. Since most state actors have not recognized Taiwan as the Republic of China, the American military support will make the United States look like the actor, which seeks war. However, I assume that Beijing's talk about annexing Taiwan is a strategic bluff of Chinese policymakers to keep America away from the Chinese periphery. I do not believe that China will establish a blockade over Taiwan for another reason: America is still enjoying strategic preponderance in the APAC. Taipei will become part of China once Beijing succeeds in pushing Washington out of the region. Until then, China will continue to provoke the United States as Sun Tzu has written in the Art of War *if your opponent is of choleric temper, seek to irritate him. Pretend to be weak, that he may grow arrogant* (Tzu 2012, 10).

Is Beijing less concerned about its survival than Washington is?

None of the above, but more pragmatic – yes. This book joins the argument of Yong Feng that despite the wide range of views existing along the realpolitik-idealpolitik spectrum in the Chinese conception of national interests, the dominant thinking is still realist (Feng 1998, 322). However, an essential facet of the Chinese strategic culture that is less discussed in academia concerns the existence of what Scobell defines as the "third bureaucratic entity": the People's Liberation Army (Smith and Paul 2021, 1). When analyzing the latest trends in CCP Politburo's discussions, Scobell's theory also depicts the Chinese worldview as a *nested* system of four circles: mainland China and its claimed territories; China's immediate periphery, consisting of fourteen neighbors; the APAC neighborhood, and the world beyond (Scobell 2002, 26). Scobell is correct in his claim that the strategic culture of China embodies an amalgam of legalist/parabellum hard realpolitik and Confucian/Mencian idealist strand. It is a realist explanation of a realist foreign policy and thus, completely relevant to contemporary China. The fundamental question, which follows that explanation, is can we employ the standard realist approach to infer the basic implications of China's strategic culture. My answer is that the realist paradigm could provide plausible predictions about Beijing's behavior, but only partially. Scobell's analysis, therefore, is a bridge between the realist explanations of China's grand design and Feng's detailed exploration of Chinese political culture.

Kissinger points out that in the Chinese view, the world order reflects a universal hierarchy, not an equilibrium of competing sovereign states (Kissinger 2014, 127). China is the Middle Kingdom, the Emperor's "All But Heaven," of which Beijing has formed the central, civilized part, inspiring and uplifting the rest of humanity. So far with the similarities between the American Manifest of Destiny and the Sinocentric view of Beijing. American political culture is messianic and extrovert in its struggle for global liberalization, while the Chinese pursue a policy of prestige through inspiration. In contrast to the Monroe doctrine and Theodore Roosevelt's social Darwinism, Chinese foreign policy seeks to promote tributary diplomacy and deter its adversaries economically. A difficulty arises from Kissinger's use of universal hierarchy to describe the Chinese worldview. China's hierarchical vision, however, does not correspond to the liberal paradigm and its aspirations to alter the international anarchy. In contrast to liberalism, Confucianism advocates social harmony and centralized hierarchy to secure the domestic political order. Thus, we cannot apply the Western concepts of realism and liberalism to the Chinese worldview, which envisions Beijing as the sole sovereign government of the world. I assume that the most accurate definition belongs to Kissinger, who envisions it simply as Sinocentric (Kissinger 2014, 130). Some would argue that we could identify Sinocentrism with nationalism. Chinese nationalism constitutes a considerable part of Beijing's foreign policy, but I find it too simple to restrict the theoretical debate by stressing the nationalistic aspect of Chinese politics. We could call Beijing's political philosophy *realpolitik*, but only to the extent of understanding the Chinese foreign policy through the Western perceptions and its respected schools of international relations. Only if China truly embraces the pattern of U.S. Foreign Policy its worldview will abandon Sinocentrism. My concern is that regardless of the political regime in Beijing, the Chinese will hardly adopt the Western system of values as it contradicts their universal attitudes.

Another popular myth about Chinese leadership originates from the assumption that China's leaders are communist dictators who follow the steps of their Soviet predecessors. Although socialism with Chinese characteristics is the dominant ideology of China, Feng suggests that the belief system of the Chinese leaders predetermines state behavior and that Xi Jinping's comprehension of the political universe may move towards a cooperative direction although his strategy of achieving goals would be more assertive or conflictual (Feng 1998, 325). The incumbent leader of China definitely fits Feng's explanation. Xi Jinping is more cooperative on a global level but less inclined to compromise the Chinese national interests when facing opposition from Beijing's adversaries. In addition, I assume that Xi's foreign policy embodies two aspects that make his leadership pragmatic.

First, Xi Jinping's pragmatism derives from the centralized political system of China. However, centralization in China does not reflect the Soviet approach to foreign policy, which was idealistic and focused on the utopic vision of Marxism-Leninism. When the Qin dynasty laid the foundations of the Chinese Imperial tradition, Emperor Qin Shi Huang abolished the feudal system, following the legacy of Mencius, who considered unification pathway to peace (Wilkinson 2000, 10). Emperor Qin was one of the most pragmatic rules of China due to his rational strategy to make alliances with distant states, but attack those, that was near (Wilkinson 2000, 55). Although Mao initially opposed any Confucian interpretations of Chinese politics, he refined Qin's doctrine and even applied it to strengthen the authority of the ruling Party. We could see the same tactics used by Xi in his efforts to reunite the People's Republic by ceasing the Hong Kong protests and by the accession of Taiwan. In Chinese, the word for "world" expresses the literal explanation of "all beneath the sky." (Youlan 1948, 25). One should distinguish, however, between the world in general and the Sinocentric concept of the universe that unites all people of Chinese blood. Western theoreticians would call that nationalism, but for China, the reunification of all Chinese is essential for establishing peace "under the sky." Therefore, the pragmatic leader will unite the nation, before going to war against its enemies.

The second facet of Xi's pragmatic approach refers to politics itself. Chinese philosophy advocates self-cultivation and encourages men to engage in politics (Youlan 1948, 75). The image of the Chairman is less ideological than the Soviet Cult of Personality. If the Communist Party of the Soviet Union had invested in leaders, who were less pragmatic but more ideologized, Beijing's policymakers would have established a completely different mechanism of meritocracy that tolerates the most confident and audacious members to become *statemen*. Ideology is essential to the development and the cultivation of the leader, but pragmatism, personal skills and accomplishments occupy a central place in selection. Moreover, the political engagement of the Chairman stresses less theoretical than on practical commitments to the nation and the party. Instead of digging into their vision of China, Chinese leaders focus on the practical policies through which they intend to achieve results. I doubt that a Chinese policymaker will use Marxism to describe the future of China without first describing the tools with which he intends to make his nation more prosperous and independent, not just to make it great again. For the pragmatic leader, ideology can be the source of legitimacy, but it cannot serve as the inspiration for foreign policy. The Confucian view of the ruler constitutes another aspect of Chinese pragmatism – authority. Xun Kuang's interpretation of Confucianism presumes that the ruler-sage should unify the minds of the people and lead them to the true way of life, in which there is no place for disputation or argument (Cheng and Peng 2008, 60). Western scholars have already named Kuang's concept *pragmatic authoritarianism* (Kuang 1994, 112). The Chinese leadership is explicitly durable to political fluctuations that have outlived historical authoritarian governments such as the Soviet Union. We can trace the roots of that connection in the amalgam that exists between the centralized political authority in China and its pragmatic decisions, which advocate the adaption of economy, culture, and foreign policy to the changing political realities. In similar to the Qin's doctrine, unification, control and leadership are the aspects of pragmatic, which, as the history of China shows, possesses high durability against collapse (Huang 1995, 60).

To conclude, I assume that many scholars would tempt to blame me for calling democracy less pragmatic than authoritarianism. The purpose of this book is not to define which form of government is better. It is important, however, to highlight that liberal democracies, after the Cold War, are more likely to trade pragmatic foreign policy for hegemony instead of sticking to realpolitik. In 1989, Fukuyama argued that the end of bipolarity is the end of human evolution and the universalization of Western liberal democracy as the final form of government (Fukuyama, 1989, 4). Fukuyama's assumption insisted that post-Cold War China far more resembles Gaullist France than pre-World War I Germany (Fukuyama, 1989, 6). I will remind the warning of Kissinger who explicitly points out that China has managed a millennial tradition of uninterrupted self-government (Kissinger 2005). Liberal democracy might have the ability to dethrone corrupted regimes and deter authoritarian ideologies, but it cannot rebuild and maintain the former. Moreover, liberal theoreticians typically focus on Hegel's construction of history but neglect the Hegelian claim that India and China lie outside the World's History as the mere presupposition of elements whose combination must be waited for to constitute their vital progress (Hegel 2004, 133). In short, Hegel claims that if Asia has traditions, China has a history. In Chinese culture, despotism is necessarily the form of government for two reasons: special interests enjoy no consideration on their own account and the government proceeds from the Emperor alone (Hegel 2004: 134). The only temptation that exists for the pragmatic leadership of China's leaders is similar to the general weakness, which lures liberal democracies: universalism. If China succumbs to the temptation of claiming and expanding its beliefs as the perfect form of government, its original tradition will perish, melted in the Hegelian spiral of absolute knowledge.

Chapter Four
The Post-Pandemic Structure of International Politics

This chapter deals with the final purpose of my research – to explain the post-pandemic world. In the first part of the book, I brought three primary and three secondary variables to construct my explanation, which I defined as coercive realism. I have chosen the term *coercive* to indicate the straightforward nature of my assumption. In this chapter, I infer three hypotheses that provide the starting point for my analysis.

My first assumption is that the post-pandemic structure of international politics will be bipolar. I define the post-pandemic nature of the international system as *nuclear bipolarity* for reasons I will further discuss when introducing my model. During the Cold War, the United States and the Soviet Union struggled to dominate the international system and challenged each other's primacy, even facing the MAD scenario. The rest of the state actors served the national interests of Washington and Moscow in their limitless and pragmatic purpose – to defeat the adversary. Non-state actors such as the European Community, NATO, the Warsaw Pact, or the Council for Mutual Economic Assistance added powerful sources of influence, which the superpowers utilized to manipulate the balance of power. In short, the bipolar system mirrored the structure of international politics. Therefore, I assume that the structural analysis is necessary and useful to design a thoughtful explanation of the post-pandemic world order. However, I assert that bipolarity in the post-pandemic age will have a *pyramidal* structure, in which the United States and China will occupy the walls alongside the rest the rest of the nuclear actors will coexist in a state of constant competition on the lower levels of the pyramid.

My second assumption is that disarmament will give way to an arms race between Washington and Beijing. Although the United States and Russia advocated arms control under the mask of multilateral cooperation and mutual security agreements after the Cold War, I do not expect China, in the next ten to twenty years, to become part of any future accords. Beijing is a rational actor and pursues a policy of prestige, but Chinese policymakers are aware of the fact that arms control will prevent China's rise. Moreover, I believe that most of the existing agreements are outdated and ineffective due to the increasing tensions between America and Russia. My claim is that if the United States wants to deter China effectively, Washington should think of providing nuclear support for its allies in Asia. Some would argue that deterrence through nuclear proliferation could lead to MAD. However, I consider MAD highly unlikely but yet, possible, for a simple reason: although realism believes that states are rational actors and though they struggle for power, a very few policymakers are overobsessed by power. For example, nuclear mushrooms can serve as inspiration for leaders like Putin, but in reality, rational decision-making always prevails over reckless behavior.

Third, I argue that most non-state actors will primarily serve the national interest of the United States and China. Military alliances like NATO are likely to become less effective and even unproductive if the allies do not conduct an institutional reform. Integration *suis generis* communities like the European Union will provide legitimacy for their Member States, but without armed forces, Europe will be vulnerable to external threats such as hybrid warfare or cyber-attacks. Security agreements will not cease to exist as long as they benefit the national interests of the poles. For instance, economic entities are likely to evolve at the expense of political cooperation since Washington and Beijing will have to take responsibility for the world economy. My assumption is that state actors will be central to the post-pandemic structure of international politics and that great powers will be less likely to cooperate unless their survival is at stake. Nevertheless, their efforts will be less inclined to establish a new generation of non-state actors instead of investing a significant amount of resources to defeat the adversary.

Assumption four refers to the policy of values that occupied a central place in U.S. Foreign Policy after the Cold War. Although soft power and culture will still exercise a considerable influence on the adversary's behavior, I assume that the United States and China will be more likely to resolve international conflicts through using hard power. There is a growing discussion about warfare and its nature, evolving into non-conventional or *hybrid* forms. Although hybrid warfare poses a challenge to the foreign policy of state actors, my concern is that hybridization of war coincides with soft power through which a state actor seeks to influence the foreign policy of its opponent. Cyberwarfare, on the other hand, is far more capable of causing damage than hybrid strategies and presents a bigger concern for state actors. The evolving nature of war, however, does not predetermine the death of conventional warfare. Both United States and China possess destructive capabilities that are less likely to end the world but more probable of being tested when Washington and Beijing demonstrate power.

Finally, I believe that the cooperation under the security dilemma, which dominated the Cold War security architecture, is likely to evolve into confrontation. China will be far less cooperative than the Soviet Union for two reasons. First, Washington's behavior towards the rise of China is warlike because America will not tolerate peer competitors in the APAC. Under these circumstances and considering that China does not participate in arms control, Chinese policymakers will hardly follow the logic of cooperation. Second, deterring China will require a skillful strategy, which, I assume, does not always coincide with containment. Although containment from the Cold War era could serve American foreign policy, its potential to negate Chinese global advantages is doubtful. Instead, the United States should elaborate on an alternative approach, which combines the conventional tools of containment with offshore balancing.

In the final part of this chapter, I discuss a few plausible scenarios for the post-pandemic age. My first conclusion is that the present state of the international system is far from that of the Cold War. Instead, I have chosen to call the New Grand Chessboard a four-scenarios game for the reason that, according to my explanation, the ultimate purpose of the United States and China will be to negate each other's resources of influence and to neutralize any advantage that might serve another great power to emerge. The second conclusion of this book is that if the United States wants to deter China, Washington should abandon the struggle for liberal hegemony and pursue a combined scenario, which I define as *offshore containment*. Finally, I conclude that if Beijing strives to win the competition with Washington, China should abandon the temptation of orthodox Communism and stick to political meritocracy and pragmatic leadership. To survive the clash, Chinese decision-makers should employ more elements from the traditional culture of Ancient China and integrate them into Chinese foreign policy. Thus, China will pursue the policy of *silent cultivator*, which will provide it with the resources to negate the major American advantages.

In this section, I will explain my vision of post-pandemic bipolarity. Liberal scholars will tempt to object that pyramid presumes hierarchy rather than anarchy. Even so, my explanation does not deal with political geometry. I have chosen to employ the pyramidal model for two reasons. First, structural realism provides the methodological core of my research and thus, I have found it useful to construct a pattern that depicts political relations among nations as a pyramid. Second, structural realism assumes that the international system is anarchic because there is no governing body above state actors. Therefore, I exclude international bodies from the pyramid because I assume that they serve and thus, reflect the national interests of state actors. A governing entity might hold a legal personality, but its behavior mirrors the foreign policy of the Member States. International law provides legitimacy for international organizations though it does not explicitly define if they enjoy the same sovereign rights as state actors. Therefore, I assume that, although non-state actors interact and affect world politics, they should remain outside of the pyramid as substitutes for state behavior.

Setting the model: the pyramid of balance

My central contention is that the international system is pyramidal, and embodies a number of variables that have both qualitative and quantitative character. For the purpose of this study, I use maths as a source of empirical data because I believe that, in the case of numerous variables, the quantitative methodology can most accurately assist in defining the post-pandemic structure of international politics. Although this approach is poorly developed in the theory of international relations, I find it expressive for two reasons. First, it makes it possible to assess the relationships between the variables in the study, which, as Waltz highlights are central to one's study (Waltz 1979, 14). Politics, power and anarchy play a crucial role in the realist explanation of international relations, but I believe that their graphic expression will help better understand the coexistence of the variables. Second, the logic of maths allows to better calculate the balance of power in international relations. My quantitative research includes formulas based on statistics and empirical information. However, Waltz reminds us that when the variables become very appropriate, there should be a unified model that demonstrates how explanations work (Waltz 1979, 16). Third, the pyramid, of all the geometric shapes, provides me with a relevant approach to introduce my explanation. The selection of this polyhedron also reflects the relations that exist between state actors in the international system. Finally, I would like to make it clear that this book does not deal with theories similar to Maslow. The source of inspiration for this model is Kenneth Waltz's structural approach to the explanation of international relations. Thus, I assume that the post-pandemic balance of power can be depicted as a hexagonal pyramid, which combines three groups of variables.

In addition, before deriving the formulas, I make a few clarifications, by which I seek to refute potential criticisms of my explanation. First, I assume that the pyramid is hexagonal and that it embodies the structure of the international system. This does not mean that the system exists in perfect balance or that the introduced variables, in the sense of state actors, have an equal chance of defeating others in potential conflict. The geometric shape that builds the pyramid in the straight geometric progression is a reflection of the realistic assumption about the anarchic nature of the international system. Therefore, the base area of the pyramid is not determined by the simple existence of the state actors but by the direction in which the confrontation between states will take. The polygon on which the pyramid rests is a hexagon because I assume that state actors in possession of weapons of mass destruction (WMD) have the destructive capabilities to achieve Mutual Assured Destruction (MAD). For example, North Korea's military potential cannot be compared to that of the United States, but that does not mean that Pyongyang could not provoke a US-China military conflict that could lead to MAD. At the same time, I acknowledge that not all states in my model are superpowers. I accept that the post-pandemic world will be bipolar, but along with America and China, I assert that nuclear powers will also play a central role in the post-pandemic structure of international politics. Although a state actor may not be a superpower, if it possesses WMD, it could still serve as a global balancer in international relations. Finally, yet importantly, my model does not deal with absolute values. Variables and aspects of the pyramid can switch places depending on how the balance of power in the international system evolves.

My model is limited in four ways. First, this book does not seek to introduce a universal theory of international relations. Second, the model is limited and adapted to the post-pandemic realities. The structure of the international system in the 1990s and more particularly after September 11, differs from the post-pandemic structure of international politics due to the change in the balance of power. Therefore, my model can serve as a starting point for calculations only in the years after 2020. Third, my explanation is not based on historical case studies, although one can use such to provide parallels with the Cold War. My explanation does not address world politics only in terms of history or geostrategy, as it combines quantitative with a qualitative methodology. My assumption is that the formulas I use reflect the anarchic nature of the international system, beyond which anarchy will evolve into chaos, which, I assume, is a condition similar to MAD. Finally, the Pandemic is not a variable of my research but rather a historical framework. In my theoretical explanations, which I discussed in the first chapter of this book, I introduced three variables – politics (dependent), power (independent) and anarchy (intervening), which I will further operationalize within the pyramid. In truth, the structural model I offer employs elements from previous theories. However, I mentioned at the beginning that it is not possible to construct a concept without learning from previous explanations. The theories I employed provided me with a robust theoretical framework for my research. Therefore, this book does not duplicate or reinvent older explanations but rather refines or develops them.

There is a body of literature that seeks to explain the structure of the international system as a pyramid. I have found it useful to offer a critical review of concepts, which follow a similar logic to my study. Most of the pyramid explanations, however, are as clear as misguided. I begin with the theory of Rosecrance, who offers a pyramid concept to explain the rise of China. Rosecrance states that Great Britain was at the top of the international pyramid of power in industrial terms but did not seek to exercise that power (Rosecrance 32, 2006). The depiction of the structure of the international system as a pyramid, in which great powers occupy the top, expresses the common approach of most authors to consider major variables in their studies. However, such structural models do not provide us with empirical explanations of state behavior. Although my research also considers power an independent variable, I believe that defining the position of great powers in the international system does not enough does not provide us with a clear image of how the balance of power would change. In short, static models are insufficient to offer a plausible explanation of the international system. For example, we state that at the moment the United States is the most powerful nation on the earth and thus, it occupies the apex of the pyramid. The problem arises from the constant dynamics in which the international system finds itself, which is currently shifting the balance of power in China's favor. Therefore, Rosencrace's approach can serve to geometrize the British primacy but fails to explain how multipolarity shaped Britain's behavior in that particular historical period.

Alexander Ossiander introduces a similar approach to the structure of the international system by analyzing the Peace of Westphalia and the emergence of sovereignty. Ossiander's concept differs from Rosencrance's with its emphasis on world politics as a derivative of states behavior. By assessing the historical legacy of the Swiss adventurer Johannes Burkhardt, Ossiander argues that the Habsburg Empire occupied the top of the pyramid in 17 century because it had long been the most obvious contender for top rank in Christian society. They had tradition and legitimacy on their side. Therefore, their combined dominions not only were more extensive than those of any other dynasty but had been acquired (at least within Europe) very largely through nonviolent means, especially marriage (Osiander 262, 2001). Ossiander concludes that war, like religious and ideological propaganda, was central to the definition of where the top of the pyramid lies. Although I recognize the validity of Ossiander's model, it is arguable to what extent religion and ideology affect political relations among nations at present days. Realism believes that soft power by itself is not enough to drive states' foreign policy. Ossiander's structural analysis offers a better vision of the international system but misjudges state behavior and the balance of power.

Michael Brecher refers to regional security in Asia as a unique pyramid of power, which takes the form of bipolarity, with two superpowers acting at centers of decisions, military organization, economic coordination, and diplomatic cooperation involving a large segment of the system – though not all its members (Brecher 1963, 215). Although the pyramidal model for Brecher provides us with a starting point for a more detailed explanation of the balance of power, it fails to operationalize a few variables. First, the pyramid of power is a model which introduces only one aspect – the influence of state actors in world politics.

After distinguishing superpowers from other international actors, Brecher does not assess deeper variables such as the reasons for the rise of China. Second, the pyramid of power is applicable only to the period of the Cold War, and I assume that it cannot serve as an explanation of the post-pandemic world order. Although the bipolar confrontation between Washington and Beijing reminds us of the Cold War bipolarity, my concern is that some aspects differ, such as the security dilemma, Chinese foreign policy, and the striking polarization in American society. Brecher's pyramid can explain the U.S.-Soviet bipolar world, but is insufficient to assess the post-pandemic structure of international politics.

Andreas Antoniades offers a theory of hegemonic analysis, which envisions hegemony as a four-sided pyramid, which signifies the dynamic, antagonistic, and ever-changing relations among the different movements of power within a hegemonic order (Antoniades 2008, 14). It is a concept that examines the balance between hard power (coercion) and soft power (attraction) in U.S. Foreign Policy. The authors typically refer to the United States as the *hegemon*. The holistic approach of Antoniades suggests that the base of the hegemonic pyramid embodies *life*, or in other words, the struggle of state actors for power. Although the author employs structural analysis to operationalize the variables, Antoniades' model explains only the behavior of the hegemon without assessing the balance of power. I assume that the hegemonic concept will be applicable to future hegemons, but I doubt that it can provide a further explanation of the post-pandemic bipolarity. Finally, Antoniades summarizes the tools of hard and soft power, introduced earlier in the IR theory by Joseph Nye, without explaining whether hegemony has positive or negative consequences for the United States. The equations used by Antoniades are a perfect expression of the validity of his theory but my conclusion is that a pattern cannot explain the structure of international politics without assessing the foreign policy of the other state actors.

In his notable theory of international relations, David Lake states that despite all aspects of authority, all treat hierarchy as a structural characteristic defined by coercive capabilities within either a global or regional system organized into a single pyramid for all relevant states (Lake 2011, 60). It is arguable, however, that the pyramidal structure of the international system always presumes hierarchy. The one-dimensional pyramids might envision the system as a hierarchical entity with separate layers but as Kenneth Waltz reminds us "Peace is a fragile concept" (Waltz 1988, 260). History shows that international organizations seldom use their mechanism adequately for conflict resolution and peacebuilding. Even liberal scholars, who criticize Waltz's theory for being insufficient to explain states behavior, agree that only state actors can exercise soft and hard power in its fullness (Nye 2021, 201). My concern is that envisioning the international system as a one-sided pyramid or a triangle does not provide a profound vision of its structure. Morgenthau highlights that despite superpowers having control over world politics, the struggle for power is central to states behavior (Morgenthau 1985, 112). In short, one-sided pyramidal models are insufficient to explain the structure of international politics. Hierarchical models reflect power relations between international actors but fail to explain how those interconnections could lead the world to MAD or how political relations between nations affect conflict resolution. Static hierarchical models are applicable to the nature of state, which is much more similar to Kant's eternal peace than to the geopolitical realities of the post-pandemic world.

The best argument of my theory belongs to Robert Gilpin, who suggests that no power can stay atop the world pyramid for any great length of time (Gilpin 181, 156). Is it, then, reasonable to assume that we can envision the international system hierarchically? The answer of this book is no. Therefore, I argue that the system of international relations resembles a *multi-dimensional* pyramid rather than a simple triangle: the apex of the pyramid expresses power, the independent variable in my research and the base area equalizes with politics, the dependent variable in my study. Anarchy – the intervening variable – infuses the pyramid, which predetermines its multi-dimensional nature. Some would argue that if the apex expresses power, superpowers should occupy the top of the pyramid. Such a claim might be applicable to the liberal paradigm, but realism rejects it, reaffirming the statement of Gilpin that no eternal great powers. Liberal scholars, who criticize Gilpin's theory, also fail to explain why an absolute and omnipotent power has never achieved permanent dominance in international relations. Therefore, the struggle for power is constant, not its possession. One-dimensional models collapse when the international system transitions from multipolarity to bipolarity, or from unipolarity to bipolarity. History offers no better example than Rome, which has ruled Europe but finally has fallen in the hands of barbarians.

To sum up, I assume that the existing pyramid concepts of the international system provide a starting point for its explanation, although they face significant methodological limits. First, one-dimensional models do not take into account the multidimensional nature of the system. The one-dimensional pyramids explain how superpowers control world politics and affect minor actors. However, they do not explain what happens if one superpower challenges another. One-dimensional models do not address the security dilemma, limiting confrontation between state actors to the use of soft power. Indeed, in a nuclear world, it is impossible to fight a war, as nations fought in 19 century. However, war is part of international politics, and to exclude it as an option would be naive. Second, one-dimensional models reduce all tools of foreign policy to hard and soft power. I find this misleading, and I think that a more detailed look at the offensive abilities of state actors is needed to explain their behavior. When two superpowers confront, the survival of the international system is often at stake. Nuclear arsenal and conventional military, however, do not share the same proportion of hard power. The same logic applies to diplomacy and attraction in terms of soft power. Third, one-dimensional models typically relate the foreign policy of state actors to an essential variable in international politics – power. Although it is the ultimate purpose of states to maximize their capabilities, it is important to highlight that there are no omnipotent states. The United States is the strongest nation in the world, but even its power has limits, which I discussed in the previous chapter. It is paradoxical that sometimes the omnipotence of one superpower causes another rising power to challenge the supremacy of the former. After discussing the methodological limitations of my theory and those of the existing concepts, I proceed to the operationalization of the main variables in my model, which I call the *pyramid of balance*.

Assessing the primary variables

In the first chapter of this book, I inferred three variables that constitute the body of my research. I begin with power, which is the independent variable in coercive realism. Power is at the apex of the pyramid for two reasons. First, the lateral edges of the pyramid meet at the apex as all state actors struggle for power. Regardless of their ideology, states are equally inclined to defend their security. Second, the apex is located above the base area, which reflects the realist belief that power man's control over minds and actions of other men (Morgenthau 1985, 13). The emergence of rising power and its struggle for global leadership is determined primarily by its capabilities to exercise hard power. Some would argue that the pyramid would have a different view depending on whether the world was bipolar or unipolar. Although the structure might differ, my claim is that the apex will also indicate power because all status-quo states seek to preserve their primacy. In a nuclear age, moral, on the other side, has little to do with politics.

The dependent variable in my model is politics. It combines the short-term and long-term goals of states foreign policy. I assume that whatever the purposes of an actor's policy, its ultimate purpose is maximize its resources and to accumulate more power at the expense of others. Politics covers the center of the pyramid. Of all the resources, available to state actors, I find the nuclear arsenal of most crucial and decisive for their status, because it gives them the opportunity to manipulate peace and war in international politics. Nuclear powers are the actors which, in their struggle for power, can lead the world to MAD, and so their desire to rule the system could be its undoing. Henceforth, I assume that fear is the only deterrent that keeps them from resorting to total war. Combined with the realist assumption that states are rational actors, I conclude that their foreign policy presupposes real expectations of how an international conflict would develop. One would argue that my model is limited because it does not take into account what would happen if nuclear weapons fell into the hands of a non-state actor. My assumption is that state actors will not be willing to voluntarily delegate their nuclear sovereignty to an international organization because if there were such an option, it would have already happened. For instance, the United States and Russia succeeded in removing nuclear weapons from Ukraine and South Africa but failed to involve China in nuclear arms control. Besides, most arms control formats are outdated and irrelevant to the post-pandemic world order. Other arguments typically relate to scenarios in which terrorist groups acquire nuclear weapons. My concern is that terrorists cannot construct or acquire nukes unless being provided with resources by a state actor. However, I do not think that a rational actor would entrust WMD to terrorists, and therefore this cannot happen. For example, ISIS gathered a set of IT experts when it emerged on the ruins of Al-Qaeda. Yet, it did not develop its nuclear arsenal. The same logic applies to Al-Qaeda, Muslim Brotherhood, Hezbollah and other terrorist networks. The possibility of terrorists acquiring nuclear weapons would unite state actors to such an extent that adversaries such as the United States, Russia and China would do everything possible to prevent terrorists from getting the bomb. Finally, the main purpose of terrorism is to harm civilians, not to destroy states. The messages of political Islam that the West must be weakened as a declining culture and that Islam's ideology must prevail over Western values are as utopian as the claim that ISIS destroyed Palmyra for religious reasons. The artifacts of the ancient city were removed not because they were a symbol of non-Muslim culture but because the monuments went to the black market, which infused a substantial financial resource into the accounts of ISIS.

This leads us to the intervening variable in my research – anarchy. Anarchy intervenes to prove the realist claim that international conflicts stem not only from the desire of states for power, but also from the structure of the international system. Anarchy fills the pyramid of balance, and intersects the apex with the base area. Mearsheimer is clear when outlining in his first assumption that anarchy does not mean chaos but a lack of central government to run states (Mearsheimer 2001, 10). As I explained in the first chapter of this book, international bodies have failed to exercise power, precisely because they do not have the potential to alter the anarchy. History shows no better example than the tragic end of the League of Nations. If we lived in a world of values where beliefs dictated world politics, maybe Kant's project of eternal peace would come true, or at least Jimmy Carter would win a second presidential term during the Cold War. However, the short peace of the 1990s has shown that once a country has enough resources to oppose the status quo, it will do so, whether it uses realpolitik or sinocentric foreign policy. Those who blame realism for being cold and rational should remember the optimism with which the liberal world welcomed the collapse of the Soviet Union and how all that optimism went away on September 11.

Assessing the secondary variables

The first group of variables is the state actors, which correspond to the lateral faces (the walls) of the pyramid: the superpowers United States and China, and the rest of the nuclear powers. In opposition to most theories, I do not consider arms control central to methodology due to the nuclear diplomacy of China. Although Beijing has joined the nuclear non-proliferation treaty, it is unlikely for arms control to affect Chinese foreign policy toward the United States. The pyramid of balance is a polyhedron pyramidal structure composed of six triangles, which denote the nuclear concert. The first triangle is the United States, which I assume will maintain its global primacy for the next 50 years. The second triangle is occupied by China, which moves towards reaching parity with Washington. The third wall of the pyramid is occupied by Russia, which will act as provoker in world politics. The position of a provoker will allow Moscow to influence world politics without directly confronting the United States and China. The fourth lateral face of the pyramid consists of Britain and India, which are in possession of WMD. London's aspirations for reviving the "Rule Britannia doctrine" are central to U.S. Foreign Policy and the Big Five. India is a strategic outpost for the Western influence on the Southern Chinese border, however, still hesitant in its foreign policy towards London and Washington. The fifth wall is France, nuclear power, and alongside Germany – the driving forces of the European integration. Finally comes the face of nuclear powers such as North Korea and Pakistan, which, although rational actors, are on the verge of gaining destructive capabilities that will lead the leading forces to comply with them. Although Iran could be placed in this triangle as a state of nuclear concern, at this stage I will refrain from doing so due to its lack of WMD.

The second group of variables includes the ultimate resource available to state actors to affect international politics – nukes. I assume that they occupy the lateral edges of the pyramid, which outline its base. My claim is that resources of global influence in the post-pandemic world include nuclear arsenal, conventional military, emerging technologies, coercive diplomacy, smart power, and economics. I suggest that the nuclear arsenal is central to one's ability to exercise power in world politics for a simple reason: nuclear confrontation could lead to MAD. A state actor, which acquires nuclear weapons becomes a nuclear power, while nukes more or less serve as a buffer against the outbreak of World War III in a world where policymakers slowly become more obsessed with power and less rational. Therefore, the lateral faces of the pyramid consist of nuclear states and do not limit their expression to the poles. The conventional military will still play a crucial role in the post-pandemic security architecture because when diplomacy fails, sophisticated weapons prevent state actors from going to war. By conventional military power, I mean basic capabilities such as Army, Navy, Air Force, and military budget. Emerging technologies presume, above all, the ability of a state to influence another actor through cyber technologies – hacking, hijacking, data leaks or sophisticated weapons in terms of Space Force. Although the aforementioned resources are not equally present in all lateral faces of the pyramid, I believe that countries like Japan have the opportunity to influence the policies of other actors no less effectively and technologically than China and Russia. European countries such as France, on the other hand, have adopted cyber strategies within NATO according to the principles of the rule of law, which prevent the state from interfering with the private sector. Another lateral edge of the pyramid is coercive diplomacy, exercised mostly through economic sanctions. In a nuclear world, where total war is tantamount to MAD, it has become appealing for global actors to impose sanctions on each other or third states. For instance, seven years after the annexation of Crimea, the United States and Europe have not yet lifted the sanctions on Russia, which, although partially effective, have not returned the peninsula to Ukraine. Moscow has repeatedly responded to sanctions, far from affecting the West's economic interests. However, the logic of coercive diplomacy does not apply to China, where economic sanctions would have a detrimental effect on Western economies. I incorporate smart power into the pyramid of balance because my assumption is that soft power, although secondary to hard power, is still central to great powers' ability to affect the foreign policy of other states. However, my claim is that soft power is effective only if it is applied alongside hard power (Ivanov 2020, 50). Although smart power is primarily a U.S. Foreign Policy tool, China and Russia, and to some extent, Britain and Europe, have the potential to manipulate the attitudes of their adversaries. States in possession of nuclear weapons are also inclined to employ smart approaches in their foreign policy. For example, the nuclear diplomacy of North Korea keeps America in constant fear that Pyongyang could launch a preemptive strike on the U.S. allies in the APAC. Economics is the last edge of my equation. One would argue that of the actors, only the United States holds the main reserve currency, along with China, Japan, Britain and the Eurozone countries. Even so, the currency is not the only issue influencing foreign policy. Inflation in Russia and the devaluation of the ruble do not prevent Moscow from maintaining high military capabilities, such as its missile defense and early response system, which is already causing alarm among the European allies. The Indian rupee is not a reserve currency, but few would deny that India is an economic giant and an unwitting ally of the United States against China. North Korea and Iran, whose economies exist in isolation from America, are devoting enough to sustaining and developing their nuclear projects. In other words, even if the lack of resources distorts the power capabilities of an actor, other opportunities for influence compensate for it.

The third group of variables involves *imperfect rationality*. Therefore, the base area of the pyramid, which traces the roots of the base edges, determines the rational limits of the nuclear states' foreign policy. In a nuclear world, affected deeply by the hegemonic behavior of the unipole, humans are far from perfect, even when possessing the deadliest weapons in history. Given the fact that my model is a hexagonal pyramid, this leads us to the conclusion that its lateral edges could be flexible in shape. Therefore, each of the lateral faces of the structure can lead to its collapse, as long as the state has the necessary resources to do so. In the event that the balance of power tilts in favor of one or another superpower due to the availability of a scarce resource, the foreign policy of one actor can deform the pyramid and make the threat of MAD more realistic. Therefore, I consider the risk of MAD as real, although the state actors, being rational, pursue a policy of survival. Moreover, my assumption is that it is precisely that policy, which could lead the world to MAD.

Finally, I address the potential criticism that the pyramid of the balance does not explain states behavior. In contrast to most of the existing models, and more particularly – to the one-dimensional ones, my pyramid seeks to provide an explanation for the structure of international politics and the behavior of states after the Pandemic. It combines the basic configurations that will shape the post-pandemic world and introduces plausible scenarios for their development. In addition, despite my model does not pretend to be universally valid, I assume it is theoretically robust precisely because we do not have enough empirical knowledge to predict the end of the Pandemic. Thus, I need to proceed with the examination of the pyramid's aspects.

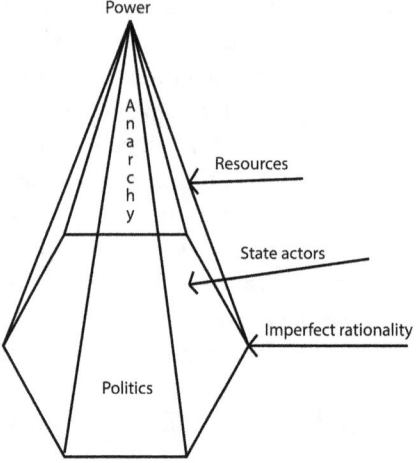

Figure 1: The Pyramid of Balance: Variables

Defining the aspects

The three variables I have introduced to explain the structure of post-pandemic policy presuppose the existence of dependencies that can be used to calculate the balance of power in the international system. I contend that the balance of power in international relations predetermines its nature, which cannot be defined simply as unipolar, bipolar, or multipolar. My assumption is that along with the number of poles, the nuclear arsenal of the international actors will occupy a central place in the post-pandemic balance of power. By nuclear powers, I mean state actors, which are in possession of nuclear weapons. For example, in the bipolar model, in which the United States and China are the poles, Russian and Britain, considering their nuclear arsenal, can also take the position of balancers in the relations between the superpowers. Moreover, I assume that, in the context of conflict resolution, balancers will often play a much more crucial role in resolving disputes than the poles. Russia's role in the Syrian civil war is an example of how a state actor that does not have the capabilities of the United States and China, has managed to benefit from the geopolitical situation in MENA. Henceforth, in this section, I will define the aspects of my model, which explain how the poles and the nuclear powers will shape the post-pandemic structure of international politics. In order to offer a more plausible explanation of the model, I begin with the ideal type of right hexagonal pyramid.

The first aspect denotes the apothem of the pyramid. Since it is a right hexagonal pyramid, I signify the apothem with a. In maths, the apothem of hexagonal polyhedron indicates the segment from the center of the polygon, on which the pyramid is built to the middle point of any side of the base area. I argue that in my model, the apothem corresponds to a defensive posture or the probability that an actor will fall into a position, in which to defend itself (Jervis 1978, 198). My model borrows this term to calculate the possible development of a conflict scenario and what resources a state actor would use to maintain its defense. To measure the extent to which states tend to defend themselves, I employ the Pythagorean theorem to define a. After dividing the hexagon that constitutes the base of the pyramid into six triangles, I assume that each of them is equilateral, and therefore, I can calculate the apothem using Pythagoras. In the formula, I assume that the apothem of defensive postures (a) is the sum of the defensive advantages of a state, which in sum with the realistic chance of a state to win the conflict is equal to the most probable scenario of the confrontation. My formula is based on a realistic understanding that states are rational actors, and their quest to achieve victory or manipulate the balance of power reflects the real judgment of whether they can win against their adversary. Therefore, it is logical to sum up the desire of states to confront, combined with a realistic assessment of their ability to calculate whether a conflict is possible and what is the most likely scenario for its development. Given that in the post-pandemic world, the international system is anarchic and that countries are in a constant state of competition, I conclude that the balancing pyramid cannot exist in perfect condition.

This brings us to the second variable in my model – slant height *(s)*. In the pyramid of balance, s is the distance from the base area of the pyramid to the apex along the center of the lateral face. I equalize slant height with offensive postures, which are defined as the position of one actor to attack another (Jervis 1978, 198). I borrow this term to explain whether it is possible for one state actor to attack another and, if so, how offensive postures will affect the balance of power. In math, slant height can be calculated with a given height and apothem. In my theory, however, slant height is computable and denotes the MAD scenario. One would argue that by doing so, my model limits the geopolitical outcome to one option. This would be the case if I assumed that the pyramid of balance was right by definition. However, I believe that, in a confrontation between state actors, the shape of the pyramid undergoes a deformation, which could lead to MAD. Therefore, when two nuclear states come into conflict, regardless of their nature – economic, diplomatic, or military – the confrontation can lead to the collapse of the international system, the balance of power favors the stronger actor. The more the slant height of the surrounding wall increases, the more walls of the pyramid deform and recline, and the apex gets closer to alignment with the lateral edges, so the states get closer to MAD. I assume that an additional inclination will lead to the eventual collapse of the pyramidal structure, and consequently – to total war. At the same time, the height of the surrounding walls is also changing, which means that they have a holistic view of the conflict. Although the resources are basically the same and therefore its size is not deformed, the probability of MAD depends on the length of the slang height. If the pyramid of balance collapses, the surrounding walls will also fall apart. I calculate the probability of MAD using the standard slant height formula, which again employs the Pythagorean theorem, given that the base area is a regular polygon.

The third variable involves the height of the pyramid – h. In mathematics, height indicates the distance from the apex to the base, depending on the type of the pyramid. In its ideal shape, I argue that the height of the pyramid indicates the offensive capabilities of the states. Analogically, with given apothem and slant height, we can use Pythagorean to calculate the height of the pyramid because the static shape of the geometric body is right and hexagonal. Therefore, I can employ the standard formula and apply it to one of the equilateral triangles, which constitute the lateral faces. Since anarchy dominates the pyramid of balance in the absence of the intergovernmental body, the calculation of the height will indicate the national interests of the state actors, which connects the apex of the pyramid with the base are.

The last variable refers to the base sides of the pyramid, which I indicate with b. In the calculation of the base area of the right hexagonal pyramid, the base sides mark the limits of the regular polygon. Similar to h, base sides indicated the defense capabilities of the states. In a right hexagon pyramid, where the lateral faces are isosceles, we can easily calculate the base side by utilizing a standard formula. If not, a more complicated equation will give us the final value. Since all states in the pyramid are part of the nuclear concert, they are in possession of nukes. However, it is important to highlight that the pyramid will not be right as nuclear powers differ in their capacity.

Inferring the postulates

Before calculating the security dilemma, I will outline a few postulates that I believe will be valid for the post-pandemic structure of international politics. I do not use the word "axioms" because my statements do not claim universal validity and follow the limits of my model, which I set at the beginning of this chapter. I believe that the derived variables and aspects lay the foundations of a theoretical model that can provide explanations for the post-pandemic world order. Thus, I use the tools of mathematics as much as they can help the quantitative aspects of my research.

Postulate 1: States will remain the primary actors in the post-pandemic world order

This book does not deny the potential of international organizations to mediate disputes or exercise soft power. However, the pyramid of balance involves only state actors, as only they have the sovereign capabilities to exert power and maximize their resources. Serving the national interests of their members, international organizations are an expression of common will and cannot reach the same degree of rational foreign policy as states. My conclusion is that peace and war in the post-pandemic system will serve the interests of the United States and China and the nuclear powers involved in international conflicts. If Washington endorses the concept of offshore balancing, introduced by Mearsheimer and Walt, U.S. Foreign Policy will demonstrate a typical example of husbanding American power in favor of the U.S. national interests. If Beijing develops its policy of silent cultivator, it will be transformed into an instrument of tributary diplomacy that will help Chinese leaders to neutralize Beijing's adversaries and to undermine the U.S.-led system of alliances. My model presumes that Moscow is unlikely to rise to the status of a global power equal in capacity to the United States and China. Moreover, I believe that Russia will take the more comfortable role of mediator in the international system. Mediating between Washington and Beijing will allow it to defend its national interests on an equal footing with America and China and to reap the benefits of the conflicts in which they are involved. How successful this strategy will depend on how stable Vladimir Putin's administration is and who will succeed him. Actors who will collaborate with the United States include Britain, France, Japan and, to some extent, India. Washington will be opposed by Iran, Pakistan, and North Korea. The emerging bipolarity does not mean that domestic insurgencies cannot occur within those blocs. It is quite possible that the positions of Washington and Brussels differ on various issues, the way Beijing is trying to control Pyongyang's nuclear program. However, I believe these differences will be much less important than the bipolar opposition, which will inevitably lead the minor actors to take sides.

International bodies, on the other hand, will reduce their influence for several reasons, the first of which is the lack of military capabilities. For years, Europeans believed that true reunification of the Old World would occur when the community finally moved towards giving more sovereignty to supranational institutions and stepping up their politicization. My statement is that the true unification of Europe presupposes the creation of European armed forces. The European Union is a unique community that enjoys the advantage of operating with the second most common reserve currency – the euro. Europe has a stable economic framework, a healthy social policy and free movement between member states. Without the armed forces, however, Europe will not be able to act as an independent actor in the post-pandemic system of international relations. Russia will forever remain the scarecrow of Eurasia, and NATO's differences will widen until the Alliance needs to be thoroughly reformed.

Second, the UN also needs reform. For years, several countries, including Japan and India, have been urging permanent members of the Security Council to include more countries on a rotating basis. If this does not happen, the organization will probably follow the fate of the League of Nations. The differences between the permanent member of the Council will become so great that the decision-making process will be blocked. We are currently witnessing such a process, as many UN resolutions do not pass due to the Chinese and Russian vetoes. The organization is, of course, unanimous in its decisions on threats such as global terrorism, arms and human trafficking and crimes against humanity, but much of the decision-making process has been blocked due to divisions among the permanent members of the Security Council. From a peacekeeper, the UN can easily become a provocator of conflicts. The best opportunity for the organization to reform is if it accepts more countries by the Permanent Council, and in order to compromise, this can be done on a rotating basis. Otherwise, the UN will not survive in its present condition, in the era of bipolar confrontation in which Washington and Beijing will not compromise in their foreign policy and will not tolerate the rule of international law over their national interests. Second, the UN will not be able to adequately secure global stability in a world where peace and war will serve the interests of the nuclear powers. The history of the Cold War shows that when the superpowers clash, the UN has little if any, role in preventing MAD, which is the real threat that can lead to a zero-sum game for all nations. This is not to say that the organization is ineffective in preventing crimes against humanity. But let us not be deceived that it will have the full mandate to act in the same way as it did in the Srebrenica massacre when China was still rising and Russia was still weak after the collapse of the Soviet Union. Third, the UN member states have adopted the Charter of the organization as sacred. But there are no absolute values in international politics, because even the great powers come and go. The UN arose as an idea to prevent World War II and failed in its mission because it had no actual potential to eliminate the preconditions for another global confrontation. The UN is on the verge of failure because it does not have the tools to assure the world that it will prevent total war between the United States and China. The easiest way would be to make the organization's resolutions binding, but that idea failed after terrorists hit the United States. It is also debatable to what extent the UN can take rational resolutions given its cumbersome bureaucratic structure and its claim to be the only universal global organization.

Third, NATO also needs to reform. Since September 11, the Alliance has embarked on huge and costly global commitments, many of which have turned to be quite detrimental to the national interests of the allies. With the potential accession of Ukraine to NATO, its stability will be even more threatened as its borders will clash the Russian. I assume that reform of Article Five is needed to set reasonable criteria for who can receive direct support from the allies and to what extent the collective defense will apply to hybrid threats and cyber warfare. I believe that the criteria should follow three principles: shared burden, shared defense, and shared modernization. Countries that refuse to pay, develop and modernize their armies should not be able to enjoy all the privileges it provides because such states will simply be passive consumers of security without offering any contributions as actual allies. If NATO does not reform but continues to expand to the East, to say, in the next twenty years, it will become completely ineffective against Russia. If that happens, the effects and repercussions of what has happened will ultimately undermine the European trust in its American allies. The ultimate test for the Alliance is Stephen Walt's theory, which defines three conditions under which an alliance would disintegrate: changing perceptions of threat, declining credibility, and domestic politics in terms of regime change, ideological divisions, domestic competition, or socio-demographic trends (Walt 2008, 158–164). Of all preconditions, I believe that declining credibility is of crucial importance. The Alliance has shown that it is resilient to changing threats since the end of the Cold War since the image of the enemy has evolved from the Soviet Union through global terrorism to Russia and China. Given that the world is moving towards *nuclear bipolarity*, we can expect a long life for *reformed* NATO. Domestic politics seems like a risk to the Alliance, but to the extent of populism, which depends on the electoral preferences of the nations. While Donald Trump was in the White House, there was a talk that the United States could leave NATO if there were no shared funding because and thus, Alliance would not benefit American national interests. However, the majority of American policymakers rejected this proposal because they believed that the losses from the U.S. withdrawal would outweigh the benefits. France, which has been pessimistic about NATO since its foundation, has often expressed disapproval of U.S. Foreign Policy towards Russia. However, it is far from realistic for Paris to withdraw from NATO due to its temporary frictions with the United States. French politicians will not benefit from the isolation of Germany, which would mean the rise of far-right nationalism in the country and the collapse of Europe's security system. With American troops in Berlin, Germany is a loyal Member States of the Alliance, and its non-membership is out of the question unless America withdraws from Europe. Germany is the most powerful economy on the Old Continent and could become the cornerstone for the future European army. However, this will mean the end of the European project as countries like France will also prefer the path of self-development rather than that of cooperation. The countries of Central and Eastern Europe will remain in the Alliance as the United States has an interest in having a military presence in regions such as the borders with Belarus and the Black Sea. U.S. national interests in Eastern Europe will be lasting as long as Russia has a presence in Crimea and claims the rest of Ukraine. Therefore, the disintegration of NATO due to domestic politics is possible only with the return of nationalism in Europe. Although the nationalist movements of the Old Continent are strong, political elites are unlikely to listen to them for one simple reason: money. Values can be a scarce resource of political PR for voters, but rational decision-making requires a clear assessment of how much the benefits of withdrawing from a community outweigh the losses. Voters in Eastern European countries such as Bulgaria and Romania are often enthusiastic and unanimous about their rejection of Western liberal values, but official statistics show more than 60% of the population supports NATO and EU membership because of the financial support that Russia cannot offer. Declining credibility is the only stone that can overturn the Alliance's tank. Therefore, the United States should demonstrate limited commitment to Europe, with a clear emphasis on the shared burden. A Shared budget, on the other side, is the starting point for limited commitment and offshore balancing, and once Europeans create their own armed forces, one could consider delegating some of NATO's functions to European command, a thesis Mearsheimer defends in his articles (Mearsheimer and Walt 2016, 70). Furthermore, it is debatable to what extent the American national interest runs counter to the European presence while Russia threatens to push its borders with the alliance. Moscow has strong instruments of influence in the post-Soviet space, and parity with the United States should not be binding in risk assessment. Along with NATO's structure, its capabilities also need reform. Without increased cyber tools and opportunities to combat ideological propaganda, the Alliance is vulnerable because these threats do not fall under Article Five. Therefore, the allies should develop sophisticated mechanisms to neutralize cyber threats and hybrid propaganda and prevent their spread to the United States.

Finally, the post-pandemic world will be less tolerant of regional entities such as the Organization for Security and Cooperation in Europe and the Non-Aligned Movement. Many of these bodies cannot survive without the financial support of their members and without a theoretical framework of values that they seek to preserve. My prediction is that they will need an updated vision to defend their existence and their mission in the face of emerging China. Economic formats such as ASEAN also play a central role in the global economy and the competition of great powers in the post-pandemic world. However, this book does not deal with the future of international organizations. My assumption is that in one way or another, these organizations will, to some extent, serve the national interests of the United States and China. Regional organizations are useful formats for joint action and coordination in the fields of economy, culture and politics, but their decision has a little, if any share in international politics. Each organization is dominated by a country or group of countries that promote their interests in its institutions, regardless of the common positions of the other members. The pyramid of balance can incorporate nation states without involving international organizations, which, I assume, reflect the national interests of their members. In order for an international organization to become a part of the model, it ought to acquire all the characteristics of a state, which political theory assigns from sovereignty to independence in foreign policy. But then, what would be the difference between an organization and a nation-state? This is one of the questions that liberal institutionalists who criticize Waltz have failed to answer.

Postulate 2: The ultimate purpose of the states will be to prevent mutual assured destruction

My explanation suggests that the ultimate purpose of state actors in the post-pandemic world will be to prevent MAD. When I say state actors, I mean those countries that have with nuclear weapons. Each of the walls of my pyramid outlines variables in which at least one nuclear force is present. Robert Jervis explains that according to MAD, trying to protect yourself is destabilizing because it threatens the other side (Jervis 2002, 41). Indeed, in a world where the United States does not tolerate peer competitors and where global terrorism is the only direct threat to American national security, defense is preferable to deterrence. Even the most powerful nation in the world cannot contain terrorist groups that strike in advance at any point in the world. However, it is my view that in the bipolar world of the United States and China, restraint will once again be the preferred strategy over the defense. A nuclear apocalypse is a likely scenario if tensions around Taiwan begin to rise or if Beijing decides to break the cordon formed by the United States through AUKUS. The situation is getting more complicated by North Korea's nuclear program, which has shown little willingness to engage in dialogue and which would not hesitate to test its nukes against Tokyo and Seoul. Although states are rational actors, the use of nuclear weapons is a historical precedent from World War II, and my concern is that this scenario should not be excluded. This is not to say that the threat of terrorism will disappear. It is quite possible that a new ISIS will emerge after the Pandemic ends or that part of the existing terrorist groups will merge into another Caliphate. For the United States, the challenge of China's rise is far more detrimental than the war on terror. The same logic applies to Beijing, which, in its efforts to dethrone the United States, will not hesitate to reshape its policy towards the Uighurs minorities. With Beijing's nuclear arsenal rising, Washington will have no choice but to return to the Cold War containment policy, as a direct confrontation between the superpowers will be tantamount to MAD.

Russia, which constitutes one of the pyramid's lateral faces, has the largest nuclear arsenal of all state actors. The future of Putin's administration is unclear, but I assume that Russia is unlikely to return in the 1990s. Such a scenario is as realistic as assuming that Moscow can unite Eurasia politically, militarily, and economically in the next five years. However, Russia has demonstrated an excellent record of fighting wars without risking the nuclear apocalypse since the annexation of Crimea in 2014. The main point is whether the West should risk a nuclear war with Russia to make Ukraine part of NATO. The answer to this book is no. Moscow will not resort to the use of strategic nuclear weapons unless it is attacked first. However, Ukraine's aspirations for the Alliance could trigger a tactical Russian reaction. The Black Sea, on the other side, remains a region of constant tensions, from which Moscow will not back down even with Putin's successors in Kremlin. Historically, Russia has always had claims to the region since the times of Catherine the Great, and Russian aspirations will not change even if Kremlin regime becomes friendly to the United States. However, if Ukraine joins NATO, tensions could escalate to dangerous levels. Mearsheimer notes that much of the blame for the Crimean scenario lies with the West, which for years underestimated Russia's potential to contain Western influence in Eastern Europe. With NATO's troops on its borders, Russia may become more unpredictable for two reasons. First, policymakers in Moscow are aware that if Russia does not effectively counter NATO's presence on its borders, it could undermine the legitimacy of Kremlin's political regime. Second, if Russia withdraws from the Black Sea, it will probably lose Crimea to the West at a later stage. Even if another President comes to Moscow, Russia is unlikely to compromise. My prediction is that Moscow will not withdraw from Crimea in the near future, and any challenge to the region poses a potential risk for MAD. Therefore, the rational policy for the United States is to restrain Russia's influence in the region, but only in countries that are the Member States of the Alliance. With China lurking in the Pacific, growing tensions with Russia could force the West to fight on two fronts, a tactic that has often proved losing in the past.

In the nuclear era of the post-pandemic world, APAC will play a central role in U.S. Foreign Policy, followed by Europe and MENA. If we follow Allison's logic, there are several scenarios in which the United States and China will go to war, two of which he considers most likely: a clash through Taiwan or the collapse of the regime in Pyongyang (Allison 2017, 101). Both scenarios could lead to MAD. If China decides to annex Taiwan, it would be a direct challenge to the West Coast through Guam. Washington could activate AUKUS and subsequently send nuclear submarines into Chinese territorial waters, which will most probably provoke another Cuban missile crisis. Unlike the Cold War, however, the superpowers will be far less inclined to back down for one simple reason: if Washington backs down in such a crisis, it would mean victory for Beijing, which, unlike Moscow during the Cold War, is a rising power. An American retreat in such a conflict will legitimize China's claims in the region, undermining the allied relations between Washington, Seoul and Tokyo. If Beijing imposes a permanent blockade on Taipei, this will be the most direct route to a nuclear apocalypse, as access to Guam will be facilitated and the United States will be forced to intervene.

The same logic applies to Pyongyang's nuclear diplomacy. North Korean leaders are rational-minded actors, but the same cannot be said of the military. If a military coup takes place in North Korea, it is very likely that the military will blackmail Western forces, threatening to launch pre-emptive nuclear strikes against Japan and South Korea. This will lead to an international crisis with the only possible way out – MAD. China will not allow U.S. troops near its border, and America will not tolerate Pyongyang threatening its allies. Russia's intervention in the conflict would also lead to a nuclear apocalypse, especially if the United States demonstrates the ability to retaliate. However, the ultimate challenge will come from Pyongyang, as the military regime could be unpredictable, especially if challenged by Japan or South Korea. Thus, any attempt by the West to overthrow Pyongyang should be carefully considered and comply with China's strategic interests in the region. Whatever the relationship between Washington and Beijing, they must not rule out the possibility of a military dictatorship in Pyongyang resorting to the use of nuclear weapons without rationally assessing the destructive consequences of MAD.

What would nuclear containment look like in the post-pandemic world? First off, any attempt by the other nuclear powers to include China in another arms control agreements is doomed to failure. Chinese policymakers are unlikely to ratify similar accords, at least until their country reaches parity with Washington and Moscow. In addition, Beijing is very sensitive to any talks that would limit China's rise. My assumption, however, is that nuclear agreements will be in decline. This is a process that began during the Trump administration when the

United States and Russia withdrew from a number of accords reached by their predecessors during the Cold War. One might argue that at some point the U.S. president and the new Chinese leader could agree on a form of cooperation. It is arguable if both powers will cooperate, or at least not until China reaches parity with the United States. Russia, for its part, has no use in pressuring Beijing to join nuclear arms control unless a President who fears China's rise succeeds Putin in Kremlin. However, this is unlikely because relations between Washington and Moscow have been at their lowest point since the end of the Cold War, and they will remain so while Russian troops are in Ukraine.

Lebow and Stein pose a question that I believe can serve as a starting point for explaining post-pandemic nuclear deterrence. The purpose of this book is not to analyze whether nuclear deterrence worked during the Cold War. Although their explanations serve the realities of the Cold War, I think they are applicable as a point today. The first and most critical question is the contribution of nuclear deterrence to the prevention of World War III (Lebow and Stein 1995, 158). Although there is a growing consensus on the minor importance of restraint in the outcome of the Cold War, I believe that it was the fear of nuclear war that led the US-Soviet superpowers not to confront each other. Despite the claim that the memories of World War II and previous conflicts are a strong deterrent, nothing can compare to the nuclear apocalypse and the picture in which humanity is disappearing. My claim is that this fear will deter the United States and China from bombing each other with nuclear bombs, but to a lesser extent than during the Cold War. The confrontation in the Pacific cannot be compared to the confrontation in Europe for two reasons. First, there is no NATO in the APAC. The only unifying factor for the unity of American allies is the rise of China and American predominance in the region. If Japan is given the opportunity to rearm, it will pursue a much more independent foreign policy that will inevitably provoke a backlash from Seoul. MAD is more likely due to the establishment of AUKUS, which, although similar to NATO, precludes security cooperation and is limited to America's closest allies, Australia and Britain. Therefore, security solidarity is much less than that in NATO, which makes the risk of MAD more likely. Second, unlike the Cold War, there is an actor in the Pacific who is far more unpredictable than Mao's China, North Korea. I have already mentioned why I believe that Pyongyang's nuclear program could lead to MAD. For the purposes of this section, I will add that the destruction of South Korea remains a priority for Pyongyang, whose leader has repeatedly mentioned that Seoul will always be an enemy in the face of North Koreans. If North Korea is forced to invade South Korea, the United States will have to intervene.

The second question refers to why and how deterrence works (Lebow and Stein 1995, 159). Thus, my next assumption is that deterrence will be the only reasonable strategy to prevent MAD due to its psychological dimensions. The vision that the world's most powerful nations can bring about its complete destruction is the strongest motivation for them to refrain from doing so. The psychological effect of the scenario of millions dying in a nuclear apocalypse and the ambitions of the superpowers form more or less rational attitudes among nuclear actors. Here we need to consider whether aggression as an attitude is stronger than the human instinct for self-preservation and the pursuit of power. The answer to my book is no. Although state actors seek to maximize their weapons and influence globally, and although superpowers are aggressive by definition, their priority is survival. The history of the Cold War does not point to a single example in which the United States and the Soviet Union recklessly resorted to the use of nuclear weapons without considering the options of survival and destruction. Nuclear deterrence works because the instinct for self-preservation and survival is stronger than the quest for power and a leadership.

The third issue concerns the military requirements of deterrence (Lebow and Stein 1995, 165). I assert that in the post-pandemic world, decision-makers will reach a consensus that deterrence is necessary. Hardly anyone in the United States doubts China's motivation to become a global leader. However, less attention is being paid to whether Beijing is willing to use nuclear weapons against America. On the contrary, hardly anyone in China doubts that Washington will protect its allies in the event of war. However, it is doubtful whether any President of the United States will be willing to authorize a preemptive nuclear strike against China. Military spending on containment will continue to be a priority for the United States and China, at least until the latter surpasses the former. But is it possible for the United States to stop China's nuclear rise? I think not. Beijing will continue to increase its nuclear capabilities without fear of a potential MAD because it needs deterrent force to hold back the United States. For America, the only way to counter China is to withdraw from nuclear arms control agreements, which will inevitably confront Russia and its European allies. If Washington decides to unilaterally suspend its participation in nuclear arms control, it will be able to independently develop its nuclear capabilities to stem China's rise.

Finally, it comes the political value of nuclear weapons (Lebow and Stein 1995, 170). State actors, which acquire nuclear weapons, become members of the privileged nuclear family. Peace and war in the international system are indeed a privilege of nuclear powers, and that is unlikely to change, at least until humanity invents weapons that are more deadly than nukes. It is possible that more countries like Iran will try to get the bomb. This logically raises the question of whether nuclear aspiration will have a positive or negative effect on the post-pandemic world order. My assumption is that the more nuclear powers, the more stable the containment will be and the more peaceful the world will be. Kenneth Waltz gives the example of Japan, which I believe is the only country that can effectively contain China's rise (Waltz 2012, 3). Historically, Tokyo has proven that no other country can hold back Chinese military doctrine better than the Japanese. America cannot deal with China without Japan, so the non-inclusion of the latter in AUKUS was a huge mistake of the Biden administration. Unfortunately, American policymakers are still captivated by abstract moralistic considerations, suggesting that the rearmament of Japan will have disastrous consequences for the United States. An assumption, as naive as it is dangerous for American-Japanese relations. If Tokyo is given the opportunity to maintain its limited nuclear potential, it will slow down the rise of China for decades. It is illogical to assume that Japan's military rise will threaten the U.S. allies in the region. It is just as illogical as assuming that German rearmament will lead to the marching of German troops in Paris. The history of World War I shows that military revanchism is not a rational choice and at least provokes subsequent conflicts instead of preventing them. If Japan takes the bomb, even North Korea will be forced to be more constructive in its ambitions for nuclear power. However, building Japan's nuclear capabilities can only be done within AUKUS. This will guarantee Japan's peaceful rise as nuclear power and reliable American ally in the APAC.

Finally, it is important to highlight a few obstacles that may arise to nuclear deterrence, which Robert Jervis summarizes as limits to rationality. The first limitation presents a solid evidence from laboratory experiments that much weaker, but still aggressive people, who overestimate their cognitive abilities (Jervis 2014, 20). I think this variable is valid for the political elite in the United States and China. American politicians have the habit of underestimating China as a typical communist state that withstands American power, and therefore, tend to believe that Washington can go as far as it wants. It is highly likely that the overconfidence of U.S. decision-makers forces them to think that China will not dare to invade Taiwan because it still cannot compete with U.S. military power. Moreover, Washington can hardly make a realistic assessment that China will not hesitate to use weapons against American allies in the region, especially with North Korea on its border. Chinese leaders, for their part, tend to underestimate the willingness of their American counterparts to defend the moral principles of freedom and democracy, or more precisely, the driving force behind U.S. Foreign Policy. For Beijing, the system of alliances is associated with tributary diplomacy and is equivalent to a system of dependencies. For America, asymmetric dependencies exist in alliances, but loyalty to allies dominates U.S. strategic thinking. The Americans' belief that they could defeat China to protect their allies could be the cause of military conflict. On the other hand, Beijing's confidence that

America will not risk a global war over Taiwan could lead China to a direct confrontation with Washington.

Jervis defines another cognitive process that influences deterrence as the propensity for people to avoid seeing value trade-offs (Jervis 2014, 25). The tendency of American policymakers to recognize their policies as the only acceptable alternative is not unique to the United States but also to Europe. The West-centric nature of American foreign policy presupposes narrowing down the alternatives to the one most acceptable to the leader. These attitudes are further reinforced by the fact that the President of the United States is the center of American foreign policy and, as such, chairs the National Security Council. The situation is similar to Chinese leaders, who, due to their position and political regime in the country, tend not to accept rational criticism from their advisers. When two leaders ignore existing alternatives and insist that only their point of view is correct, the voices of rational thinking fade away.

Finally, Jervis operationalizes the process of assimilating new information to people's preexisting beliefs, to see what they expect to present (Jervis 2014, 29). Politicians often do not interpret the information received in the most rational way possible. A leader's inner conviction that his personal experience will help him make the right decision can have fatal consequences for foreign policy. If American politicians choose to pursue a foreign policy toward China that draws on the American Manifest Destiny or domestic politics, Washington would be much more inclined to go to war with Beijing than with a rational assessment of the facts. Similarly, if Chinese leaders choose to follow the view that America is China's natural enemy because it maintains Beijing's historical enemies such as Japan, it could lead to war much faster than the mere belief that the two powers must fight. The problem arises from the fact that the attitudes of leaders cannot be accurately assessed. There are few who will share them openly, and even fewer researchers who would believe such a confession. Unfortunately, politicians tend to ignore the research of scientists, who persuade them not to use their personal experience and beliefs as a source of rational foreign policy. This can expose national interests and sacrifice them in the name of abstract moral principles that could further alienate policymakers from their people.

In conclusion, this book joins the view that rational containment theory could explain the future of the post-pandemic nuclear balance. However, I believe that the United States and China will seek to avoid the possibility of MAD, as both superpowers want to survive the bipolar confrontation. Potential problems may arise from the misperceptions discussed above, but I still believe that the instinct for self-preservation will prevail over factors such as overconfidence and avoiding seeing trade-offs. In the case of a real threat of MAD, one can only hope that the circle of leaders will do everything in their power to prevent World War III. History has shown that nuclear weapons have a much longer history of deterrence than aggression. I will therefore conclude that their proliferation among state actors would rather play a constructive role to secure peace in the international system.

Postulate 3: The Scorch War: towards nuclear bipolarity

The third postulate of my model states that the structure of the post-pandemic world will be bipolar. However, in contrast to the Cold War, I define the post-pandemic balance of power as *nuclear bipolarity* for the reason that the pyramid of balance includes the United States, China, and the rest of the nuclear states. Before moving on to a more specific explanation of my concept, I found it necessary to make a brief critical review of existing theories about the future of US-China relations. There is a growing consensus in the academic debate on shaping China as a pole in international relations that will catch up with the United States in the next fifty years. My book joins this theory, and I assume that rising China will be the scorch trial of Washington.

In his notable work, *Ten Lessons for the Post-Pandemic World* the prominent realist scholar Fareed Zakaria argues that the world is becoming bipolar with the United States, remaining the number one nation so far, and China, arriving as a rising power (Zakaria 2020, 193). Zakaria's statement justifies the crisis of American soft power, which transformed the United States from a rational Cold War actor into a foreign policy amalgam of soft power and liberal hegemony, which, according to the logic of Zakaria is the major problem behind America's decline. I agree. The striking polarization in American society, economic imbalances, and the policy of values have undermined the international community's confidence in America's ability to be a global leader. When China arrived on the world stage, some actors, such as Germany and France, saw Beijing as nothing more than a convenient economically to help them become more independent of the United States. Although these perceptions were quite wrong, given China's tributary approach, many of America's allies no longer see Beijing as a small power that has no potential to lead the world. The behavior of other countries towards China is like a pole in the international system, and attitudes among large economies take into account the global role of Chinese investors in world markets. The soft power that has sustained U.S. global leadership for years and maintained the prestige of the American model has melted into China's tributary approach, which, while based on interdependence, has won supporters among American allies with its claims to social harmony and balance. Liberals will call Zakaria's theory realist propaganda, but how can they explain the divisions in the American society absent during the Cold War, when Americans were united against the Soviet threat? How will liberal scholars convince the American allies that what happened in Afghanistan will not happen again? Therefore, despite its elegant efficiency, soft power is no longer enough to guarantee the global prestige of the United States and to strengthen its role as a pole in the international system.

A particularly punctual observation of Zakaria is his envisionment of China as a superpower, which differs from the USSR in terms that it is militarily under the United States, but economically and technologically is already a peer-competitor (Zakaria 2020, 201). Liberals often see China as another communist and an ideological obstacle to the global leadership of liberal values, believing that Beijing will end like the Soviets. I deny this statement. The Chinese approach I discussed in the previous chapter is much more sophisticated and multifaceted than the Soviet one. Beijing is not seeking absolute hegemony to pursue the supremacy of values, war, economy and culture. Although China seeks military parity with the United States, claims Taiwan and pursues economic leadership through tributary diplomacy, Beijing recognizes the danger of over-expansion due to its vast history of ups and downs. More and more scholars agree that China's rise is in fact, the return of Beijing as a great power, not so much the emergence of a global actor. However, unlike the Soviet Union and the United States, China knows the cost of failure and therefore has a long-term strategy that pursues leadership without hegemony. Some would argue that leadership without hegemony is impossible. This is true in Western thinking, but in Asian culture, leadership is a matter of honor, not colonization. This, of course, does not mean that China is not pursuing an offensive strategy and that China's claims of growing influence are unrealistic. To sum up, one should distinguish between the straightforward approach of the USSR and its claims to world ideological hegemony and the clever approach of China, whose tributary diplomacy, combined with its technological rise, operates under conditions of liberal hegemony.

Zakaria's theory recognizes that although tensions between China and the United States are inevitable, conflict is not (Zakaria 2020, 212). I agree. Given the fact that the main task of the superpowers will be to prevent the MAD, Beijing and Washington may find themselves on the brink of nuclear war, but it is far from inevitable. Zakaria gives hints for one essential Chinese weakness – its neighbors, though this is unlikely to happen given America's tough policy of rejecting Japan's rearmament and the stable Chinese support for the North Korean regime. Moreover, North Korea's nuclear ambitions will make it impossible to contain China unless Tokyo acquires nuclear capabilities under AUKUS. My assumption is similar to that of Zakariah, who admits that the Cold War is preferable to direct confrontation. Unlike him, however, I believe that the Cold War is not just preferable, it is necessary. I argue that if the United States seeks to survive the bipolar confrontation with China, it must provoke a new Cold War. My statement is also different in another aspect – I believe that the armed race between Beijing and Washington will not be cold but rather *scorch*. I use this term to emphasize the nature of the competition itself. If the US-Soviet conflict was cold because there was no direct military confrontation, the American opposition to China would scorch, for one very simple reason that Zakaria points out in his works: China is more fully part of the international order than the Soviet Union ever was (Zakaria 2020, 215). The MAD is much more likely, and each of the two superpowers will be preoccupied with destroying the enemy's resources, and less restraining it ideologically. I call that equation *nuclear bipolarity*. My assumption is that ideology will have very little if any, role in nuclear bipolarity due to the fact that soft power is diminishing at the expense of the likelihood of eventual military conflict between the United States and China. Thus, a Sino-American conflict cannot utilize a policy of values, it will have to undergo through the scorch trial of another bipolar confrontation that will have only one winner.

Richard Maher offers another interpretation of the post-pandemic world order, claiming that U.S.-China bipolarity will differ in some crucial respects from U.S.-Soviet bipolarity during the Cold War (Maher 2018, 498). Although the author is correct that China will not surpass the United States in the near future, it is debatable whether Beijing needs to achieve military parity with Washington in order to define the world as bipolar. Barry Buzan clarifies that in the bipolar scenario, the question is whether there will be a power transition crisis or the U.S. and China can find a way of living together (Buzan 2012, 165). There are misleading predictions about the Sino-American powershift crisis, arising after a large-scale military conflict. I find this explanation irrelevant to the nuclear age. My opinion is that the transition crisis has already begun and that it has the following aspects. The first concerns the Pandemic. There is a growing trend in academia to underestimate the global impact of the Coronavirus Pandemic. However, the Coronacrisis has questioned vital principles that have dominated the liberal international order: freedom of movement and the privacy of personal life. Along with the objective consequences that led to increasing death tolls, there were conspiracies that I consider unnecessary to explore in my book. Speculations about China deliberately and premeditatedly causing the Pandemic to oust the United States as a global leader and strike at its allies have successfully gained momentum in the West, sparking a wave of Asian hatred. Rational-minded politicians would seldom agree with such a statement.

However, the Pandemic was not so much significant in its objective consequences as in the impact it had on people's psychological attitudes, especially in democracies. The limitations and obstacles that COVID has caused to developed societies have proven that even the most advanced countries can be put in a blocked position. And although the world has begun to recover from the Pandemic, academic consensus suggests it will never be the same again.

The second aspect is the general crisis of representation in democracies and the rise of populism. The United States and Europe, as the most advanced democracies, have faced many challenges that have brought their political systems to question their own validity. The Capitol Insurgency and the subsequent impeachment against Donald Trump proved that the American political system is in a deep crisis, which stems from economic inequality in the country and political polarization among Americans. America has never been so divided as it is now. Although President Biden's attempts to bridge the divide have been successful, it is very likely that more populist leaders will follow in Trump's footsteps. Racial segregation, poverty, and social injustice continue to erode the living body of American society, which inevitably influences U.S. Foreign Policy. In Europe, populist leaders such as Victor Orban continue to corrupt European integration and promote Europhobia among some influential actors, such as Poland and Italy. After Brexit, the future of the European Union is undergoing a major reform of the Union's institutions and the strengthening of solidarity between member states. Against the backdrop of the crisis in democracies, China continues to reap success, providing a formula with dubious relevance but tempting value – social harmony and the right of every nation to pursue its path of development. Experienced democracies can discern the risks and benefits of this approach, but minor actors looking for a role model are much more susceptible to the Chinese model, seeing what is happening in developed democracies. Economic cooperation with China does not mean accepting Chinese culture or converting to communism. It leads to interdependence with the Dragon but does not imply acceptance of the values that Beijing upholds internationally. Therefore, China's rise is partly due to the crisis in which democracies find themselves.

The third aspect of the crisis is the decline of the global liberal order. This book does not defend the thesis that the United States is declining. It is my view that America will enjoy its global role in the near future, but that the global liberal order is dying. The roots of this process can be traced to the 2016 U.S. Presidential election. My assumption is that the decline of the liberal order will continue until the point where China reaches parity with the United States. In a world of nuclear bipolarity, Washington will be forced to act under the dictates of realism (Mearsheimer 1994, 40). This means that America must abandon its policy of liberal hegemony and devise a mechanism to deter the Chinese realpolitik. The decline of the global liberal order does not mean the disappearance of globalization or the diminution of the importance of human rights. If Washington behaves as a hegemon, it will accelerate China's rise and deepen the crisis of democracy. In the global liberal order, the belief that the spread of human rights and democracy would ensure peace dominated U.S. Foreign Policy. Under nuclear bipolarity, the conviction will be that peace and war serve the interests of global actors – a truth that realism has long rediscovered during the Cold War. China may not formally surpass the United States as a global power, but Beijing's influence over American allies is Europe large enough that Washington cannot respond adequately to Chinese provocations. If the liberal order had a future, Beijing would develop into a closed state, similar to the former Soviet Union, and despite its economic influence, it would not openly challenge America. With its economic influence and stable presence in international economic organizations, China is an unavoidable factor and it is only a matter of time before this influence is transformed into a political one. The last instrument that could serve the United States to reverse the balance of power in the Pacific was the Trans-Pacific Agreement, which would block China's economic intervention. Ironically, unilaterally suspended by the U.S. President.

Stephen Burgess concludes that by 2030, the growth of China's economic and military power means that the country could be more powerful than the United States in Asia (Burgess 2016, 140). I assume that there is only one scenario that could prevent China's rise in the coming decades – war with the United States. If politicians in Beijing decide to go to war with America before reaching parity with the latter, China will lose badly to Washington, with the potential threat of MAD. However, my assumption is that if there is a Sino-American conflict, the United States will attack first. Burgess is partly right in his conclusion, except for the historical period he points out. I believe that China will need 50 years to catch up with the United States in the region for a simple reason: the U.S. military presence in the region is increasing, which increases the risk of military conflict between Washington and Beijing. Moreover, China's rapid rise will be significantly slowed down if Japan gets nukes, which I consider unlikely given America's attitudes on this issue. In any case, China is emerging as the dominant power in the Pacific, and in the distant future it will push America out of the region. There is a third, less-discussed scenario where China annexes Taiwan sooner than expected, with no U.S response. However, this development is very unlikely because, at least while Biden is in the White House, Washington is fully committed to defending Taiwan.

Yan Xuetong, one of China's most prominent IR scholars, introduces the argument that bipolarity will mark the confrontation between China and Russia on one side, and the United States on the other (Xuetong 2013, 12). The distribution of power in the international system is central to states behavior. My assumption is that Moscow will continue to be Beijing's primary partner against Washington, and I doubt that Russia can reach parity with the United States and China. The Eurasian continent is politically and militarily divided, which prevents the Kremlin from regaining the influence it had during the Soviet era. Moreover, Russia has a strong sentiment to revive the Soviet Empire and regain its status as a superpower. However, Moscow benefits far more from its position as a regional provoker in world politics, avoiding direct confrontation with Beijing and Washington, but reaping lasting benefits. Russia is also of interest to China because of its economic potential and the natural resources it has. Moreover, the Siberian region is a starting point for deterring Japan, which has territorial disputes with both countries over the Kuril Islands. I believe that the question that Xuetong raises is key to peace in the post-pandemic world – how to distribute power among states? I outline two configurations.

The first configuration involves the distribution of influence through global financial institutions. The dollar and the yuan are both reserve currencies, allowing the United States and China to print more money and thus support their foreign policies. Therefore, trade wars between Washington and Bejing and clashes within international economic organizations could have detrimental effects on the global economy and lead to a new financial crisis. There is a precedent in the relations between the two countries for the successful distribution of economic levers – the agreements between Presidents Barack Obama and Hu Jintao. In their conversation in 2018, they rejected the war as a means of regulating U.S.-China relations and concluded that the distribution of influence in the world economy implies a division of presence and leadership in international economic institutions. The financial peace that the heads of state have achieved has allowed U.S.-China relations to develop peacefully, which, of course, has not prevented China's rise and America's recovery from the global economic crisis.

The second configuration refers to the distribution of power in terms of regional influence. Regional security will be the most complicated priority for superpowers in the post-pandemic world, as the United States rejects the decline of the unipolar world and China tends to act as if it has already surpassed Washington. My assumption is that the United States and China should divide the world if they seek rational confrontation instead of MAD. If America continues to pursue a policy of status quo, trying to maintain the unipolar model, it could face the alternative of fighting a war against China. If Beijing invades Taiwan without acknowledging Washington's system of alliances in the APAC, it could suffer a heavy defeat. In both cases, the danger of a nuclear holocaust is real, given that both countries are not inclined to divide the world into spheres of influence. Moreover, in order to divide the world, China must have the military and political power to ensure that it can control its sphere of influence. The likelihood of division depends on the leaders of both sides. The more antagonistic they are to each other, the less likely they are to compromise on what the international system will look like in the future. Although both forces are reluctant to seek constructive agreement, it is my view that at some point, fear of the MAD will force them to share the world, if not voluntarily, then naturally. However, the economic division must precede political division.

Suisheng Zhao argues that although structural realist prediction of the inevitable conflict is a fallacy and the Cold War analogy is a distortion of the Sino-American relations today, the emerging bipolarity has helped intensify the US-China rivalry, leading to misplaced hostility and the attempts to force their allies and partners to take a side (Zhao 2021, 2). Zhao touches on an important component of Chinese foreign policy that is vaguely affected or often denied in frequent geopolitical analyzes – the lack of a system of Chinese alliances with satellites or allies to share Chinese principles. First of all, we must clarify that China does not claim to promote universal principles such as those on human rights and democracy. Moreover, my contention is that China does not need them, and therefore accepting this point as a starting point is quite misleading. The export of values is a liberal approach to foreign policy that dominated the United States after the Cold War and claimed that democracy was the final form of government. The Chinese tradition, being Sinocentric, denies the universal universality of a doctrine and accepts that China is the center of the world. For China, forming alliances and taking satellites is expressed by tributary diplomacy, which binds foreign nations with the obligation to pay homage to the center of the universe. Dependence on the center guarantees peaceful relations with it until the two countries enter into a conflict similar to the one in which Washington and Beijing are currently. Despite numerous criticisms of human rights, China remains the West's largest trading partner, placing liberal democracies in the position of tributary partners honoring Beijing. In such circumstances, China's foreign policy does not need allies or satellites to secure its global influence. Therefore, we can define China as a great power long before it reached de facto parity with the United States. Therefore, the division of the world between Washington and Beijing will not express the classic division of the Iron Curtain era but rather will reflect the vision of the two countries on the distribution of financial belts in the world.

The second line that Zhao distinguishes in his concept is China's partnership approach, which advocates the establishment of an anti-American axis, consisting of major American adversaries such as Russia and Iran (Zhao 2021, 4). Furthermore, he suggests that the bipolar confrontation between the United States and China is unlikely to end with the disintegration of one of the powers – a thesis that I also support in my book. The question of whether the alliance system or tributary diplomacy is more cohesive will be clear in the future when Beijing reaches Washington's global influence. In my opinion, the two strategies are equally effective because the complex network on which they are built excludes the national interests of the counter-camp. In this sense, the spheres of influence of the United States and China will not resemble the spheres of the Cold War, in which the superpowers dominated their allies and satellites ideologically, politically and economically. The Scorch War will be a condition of bipolar confrontation, in which each of the state actors will act according to his national interest, on the principle that Zhao states as the friend of my enemy are my friend (Zhao 2021, 5). I will continue to look at the two superpowers that I believe will play a key role in the structure of international politics in the post-pandemic world.

Postulate 4: The decline of Uncle Sam and the rise of Columbia

IR scholars like the personification of Uncle Sam. However, I assume that Columbia has already replaced Uncle Sam as a personification of the United States. In the aftermath of the Cold War, Uncle Sam, who symbolized the American hard power, shifted to the slight impersonation of Columbia. Furthermore, with the Soviet Union defeated, the image of Uncle Sam melted into the soft power of attraction. Joseph Nye, who elaborated the concept of soft power and who, together with Robert Keohane, introduced the theory of interdependence, sought to identify those transformations with unipolarity. Indeed, American power has become soft. Following the tragic events of September 11, Uncle Sam returned for a while to heal the wounds inflicted by terrorists but then gave way to the image of the American pacifier Columbia, whose mission was to rebuild broken governments and promote democracy. One might argue that the incarnation of Uncle Sam is less attractive than that of Colombia. Even so, soft power proved insufficient to prevent China's rise. When Mighty Columbia first clashed with China, Washington realized it had fallen prisoner of its own interdependence strategy. Beijing exercised soft power to establish dependency relations between the United States and China. In 2022, America still surpasses China in all military aspects although it has not escaped from the prisoner's dilemma of fighting a war against Beijing.

However, the decline of Uncle Sam does not mark the end of American power. The United States is still the most powerful nation in the world, and as such, I believe that it is at the apex of the pyramid of balance. Washington possesses advanced military technologies and powerful destructive capabilities that allow it to intervene at any time, anywhere. The U.S. dollar is still the main reserve currency and the strongest economic instrument on the market. American diplomacy enjoys a strong system of alliances that, although shaken by Trump's foreign policy, still deter the major American adversaries. The United States also has the world's second-largest nuclear arsenal, which is a powerful deterrent to actors who would plan a preemptive strike against America. The undeniable advantages that Washington has in terms of resources, geographical location and neighbors minimize the risk of attack on American soil. In addition, there are several temptations facing the United States that Americans must overcome if they are to win the confrontation with China.

America must break with the legacy of liberal hegemony, and more particularly, with that of the hawks, who encouraged Washington to send its troops abroad and to spend billions on exhausting military campaigns. This is not to say that the importance of human rights and democracy should be neglected. But does America need to be merely responsible for them? Should American soldiers build democratic regimes at the cost of their lives? If the export of democracy has benefited U.S. Foreign Policy, why do its biggest failures refer primarily to democratization? It is time for Washington to recognize that in a bipolar world, the export of democracy will not work well for the United States. On the contrary, it nurtures the roots of China's soft power, which portrays America as an expansionist power, aggressively trying to impose its values on all nations. The Chinese claim may sound naive and foolish in the ears of liberal democracies, but for nations where democracy has never ruled, the idea of the aggressive Columbia, which seeks to convert nations, sounds tempting. When the United States withdrew from Afghanistan, China welcomed the Taliban's choice of development, although Kabul refused to cooperate with Beijing. However, if the United States intervenes again in the Middle East, it could lead to a new military fiasco as the country is economically exhausted and political life is in a state of inequality and polarization (Zakaria 2020, 220). What would happen if Washington stuck to the policy of liberal hegemony? Many realists warn that the consequences for the United States will be detrimental because the concept of liberal hegemony no longer exists. John Mearsheimer is not the only realist to confirm the demise of liberalism. Unlike politicians who face reelections and neglect the predictions of the realist scholars, academia is looking for objective truth based on empirical observations. I assume that if the United States insists on pursuing a policy of liberal hegemony, it will face the following failures.

First, the polarization in American society will increase, which will deprive politicians in Washington of the ability to adequately defend the American national interest. If, in the early twentieth-century Americans were vaguely involved in U.S. Foreign Policy, and if in the midst of the Cold War Washington's foreign relations were simply a denial of the communist Soviet Union, more and more American taxpayers are less likely to share their financial resources for expensive military campaigns overseas. American public opinion is becoming increasingly hostile to the idea of the United States establishing and maintaining a global military presence, at least because it costs American lives. Democracy presupposes pluralism and empowers citizens to take their policymakers accountable for their actions. The greater threat to American democracy is related to economic inequality in the United States and the demise of the middle class – a proper observation that Zakaria discusses in his book (Zakaria 2020, 225). The liberal wing of American politics has always defended social justice and the right of citizens to social equality. Such political rhetoric would be praiseworthy if its actions did not indicate otherwise. The extreme rhetoric of some leftist movements, as opposed to far-right factions that preach xenophobia and racism, is destroying the driving force behind U.S. Foreign Policy – American unity. The greater the polarization in American society, the more vulnerable America is to Chinese soft power and Russian smart approach. The Russian interference in the 2016 Presidential election is a perfect example of how American democracy could perish. Evidence of this interference was found at a later stage of the investigation, but in my opinion it does not matter whether the election was the subject of a cyber attack. The basic point was that on the election eve, public opinion was severely divided. While Hillary Clinton had a clear advantage and garnered the support of most Americans, the divisions in society, combined with the Russian propaganda, created an electoral vacuum that was filled by Donald Trump's supporters. One might argue that Trump's victory is due to specific aspects of the American electoral system, and more particularly, the existence of the Electoral College. Even so, few would reject the claim that Russia repeatedly interfered indirectly in the election and managed to divide public opinion, raising the Duginist thesis that liberal elites were responsible for the American decline. The dividing lines that emerged after the election continued to polarize society and eventually escalated into the 2021 Capitol Attack, in which a group of extremists attempted to burn the legacy of the world's most developed democracy. If the future Presidential administrations succumb to the temptation of pursuing liberal hegemony, a subsequent division of the Americans could completely block the American political process.

Second, the United States will lose to China if it relies primarily on soft power. Beijing has a well-established mechanism of countering the American soft approach, and it works in regions where the United States is losing its influence. Scholars typically indicate China's economic growth as the primary source of Beijing's power. Although I find their assertion reasonable, China's economic expansion is far from its strongest advantage. The secret of China's foreign policy lies in the pragmatic leadership of the Chinese leaders. Although China has not yet reached parity with the United States, Beijing is shifting the use of soft power to the economic sphere and, to some extent, to Chinese popular culture. Beyond soft power remains China's millennial record of manipulating its adversaries by pitting them against their allies. For instance, Europe, America's most trusted ally in the Western hemisphere, stands at a crossroads. Economically, the European Union is highly dependent on China, and militarily and politically – on the United States. Although NATO allies are unanimous on Russia and China, posing a challenge to the Alliance's security, we cannot deny that the economic interests of European countries in China have a significant impact on the foreign policy of France and Germany. When the United States imposed sanctions on Nord Stream because it feared Russia's growing influence on the old continent, Germany opposed the decisions taken by the Biden administration. Berlin and Paris have always been united within NATO, but their interests do not coincide with those of the United States when it comes to energy security and trade relations with China. In other words, America's allies with Europe stand firmly behind the United States because of their military dependence on Washington, but are more susceptible to China's strategy for tributary diplomacy due to the attractive rhetoric of Chinese investors.

America's soft power cannot prevent the rise of China for another reason: Russia's growing influence. Liberal scholars often argue that Moscow and Beijing cannot offer an alternative to liberal democracy. Although I hold this view, it is hard to deny that there is a difference between a soft power that imposes a certain pattern of behavior and one that gives each nation the freedom to choose its own path of development. Universal models are failing not merely because their ideological alternatives are more resilient. Liberal scholars would argue that a pattern is universal when it secures the balance of power and ensures lasting peace. However, I assume that universal models are myths debunked by Kenneth Waltz, who criticized the optimistic ideas of Kant. In the years since September 11, U.S. Foreign Policy has evolved into a smart approach combining the tools of hard and soft power. The essential mistake of hawkism was that it ignored the realistic warnings of Robert Jervis, who stated that soft power was not enough to be the driving force behind American foreign policy (Jervis 2009, 190). Thus, Moscow and Beijing did not need to offer an alternative model of development. China waited for the soft power of America to weaken so that the United States could no longer fulfill its global commitments. As Washington began to take a more selective approach toward its allies, China took advantage of this policy to further compromise America's soft power of attraction. For example, at the founding of AUKUS, President Biden said that Japan would not be able to join the pact, despite Tokyo's unequivocal wish to become part of the pact. Washington's refusal posed the question of what the future of Japan's defense strategy will be and how it will respond to China's rise. The United States has a number of obligations to Tokyo under Article 9 of the Japanese Constitution, but to what extent would Washington fulfill its commitments to Japan? What if the exclusion of Tokyo from AUKUS undermines the Japanese confidence in the United States? A realist approach would require America to enable Japan to develop its own defense capabilities, rather than relying on the soft power of American diplomacy. However, irrational fears of a resurgence of Japanese militarism hamper Washington's realistic perceptions. China's strategy to undermine the U.S.-led system of alliances in the APAC has not yet borne fruit, but it is on track to do so following transformations in the balance of power in the Pacific.

Columbia's greatest temptation is its traditional perception of China as a traditional communist state that will collapse like the Soviet Union. Proponents of soft power are among the predominant advertisers of that attitude, which focuses more on the Chinese political regime than on the prospects for military conflict. My assumption is that, even if the United States defeats China in a bipolar clash or one-on-one military confrontation, Beijing will not follow the fate of the Soviet Union. As Kissinger explains, the Chinese state tradition is not fleeting, and despite the revolution, China has managed to preserve its statehood (Kissinger 2005). China may give way, even return to a century of humiliation, but it will become a great power again in centuries to come. Can we say the same about the United States? The essential core of the American model is the strength and endurance of American democracy, as well as the freedoms of the American people, who inspire the political system of modern liberal democracies. However, as long as the United States erect walls between Self and Others, it will hinder their real perceptions of the rest of the world. The Soviet Union failed against the United States because, in its denial of democracy, Soviet leaders refused to recognize it and thus lost rational judgment of how powerful America was. The United States, like the Soviet Union, sees the Chinese model as a totalitarian remnant of the Cold War, which, although reformed thanks to Deng Xiaoping, will follow Moscow to the bottom of history. American scholars consistently reject the obvious fact that Chinese foreign policy stems not only from Marxist perceptions of the class struggle but also from traditional Chinese culture. Another part of the researchers, in an effort to simplify the Chinese model, identify it with philosophical and geopolitical categories from the European heritage of Ancient Greece and Rome. Few recognize China as the heir to a great civilization that is not just a rising power, but an empire that is returning to the world stage (Jones 2020, 2). For the United States, China is the adversary that inherited the Soviet Union. For Beijing, Washington is a major obstacle to China's rise. Unlike

Uncle Sam, who would look rationally at the Dragon on the other side of the ocean, Columbia deeply underestimates China's military might.

Although positioned at the apex of the pyramid, the United States risks losing the competition to China if it does not acknowledge that it is already entering a period of new bipolar confrontation. The sooner Washington recognizes Beijing as a serious challenge and skillful opponent, the better America's chances of defeating China. Unfortunately, America is late. My assertion is that China's rise cannot be stopped unless the United States decides to attack it, which could lead to MAD. I will discuss the MAD scenarios later in the chapter. For the purposes of this section, I will say that Beijing was given the opportunity to become a pole not without the support of Washington. Paradoxically, Columbia, involved in the fight against terrorism, opened the door for China to become a superpower, considering it its ally against the terrorists. What the United States has failed to understand is that Beijing attaches different meanings to the term "ally." For China, allied relations presuppose bilateral dependence, which, through tributary diplomacy, benefits both countries. This is the reason why we are not talking about a Chinese system of alliances, in the sense in which we understand the American one, in which relations are asymmetric and depend on the military-strategic advantage of the United States. The problem arises when it becomes obvious that many of America's allies are part of a system of tributary diplomacy that is reminiscent of the Silk Road. Therefore, for many U.S. allies, abstaining from confronting China is no longer a matter of ordinary loyalty, but of national interest. Under these conditions, the central question for the United States and China is – who would the American allies choose? Will they prefer the alliance with Columbia to the economic goods flowing from the Silk Road? A historical dilemma, which has reshaped the foreign policy of many empires.

Postulate 5: The Flying Guillotine of the Sage

Researchers like to portray China as the Dragon facing Uncle Sam in an apocalyptic battle for the Pacific. The prospect of Asian power, taking over the world's leadership confounds the Western world. I find those Dragon tales culturally appropriate but geopolitically misleading. In Asian culture, Dragons are a symbol of wisdom and longevity. Thus, the emphasis on their nature is not necessarily related to "slaying the Dragon" stories. Unlike the great Western powers, China has one essential advantage that allows it to cultivate its potential without revealing it. I assume that the cultivation strategy of China is unique to Asian civilizations because their traditions do not duplicate the West, as many IR scholars tend to believe. In this book, I prefer to identify China with the long-lived Sage rather than the Dragon. I will elaborate my concept by introducing a thoughtful historical comparison between China and the other great powers.

The reason China took the place of a great power alongside America is the periodic Chinese revival as such. The Roman Empire, a source of cultural and political inspiration for Western civilizations, along with Ancient Greece, experienced its rise and fall until Rome finally fell to the barbarians. Medieval Byzantium, which preserves the Roman tradition and through the Justinian Code set the stage for a new form of statehood, lived a thousand years to collapse under the Ottomans. The British colonial empire, over which the sun does not set, reached its peak in the 18th century but lost its power in the flames of the two world wars. Western civilizations follow the Hegelian spiral, but unlike Eastern ones, their downfall is final and irreversible. China experienced a series of historical transformations, but it still retains the Sinocentric core of Asia. The Chinese Empire went through periods of prosperity when it was united by the Qing Dynasty until its power melted away during the Opium Wars, when Beijing entered its dark century of humiliation. The pattern of Chinese civilization, however, is very different from Hegel's spiral, and therefore, my claim is Hegelianism cannot serve as a plausible explanation for China's vital historical cycle. Therefore, and due to its ability to cultivate the ancient Chinese tradition, China will not collapse and perish as a civilization, like the Western empires. In other words, it is untenable to depict the Chinese Grand Strategy as Pax Sinica, at least because we cannot *westernize* the Chinese worldview. The sinocetrism that Kissinger discusses in his writings is a geopolitical oxymoron of the hegemonic culture that dominated ancient Rome and colonial Europe. This is not to say that Beijing has abandoned its grand design for global leadership. However, one should distinguish between leadership and hegemony. Hegemons impose their values and seek to dominate the minds and actions of their allies. The leader seeks to establish a system of alliances that benefits all countries which voluntarily recognize the global primacy of their guide. A strategy, far from relevant to that of the USSR and Trump's America. In other words, the pursuit of social harmony and the Confucian approach to foreign policy does not deprive China of its pursuit of great power policy. On the contrary, they express the policies for achieving this goal in a period of time that may take decades. It is much more convenient and rational for China to wait for the demise of America than to fight a war, it cannot win. Morgenthau has repeatedly stated that conquering China is the way to victory and that peripheral military actions are not a plausible strategy against Beijing.

When a state actor or American ally becomes the subject of tributary diplomacy, it has two possible outcomes: peaceful coexistence or a flying guillotine. It is important to clarify that under nuclear bipolarity, every state actor, whether it is in possession of nuclear weapons or not, will have to maintain a constructive relationship with the superpowers, and isolation is not an option. Only Japan will be less inclined to avoid tributary diplomacy and the flying guillotine due to its outstanding contributions to the world economy. Peaceful coexistence includes the development of economic cooperation and cultural relations while respecting the national interest. A policy, which does not bind states to share certain values, although it makes their economies dependent on China. Another strategy that Beijing is likely to apply is an indirect policy of sanctions, which I define as the *flying guillotine*. In the Western tradition, the United States and Western Europe punish their adversaries through economic and diplomatic sanctions. However, China does not benefit from imposing sanctions on anyone. In the Chinese tradition, punishment does not merely imply sanctions. It also presumes a comprehensive approach aimed at undermining the economic sovereignty of Beijing's adversaries. It is a reciprocal action of interdependence, which presumes that any sanction against China and the Chinese economy will affect the economy of the other actor. President Trump's trade war with Beijing is a perfect expression of the flying guillotine strategy. Criticized for taking a hard line, Trump was adamant in his efforts to bring American production back to the United States, despite labor costs. However, U.S. sanctions have also hit Western investors because of the dependence that has existed between the Chinese and U.S. economies. Thus, the liberal concept of interdependence turned against Washington. And although the United States has endured these upheavals, it is doubtful how much smaller actors could avoid the flying guillotine.

Yet, China is not immune to the great power syndrome, which represents the greatest temptation of the Sage. Chinese traditional culture should not fall victim to orthodox communism, as this will lead to the same hegemonic desires that America is currently experiencing, and which have also failed the Soviet Union. Stalinism and Leninism are incompatible with Chinese communism, which has its roots in Mao's dialectics. Socialism with Chinese characteristics combines the legacy of Mao, Xixian's social reforms with the original Chinese tradition. China's Sovietization would be as detrimental to the country's political future as its liberalization. Beijing would not be what it is today without this unique amalgam that has provided resources to China's foreign policy and transformed the Sage into an attractive harbor for foreign investors. Soviet ideology, which had dominated the socialist camp for half a century, had the opportunity to open up to the world during the short peace under Carter and Brezhnev. Missing this opportunity, Brezhnev signed the death warrant of the USSR. In truth, the opening was practically impossible because Moscow had the tools and the inspiration to reform its communist ideology. Tsarism died with the last Russian

Emperor, and the Church was under the control of the Communists. Unlike the USSR, China has a millennial heritage that can serve as an instrument of political influence through Chinese popular culture. What is unique about China is that Chinese socialism largely corresponds ideologically to pre-revolutionary centralization in the form of the Mandate of Heaven, which would make it attractive to both Chinese and Westerners. Thus, unlike the USSR, China has the potential to form its cultural models and to offer an alternative to Western ones, which dominate the contemporary cultural attitudes. Given China's huge market, those cultural patterns will spread rapidly and further stimulate the Chinese economy.

The second problem that could alter China's rise is political liberalization. The penetration of Western culture in China might benefit the Chinese economy, but it will undoubtedly affect the attitudes of the younger generation. The soft power of Western values is an objective reflection of liberal universalism. How can China find the perfect balance between restraining U.S. soft power and Sovietization? My assumption is that the answer lies in pragmatic leadership. Xuetong is clear when he concludes that political meritocracy is the model that guarantees the continuity and pragmatism of Chinese leadership (Xuetong 2020, 102). Therefore, the Chinese Communist Party should shape future leaders in Sinocentrism. Skills, knowledge and virtues should be the basis of pragmatic leadership, alongside strong commitments to national interests. When a leader duplicates Western cultural models or attempts a Chinese Perestroika, the consequences of his reforms would be catastrophic. China will enter into another century of humiliation. When a leader seeks to copy totalitarian models like the Soviet one, it will end well for Beijing, as Sovietism will hand over China's cultural heritage. If the leader pragmatically follows the Chinese tradition, adhering to balance and national interest, he will be revered as the unifier, seeking the national prosperity of his nation.

The final temptation concerns an eventual attempt of Beijing to confront Washington militarily. China's national pride is particularly sensitive to issues such as Taiwan or its historical ties with Japan and South Korea. However, Chinese aspirations for Taiwan should not overshadow the rational logic when politicians in Beijing make decisions on the future of Sino-American relations. China's reunification with Taiwan is a long-standing purpose and it cannot be achieved in a single leader's term. Moreover, Beijing's ability to long-term planning is essential to China's rise so far, and if China decides to act impulsively against Washington, it could lead to MAD. Therefore, Beijing should adhere to its defense doctrine for two reasons. First, a direct military confrontation between the United States and China threatens will have catastrophic consequences for the world economy. Second, as important as Taiwan is to China, America still surpasses Beijing militarily and strategically and thus, Washington could intervene to protect the island from the Chinese. Weakening the United States will be a long-term but inevitable process, as is the fate of most great powers. The liberal global order, I believe, is already at the bottom of its decline, but that does not mean that America is in decline. We still do not know what the foreign policy of the next American administrations will be and whether the United States will not decide to return to the realism of the Cold War era. If that happens, China will face the daunting task of preparing for a long-term conflict that, while different from the Cold War between the United States and the Soviet Union, poses a much greater danger of escalation.

Confrontation under the security dilemma: four worlds

Before proceeding with calculations, I should make one essential clarification. When I introduced the construction of my model, I explicitly mentioned that the static shape of the pyramid serves merely as a pattern to the explanation of the dynamic nature of international relations. Therefore, what has been said so far cannot be of any use to us if we decide to calculate the dilemma in the post-pandemic world, which I assume will embody nuclear bipolarity. Moreover, even if we assert that offensive posture cannot be distinguished from the offensive, we cannot calculate the security dilemma when neither offense nor defense has the advantage. This is not a realistic formula for what the post-pandemic world will look like. In my theory, I assume that when there is a transition in polarity, the pyramid of balance deforms as the poles begin to compete, along with their allies who embody the walls of my model. I assume that the regular hexagonal pyramid could deviate into two forms, depending on the competition between nuclear powers. I clarify that due to these deformations, I use mathematical formulas that are universally applicable to the pyramids. Thus, I proceed to the explanation of the second state of the pyramid, which I call dynamic and which, I assume, will apply to the balance of power in the post-pandemic world.

The first form of deviation is an *oblique hexagonal pyramid*. Oblique pyramids emerge in bipolarity/multipolarity when one of the great powers mobilizes all its resources to oppose its counterpart. Following the logic that the pyramidal model is applicable to each case, I conclude that this form can also be used for the assessment of isolated case studies. The pyramid is not a universal model with precisely defined walls but a pattern. In a bipolar world, the more a nuclear power exercises pressure on another, the greater the risk of MAD. When the apex of the pyramid aligns with the slant height of offensive postures, the world is usually on the brink of nuclear war. History shows no better example of such deformation than the Cuban Missile Crisis, in which the United States and the Soviet Union were at their closest point to MAD. My prediction is that we can witness a similar crisis in Taiwan.

The second form of deviation is an *irregular hexagon pyramid*. In mathematics, its shape depends on how the base area of the figure changes. Therefore, the regular hexagon reshapes into irregular in the following scenarios. First, if the base edges change their size and therefore the base of defense deforms. In bipolar or multipolar models, state actors defend themselves in different ways, which can lead to numerous configurations in the polygon. Second, deformation is possible when lateral edges move towards their analogs. Therefore, if one state decides to confront another, the offense/defense balance will shift to the actor, who is more likely to win. The influence of that state will then increase and the potential of others to oppose will decrease. The parameters I derived for the unipolar world will also change because we can no longer use a regular polygon as a basis to calculate the balance of power. Moreover, when the height of the pyramid no longer coincides with its center, the balance of power changes and threatens to turn into armed conflict. Based on my geometric model, I distinguish the following worlds. In all forms of the pyramid, however, the dilemma is in a state of constant confrontation. I clarify that any change in the balance of power can lead to a powershift.

I highlighted that my model aims to explain the balance of power in the post-pandemic system, without limiting its scope to the United States and China. However, the purpose of this book is to analyze how relations between Washington and Beijing will evolve, which, I argue will determine the future of the post-pandemic world order. I have found it necessary to analyze the Sino-American confrontation, to offer a plausible prediction for the future. At the end of the section, I will look at some of the issues and objections that may arise to my model. I assume that the regular pyramid is the starting point for my analysis for two reasons. First, the United States and China have nuclear weapons, which makes the possibility of a MAD realistic. Second, even if the Sage has not yet clashed with Columbia, there is no state actor who can challenge the former to be the strongest contender for the latter.

I proceed with calculating the security dilemma. My claim is that it will be characterized primarily by confrontation, not by cooperation. The starting point for structuring my concept is Robert Jervis' concept of the security dilemma. I chose Jervis for two reasons. First, I find it rational to compare the state of the Cold War dilemma with nuclear bipolarity after the Pandemic. I also assume cooperation will evolve into a confrontation under the security dilemma, and I believe that the principles Jervis provides could serve as a further explanation of those powershifts.

The concept of Jervis explains why and how states cooperate in a system of anarchy and geopolitical competition. Jervis introduces two variables that I have also borrowed for the purposes of my model: offensive/defensive balance and the ability to distinguish between offensive and defensive postures (Jervis 1978, 211). After operationalizing the variables, Jervis concludes that cooperation under the security dilemma could result in four structures of the international system that he defines as four worlds (Jervis, 1978, 210). The first configuration prioritizes offensive, which results in a world of status quo states, which are in a constant confrontation without the ability to cooperate with each other. Jervis offers an example on the eve of World War I, when European powers constantly provoked each other and demonstrated their strength. The second world prioritizes defense, it is very reminiscent of most conflicts in history, in which the security dilemma works because offensive and defensive postures cannot be distinguished. Relatively stable, this world forces the states to cooperate, even though their ultimate purpose is to compete in the anarchic system of international relations. In the third world, there is no security dilemma, only security problems because the offense has the advantage. The status quo states can recognize their enemies, and they can also respond to threats that come from the latter. The final world refers to the safest security environment in which state actors recognize their intentions and there is no reason for them to confront each other. I believe that Jervis' model and his calculations are applicable to the pyramid of balance, and thus, I found it necessary to use his concept for the purposes of my research. Although I use similar variables, as I pointed out at the beginning of this section, I believe that in the post-pandemic world, cooperation is more likely to give way to confrontation. Relations between the United States and China will continue to strain, at least until the forces do not share spheres of influence, which, as I concluded, is unlikely to happen. Yet, since the main goal of the Washington and Beijing will be to prevent MAD, I believe that the system will still involve some form of cooperation, although limited to the world economy rather than elaborating formats of security cooperation. The Prisoner's Dilemma, Jervis presents in his article about the Cold War security dilemma serves as the main starting point for my calculations (Jervis 1978, 211). Before introducing my calculations, I will make a few preliminary calculations that illustrate the differences between Cold War and the post-pandemic world.

I have defined several variables, which I will operationalize to explain the balance of power in the post-pandemic international system. However, along with its structure, it is important to highlight that the pyramid of balance has two dimensions. I call the first one static. Although it cannot explain the post-pandemic balance of power due to ist ideal shape, I will still illustrate it as starting point for the pyramid's dynamic shape, which refer to the calculation of the security dilemma. In the static dimension, I distinguish the following aspects, which correspond to a pyramid's segments: *a (apothem) = defensive postures; s (slant height) = offensive postures; h (height) = offense; b (base side)= defensive.* For the purposes of my calculations, I denote the pyramid's aspects as follows: *apothem of defensive postures; slant height of offensive postures; the height of offense and base side of defense.* It is important to highlight again that the walls of the pyramid consist of state actors who possess nuclear weapons.

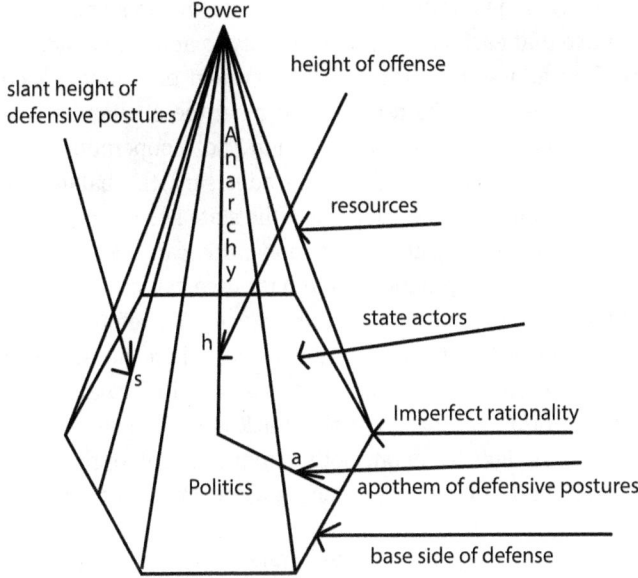

Figure 2: The Pyramid of Balance: Aspects.

The apothem of defensive postures (a) is the sum of defensive advantages of that, combined with the possible chance of the latter to win a conflict with another state is equal to the most outcome scenario from the confrontation. My contention is that defensive postures are a starting point for a state's strategy for a simple reason: realism believes that countries are primarily concerned with their survival. Therefore, within my model, state actors will seek the ultimate and rational scenario of self-preservation. The distance from the base of the pyramid to the center reflects the desire of one state actor to survive a conflict with another. Thus, it is logical, to sum up the natural desire of states to confront the realistic assessment of the policymakers, who seek the most rational scenario to survive.

The slant height of offensive postures (s) is the sum of a state's defensive advantages and the height of offense. My argument is that offensive postures are a reflection of the balance between an actor's ability to defend itself and his preparedness to attack. Therefore, in order to calculate whether a state actor is in a position to attack other states, we should first test the former's advantages in defending and attacking. Thus, the best attack is the one that balances offensive postures with the defense. If a state actor does not have a clear vision of whether its capabilities match its adversaries, it will lose to them, being forced to accept the status quo. Resources for defense and attacks are central to one's strategy, and more particularly for nuclear powers.

The height of offense (h) is the quarter sum of defensive postures and offensive postures. Thus, I prove that each country's propensity to attack depends on its potential to defend and attack. Therefore, in the pyramid of balance, each of state actors will have to maximize its resources to meet the challenges that other countries pose. This is a world of confrontation, not cooperation. If a state does not have enough resources to oppose its adversary, the balance of power will tilt in favor of the latter. On the contrary, if the state has the resources to attack, and if it is in possession of nuclear weapons, this can lead to MAD.

The base side of defense (b) is a product of the base area, which, regarding the static condition of the pyramid, shapes a regular hexagon. Therefore, I prove that states maximize their resources to defend themselves when the attack of their adversaries threatens to end with victory. In the pyramid of balance, the closer two countries get to MAD, the fiercer their attack and defense become. However, since the figure is a right hexagon, both actors have the opportunity to lead the world to MAD. The former – by launching a preemptive attack, and the latter – by retaliating.

The aspects of the pyramid allow us to make a few more calculations that can predict how the balance of power will evolve in the post-pandemic system. In mathematics, having apothem, base edge, slant height and height, we can calculate the volume, surface area, and lateral surface area. What all formulas have in common is that h and a are central to them. Therefore, the apothem of defensive postures and the heigh of offense shape the dimensions of the pyramid, which, in its entirety, embodies the post-pandemic structure of international politics. Thus, I prove that my model is relevant to the calculation of the security dilemma, which operates under certain variables. The slant height of offensive postures, and the base of defense, on the other side, can be calculated if we have the volume, the face and the base of the pyramid. The interconnection between all aspects, thus, gives me the logical right to assume that the pyramid of balance, in its dynamic dimensions, presupposes the calculation of the dilemma.

World 1: Offshore containment

The first plausible scenario is the offshore containment, in which the possibility of aggression is inversely proportional to the behavior of the states. The model will deviate from a regular to an oblique hexagonal pyramid, where the base is a regular hexagon, and the apex location does not coincide with the base's center. The main variables are as follows: constant variables – power (apex), politics (center), and anarchy, determining the nature of the post-pandemic system. The secondary variables are as follows: lateral faces (states), lateral edges (resources), and base edges (imperfect rationality). In this scenario, the right pyramid will deform into an oblique.

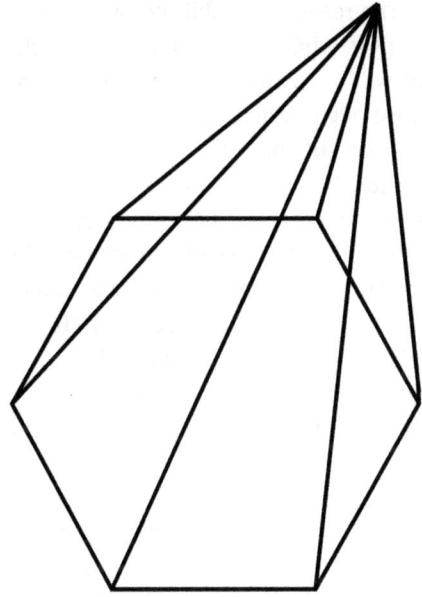

Figure 3: World 1: Offshore containment.

Proof: regular polygon, oblique pyramid

Apex is inclined, lateral faces are not isosceles, the hexagon is regular. *The apothem of defensive postures (a) is the sum of defensive advantages of a state the realistic chance of a state to win a conflict with another state is equal to the most outcome scenario from the confrontation. The slant height of offensive postures (s) is the sum of the defensive advantages of a state the height of offense. The height of offense (h) is the quarter sum of defensive postures and offensive* postures. *The base side of defense (b)* is a product of the base area, which shapes a regular hexagon. I infer that a state actor's propensity to attack depends on its resources of self-defense. My assertion is that state actors mobilize their resources for self-defense when an adversary threatens to attack them.

Conclusion

Based on the evidence, the following conclusions can be drawn. If America continues to exercise pressure on China, alongside Britain, France, and India, Washington's actions will provoke a backlash from Russia, Pakistan and North Korea. The more one of the camps tries to impose its power and press its opponent, the more the pyramid of balance will oblique. The resources mobilized by one state actor will increase the length of the side edges while the rational limits of the MAD will remain the same. This pyramid will keep two constant aspects: the apothem of defensive postures and the base edge of defense. This means that the states will have a realistic idea of the conditions under which they can win the confrontation and how to avoid the MAD scenario. Conversely, the more the slant height of offensive postures increases, the more aggressive state actors will behave. The more the height of the offense shifts to the boundaries of the pyramid, the more likely the MAD is. When the altitude finally coincides with the boundaries of the base, I assume that the threat of MAD is realistic. If we apply the equation to Jervis' concept, we identify the oblique pyramid with the "third world" in which there is no security dilemma, aggression is possible under warning, and status-quo states can follow different policy than aggressors (Jervis 1978, 212).

In a world where there is no security dilemma, aggression is possible from the United States, China, or the other nuclear powers. Moreover, the slightest conflict can ignite a confrontation between the two superpowers, which will increase the risk of a direct clash between them. Still, I assume that one of the two powers is unlikely to remain passive in the face of its adversary. Washington will not allow Beijing to approach its borders or gain access to the West Coast through Taiwan. China, while pursuing a policy of tributary diplomacy and while avoiding direct confrontation with Washington, may urge North Korea to threaten Seoul. However, if the probability of MAD becomes too high, I believe that the two superpowers will reach to a rational consensus and thus, the oblique pyramid will return to its regular form. Washington and Beijing are likely to provoke each other, but in the event of an all-out confrontation within the nuclear concert, they will cooperate so that the conflict does not escalate into MAD. However, my assumption is that both countries will prefer long-term confrontation to cooperation, and even the prospect of short peace is unlikely to be followed. I call this scenario offshore containment because both United States and China will most likely sacrifice non-nuclear regimes to avoid direct confrontation.

World 2: Bellum omnium contra omnes

The second scenario involves a series of indirect confrontations between nuclear powers. In my model, the pyramid of balance will deviate from a regular to an oblique hexagonal pyramid with an irregular base, where the base is an irregular hexagon. The main variables are as follows: constant variables – power (apex), politics (center), and anarchy, determining the nature of the post-pandemic system. The secondary variables are as follows: lateral faces (states), lateral edges (resources), and base edges (imperfect rationality). In this scenario, the right pyramid will deform into oblique. In maths, when the base is an irregular hexagon, where the sides are not equal to each other, then the pyramid is an irregular pyramid. The problem emerges from the fact that the base area of the pyramid should be calculated separately since the triangles are not isosceles.

Proof: irregular polygon, oblique pyramid

Apex is inclined, lateral faces are not isosceles, the hexagon is irregular. *The apothem of defensive postures (a) is the sum of defensive advantages of a state the realistic chance of a state to win a conflict with another state is equal to the most outcome scenario from the confrontation. The slant height of offensive postures (s) is the sum of the defensive advantages of a state the height of offense. The height of offense (h) is the quarter sum of defensive postures and offensive postures. The base side of defense (b) is a product of the base area, which shapes a regular hexagon.* A state actor's propensity to attack depends on its resources of self-defense. State actors mobilize their resources for self-defense when an adversary challenges them directly or through sanctions.

Conclusion

In world 2, the slant height of offense postures and height of offense follows the logic of intervention. The more a state actor confronts its adversary, the more the height of offense increases its length. When the slant height aligns with the walls

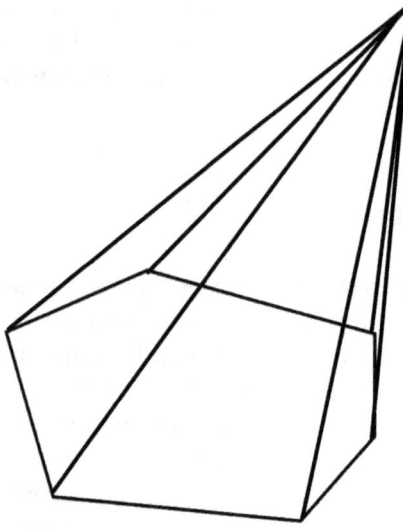

Figure 4: World 2: Bellum omnium contra omnes.

of the pyramid, the states will be on the brink of MAD. However, if the figure denotes an oblique pyramid with an irregular polygon, the base edge of the defense and the apothem of defense postures do not hold constant values. Therefore, offensive postures cannot be distinguished from defensive ones, while offense has the advantage over defense. This is the doubly safe world of Jervis, in which there is no way to get security without menacing the others, and security through defense is terribly difficult to obtain (Jervis 1978, 203).

In such a world, the United States and China will confront each other with the rest of the nuclear powers, switching sides. The conflict in Taiwan will be just the beginning of a long-term confrontation between Washington and Beijing. Europe is unlikely to side with the United States unless NATO Article 5 is at stake. The world of fierce competition between America and China will not bring peace and security, it could again bring nuclear powers one step closer to MAD. The difference with the previous model is that the other actors in the pyramid will be less aware of the rational limits of nuclear diplomacy, which may lead some of them to resort to limited military confrontation. All states, including in their allied relations, will behave as aggressors who defend their national interests without respecting their mutual agreements. In this world, it is possible that America will not respect its Article 5 commitments to Europe, refuse to defend Japan or South Korea in the event of a Chinese attack, or disregard its talks with Russia. China, for its part, could use its tributary diplomacy to mobilize U.S. allies already under its economic dependence or to prepare its nuclear arsenal for a military strike against Australia as a direct challenge to AUKUS.

India and France could refuse to support the United States against China. Pyongyang would attack its neighbors without seeking prior consultation with Beijing, and Pakistan would not hesitate to invade India because its backs are lined by the Taliban. Britain, for its part, would resume its Rule Britannia policy and encourage the further development of AUKUS, contrary to the interests of the French.

Local conflict will be a common phenomenon in such a system, and they will usually be preceded by nuclear talks between the United States and China. Cooperation would be unthinkable unless the actors have a mutually beneficial interest in doing so, but even if it does, it would be a temporary decision until the problem arises again. Nevertheless, I assume that no matter how confrontational the nature of such a system the parties will rationally judge the boundaries of the MAD. The United States and China would be the most rational in their judgment, followed by the other actors who make up the walls of the pyramid. Even nuclear powers such as North Korea, will have a clear and rational idea of what would happen if their actions provoked nuclear conflicts between the superpowers. Therefore, the confrontation between the states will be expressed above all in local crises, which will pour their tension into regionalized conflicts with a clear winner, depending on who supports whom. And although the parties are less willing to cooperate than in the first scenario, their rational thinking will prevent MAD.

World 3: Scorch War

The third scenario is a new cold war with less probability of a MAD scenario than the previous two worlds, but greater likelihood of using force in different regions. In my model, the pyramid of balance will deviate into a *convex hexagonal pyramid*, where the base is a *convex polygon*. The main variables are as follows: constant variables – power (apex), politics (center), and anarchy, determining the nature of the post-pandemic system. The secondary variables are as follows: lateral faces (states), lateral edges (resources), and base edges (imperfect rationality). In this scenario, the right pyramid will preserve its shape, while its basis will deviate into an irregular polygon. In maths, when the base is an irregular hexagon, where the sides are not equal to each other, then the pyramid is an irregular pyramid. In World 3, the base of the structure is either an irregular polygon or convex.

Proof: convex pyramid

Apex is inclined, lateral faces are not isosceles, the base hexagon is irregular. *The apothem of defensive postures (a)* is the sum of defensive advantages of a state the realistic chance of a state to win a conflict with another state is equal to the most outcome scenario from the confrontation. *The slant height of offensive postures (s)* is the sum of the defensive advantages of a state the height of offense. *The height of offense (h)* is the quarter sum of defensive postures and offensive postures. *The base side of defense (b)* is a product of the base area, which shapes a regular hexagon. A state actor's propensity to attack depends on its resources for self-defense. State actors mobilize their resources of self-defense when an adversary challenges them directly or through sanctions.

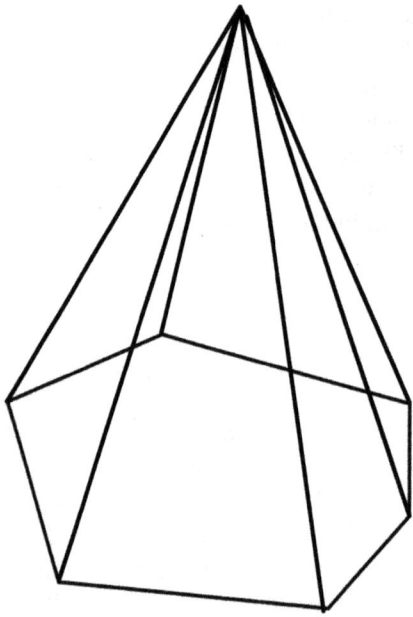

Figure 5: World 3: Scorch War.

Conclusion

In world 3, the slang height of offensive postures and height of offense are static variables, while the base edge of the defense and the apothem of defense postures are dynamic. In such a world, the desire of states to defend themselves will dominate their foreign policy. Each actor will maximize resources to protect his national security by trying to respect the rational limits of nuclear war. Although unstable, in such a world, states will most accurately realize what their capabilities are and whether they can win a conflict.

The world in question would again position the United States and China in confrontation, where they would to one degree or another benefit from the help of their allies and partners. Beijing and Washington will send clear messages about what their foreign policy will be and why they are taking such a move without demonstrating unpredictable and aggressive behavior. America and China will strive to maintain a stable balance of power, and peace will be lasting as long as both countries have sufficient resources to oppose each other. Local conflicts would arise although the arms race is unlikely to lead to a direct confrontation. Soft power will be central to foreign policy at the expense of military solutions, which will bring the system into a state where states will try to generate resources through diplomacy and cultural attraction. However, hard power will remain a major source of foreign policy, because one country will regulate its relations with others depending on whether it can defend itself against a possible attack. Such a world is very reminiscent of the Chinese concept of social harmony and peaceful coexistence, which Xuetong states in his theory of China's peaceful rise. However, its relevance is questionable to U.S. foreign policy, which aims to prevent China from becoming a superpower and seizing Taiwan as opposed to Chinese military influence in the region (Xuetong 2019, 40).

This last world would also be home to new nuclear arms control agreements of which Beijing would become a member. If this happens, it is possible that the pyramid will remain upright for a long time, at least until a new conflict arises that will separate the forces. However, I believe that this is impossible at this stage because, despite its membership in the Treaty on the Non-Proliferation of Nuclear Weapons, China aims to maximize its nuclear potential in order to achieve parity with America. Moreover, Russian military activity in the Black Sea and Moscow's attempts to deploy troops near the Kuril Islands are unlikely to ease tensions in the region. Therefore, the possible membership of Beijing in such agreements is highly questionable. This scenario is the most favorable, as the long confrontation will end with a winner. The war, however, will be Scorch as the probability of MAD will be higher than in the Cold War.

World 4: Nuclear apocalypse

States, claims Waltz, are often rational, but rarely unreasonable (Waltz 1981, 1). *Rarely*. However, a state regime, which possesses nukes, can easily fall into the hands of non-rational decision-makers. For instance, what would happen if a military coup took place in North Korea? What will be the outcome if another leader takes over in China? Some would argue that, by following the logic of nuclear proliferation, terrorist groups could also pretend to be part of the pyramid. My concern is that non-state actors cannot acquire nuclear weapons without the assistance of state actors. For instance, if Pakistan supplies the Taliban with WMD, India will be obliged to ease tensions with China. Otherwise, it is highly unlikely for terrorists to build a nuclear arsenal considering their lack of technology. The fourth scenario is the nuclear apocalypse. The model will deviate into a concave pyramid. The main variables are as follows: constant variables – power (apex), politics (center), and anarchy, determining the nature of the post-pandemic system. The secondary variables are as follows: lateral faces (states), lateral edges (resources), and base edges (imperfect rationality). In this scenario, the right pyramid will preserve its shape, while its basis will deviate into an irregular polygon. In maths, when the base is an irregular hexagon, where the sides are not equal to each other, then the pyramid is an irregular pyramid.

Proof: Concave pyramid

Statements: Apex is inclined, lateral faces are not isosceles triangles, the base is a concave polygon. *The apothem of defensive postures (a)* is the sum of defensive advantages of a state the realistic chance of a state to win a conflict with another state is equal to the most outcome scenario from the confrontation. *The slant height of offensive postures (s)* is the sum of the defensive advantages of a state the height of offense. *The height of offense (h)* is the quarter sum of defensive postures and offensive postures. *The base side of defense (b)* is a product of the base area, which shapes a regular hexagon. A state actor's propensity to attack depends on its resources of self-defense. State actors mobilize their resources for self-defense when an adversary challenges them directly or through sanctions.

Conclusion in the case of nuclear war, the position of the pyramid loses meaning, as does the positioning of its aspects. If the basis of the figure is concave, it may mean that one of the actors in the international system has lost rational perceptions of what the consequences of MAD would be. The confrontation between the United States and China will be very different from the Cold War, and there are many preconditions for nuclear bipolarity to escalate to a point beyond which there is no going back. Graham Alison provides some examples of how a war could break out between Washington and Beijing that would inevitably put the world on the brink of nuclear war.

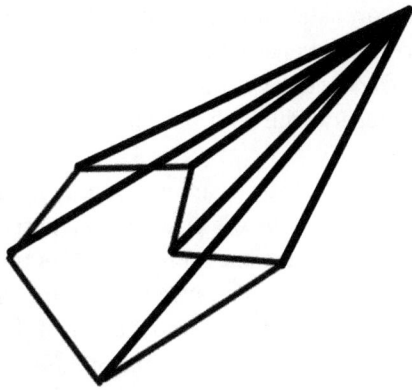

Figure 6: World 4: Nuclear Apocalypse.

Accidental collision in the sea could easily grow into a new Pearl Harbor under conditions in which U.S. and Chinese naval forces collided in the South China Sea (Allison 2017, 111). If Washington approaches the artificial islands in the region, it will provoke a reaction from Beijing because the next step could expose mainland China to an eventual preemptive attack. Allison's scenario seems increasingly realistic with the maneuvers that both fleets regularly perform at sea but is less likely to happen if Beijing is rational in its perceptions of American power. My assumption is that if an accidental collision occurs, it will be deliberately provoked by one side. If the United States causes the clash, it will favor America to increase pressure on China, blaming Beijing's policymakers for the "accident." If Beijing sets the trap, it will give America a reason to launch a preemptive strike on Chinese soil. Such a scenario reminds us of Pearl Harbor or of the German submarine, which maneuvers in American territorial waters in the midst of World War I. Alison is right that neither force would risk allowing the command down the line to collapse, leading to a zero-sum game for both countries. They will be forced to go to war, the logical outcome of which, I assume, is the MAD.

The second scenario of Alison involves Taiwan's eventual decision to declare its independence (Allison 2017, 120). I believe that of all the possible options, a war for Taiwan is the most realistic scenario for several reasons. First, if America maintains a permanent military presence on the island, it will directly threaten to strike mainland China, while if Beijing takes over Taipei, Chinese policymakers will have direct access to the West Coast. My view is that this crisis could become another Cuban missile crisis. Until China reaches parity with the United States, Beijing should avoid direct confrontation with Washington otherwise, the clash will escalate into MAD. America, for its part, must refrain from taking more commitments to Taiwan. U.S. Foreign Policy doctrines depend on the geopolitical realities that determine the American national interest, and if a politician like Donald Trump wins the U.S. presidency again, then Taipei will have to find alternative ways to defend its independence. My concern is that Allison's prediction is one step closer to becoming a reality, with both sides irreconcilable in their positions.

War, provoked by a third party, sounds less realistic as an opportunity for a clash, although no less relevant (Allison 2017, 123). Allison's example of a possible conflict between Japan and China is becoming more and more likely after the Japanese resistance to President Xi's foreign policy towards Taiwan. If Tokyo gets the opportunity to increase its offensive capabilities and reform Article 9 of the Japanese Constitution, it could be a serious cause for war with China. Still, fewer realists acknowledge Waltz's argument that the nuclear bomb is itself a source of power that allows the country to join the Nuclear Power Club (Waltz 2012, 2). Historical tales on the American side are due to a misunderstanding of how Japanese attitudes toward the United States have evolved since WWII. My claim is that the only country that can effectively contain China's aspirations for primacy in the region is Japan. The United States, of course, surpasses China's military might, but underestimates China's military strategies. Japan, which has a long historical record of military conflicts with China, could hold back Chinese influence much more flexibly and sensibly than the United States. Moreover, if Japan gets more involved in regional security, America will have the opportunity to strengthen its influence and partnership with India and thus, put pressure on Beijing on the other side of its border. However, it is doubtful that Washington alone could deal with China, which had gained sophisticated knowledge of the Pacific region millennia before the United States appeared on the map.

The North Korean Collapse is largely discussed in academia due to Pyongyang's nuclear diplomacy. Allison's assumption about North Korea's nuclear program becoming more aggressive towards its neighbors sounds quite realistic. However, I believe that the regime in Pyongyang is unlikely to collapse, or at least not in the near future. The Kim dynasty has a solid position among the North Korean military and intelligence, which makes it the undisputed leader of the country. The Supreme Leader always had the attitude to test the loyalty of those close to him on a daily basis and did not show hesitation, even when he had to eliminate members of his most inner circle. It is doubtful that South Korea and Japan would attack their neighbor because if that were possible, they would have already done so. China and Russia, for their part, have an interest in keeping Kim's regime afloat and are unlikely to put pressure on him to fall. Even if the North Korean leader's power is shaken, it is unlikely to cause a change in the country's political regime, but rather a military coup. If the military takes power and decides to blackmail Pyongyang's neighbors, then nuclear war becomes a real scenario, because if leaders realistically take their interest in retaining power, the military is not always rational, as Robert Jervis confirms in his book (Jervis 2017, 265).

The last predictable scenario – a military conflict provoked by an economic clash – has already been tested with Trump's trade war. Beijing's cyber capabilities are truly remarkable, given that Xi Jinping's military reform has helped China become the fastest-growing nation. The war of currencies will evolve in the long run and will most probably end with virtual currencies approved as the unit of payment or with the yuan reaching parity with the state dollar. However, I assume that the demise of the Bretton Woods System is unlikely to happen in the next decade. China's tributary diplomacy and flying guillotine strategy, on the other hand, cannot provoke military conflict as they work for the benefit of both Beijing and its partners. Therefore, if the United States wants to go to war with China for economic gain and friction, it will first have to overcome the opposition of many of the major American allies, which are part of Beijing's tributary system.

Objections to my approach

Before closing this section, I offer a few arguments in support of my model. I have chosen to present potential criticism as objections because I believe that the arguments most often stem from the ability of some scholars to deny or refine preceding concepts and theories. The paragraphs below correspond to the potential objections that may be raised to my concept.

Objection 1: The model is complicated and misguided

I have never argued that the purpose of this book is to examine the international system as a branch of isolated case studies such as the rise of China, the decline of the liberal world order, or the transformations of Russian nationalism. Moreover, my explanation does not claim to design a universal explanation of international politics, and it instead purports to join the neorealist family of concepts. And although my concept is hybrid and based on a complex system of geometric relations, I believe that it explains international relations better than the one-dimensional images of relations between states. My assumption is that the more complex a model is the more potential it has to explain the structure of international politics and how countries interact with each other. Although my explanation draws inspiration from Morgenthau's classical realism, it is not limited to his view of political relations among nations.

Objection 2: Non-state actors have no place in the Pyramid

Realism believes that states are the primary actors in international relations. I suppose that more remarks in this direction may come because of the European Union and my contention with it as a lateral face of the Pyramid. No other region in the world has such well-developed institutions as Europe, which is an example of a unique integration community. However, in the nuclear age of a highly competitive system, it is debatable to what extent Europe can act as a whole entity. The European Union has survived because it is being reformed and because the founding fathers of the union have laid the foundations for a step-by-step approach that seeks to create the United States of Europe. European integration is not an abstract ideology, and it has an ultimate goal – the federalization of Europe. My concern is that only if Europe truly unites it would emerge as a peer competitor of the state actors. One might argue that such contention is a manifestation of nationalism and anti-globalism. I disagree. Even in the golden years of the unipolar model, when liberals believed they had achieved the perfect form of government, no one took seriously the idea of creating a global government except conspiracy theoreticians. Despite the obvious benefits of globalization, few would deny that if the smaller actors sought to cooperate with the larger ones, the great powers would never part with their sovereignty in the name of world government. Unfortunately, under the influence of far-right groups, nationalism has become a source of ideologies such as fascism and populism. While some of these claims are not unfounded, it is unacceptable to condemn the natural right of every state actor to defend his national interest and security as a full part of the international system.

Objection 3: The explanation does not belong to a specific branch of realism

This model is not structured to be so. At the beginning of this book, I highlighted that my goal is to explain what the world would look like after the Pandemic. To this end, I have taken realistic theories as a starting point, as I believe that my explanation is closer to them than to the writings of liberal institutionalists. I doubt that any scholar would take my work seriously as a new page in realism or a theory that could explain the structure of international politics. However, I mentioned that my explanation purports to join the realist family of concepts without claiming universal theoretical validity. The pyramid of balance is inspired by theories that combine the assumptions of offensive and defensive realism without claiming to belong to a specific point. The fact that these theories differ significantly does not make my explanation less valid, on the contrary – it opens the door for further discussion. Although my research recognizes the contribution of soft power and interdependence, I believe that in the post-pandemic world, relations between states and their behavior will be more complex. Perhaps this is the greatest proof of Merschheimer's claim that false promises lead to geopolitical realities (Mearsheimer 1995, 85).

Objection 4: Maths is not international relations theory

I disagree. I do not think that an approach can be declared invalid just because it uses tools from another academic field. Waltz explicitly emphasizes that in the theory of international relations we often have to use statistics and quantitative data when the variables become more than two (Waltz 1979, 10). There are many examples of how the mathematical approach has assisted us in wargaming, so I find it appropriate to apply it to my theory. In some respects, it is limited because it does not take into account objective quantities such as angle, hypotenuse in triangles, surrounding heights, but to build a theory involving a holistic view of geometry in the context of politics will require another book. Until someone else suggests one, I think it is appropriate to use mathematics in my research instead of proving my theses with statistics that partially explain them, but fail when they have to make a deep analysis of the balance of power in the international system. In addition, I accept that my model may need improvement or correction, which I will leave for further development in other academic writings.

Objection 5: Coercive realism is a mechanical combination of different theories

I reject it. Mechanical explanations have no causal links and do not explain why they chose to connect arguments in a logical chain. My book reviews the dominant realist theories, explaining why I chose them and how I use them to construct my original explanation. If my explanations were merely a combination of theories, I would rewrite the main assumptions of the authors of the first chapter and bring them into a definition that combines them, similar to the dominant approaches in most academic papers. Instead, I chose a deeper approach that involves not only the analysis of theories as a starting point, but also their operationalization in order to derive hypotheses. In addition, I believe that the focus of my explanation – the world after the Pandemic – suggests that my approach is not to plagiarize already developed theories. It rather generates empirical knowledge to analyze the international system from now on. Although I did not have the opportunity to learn from the best authors, I decided to analyze their theories so that their legacy could ensure the legitimacy of my theory in the way that previous theories have provided legitimacy to their theories.

Objection 6: The explanation is nuclear-centric

I do not deny the nuclear-centric approach I used to delineate the world after the Pandemic. Contrary to criticism, however, I admit that nuclear-centrism does not diminish the empirical validity of my theory. It enriches it. If soft power represents the latest generation of how a country can influence global politics, then nuclear weapons, for better or worse, is a deterrent to the outbreak of World War III. Kenneth Waltz suggests that in certain situations, nuclear bombs may even play a positive role when their proliferation is regulated (Watlz 1981, 1). If he accepts that the superpowers the United States and China are the only isolated factors in world politics, then several questions remain. First, why a superpower like America was willing to negotiate with Pyongyang when it became clear that the North Korean leader was beginning to develop nuclear capabilities. Secondly, why the nuclear powers that are parties to the nuclear non-proliferation agreement are permanent members of the UN Security Council. Third, it is not necessary for a nuclear power not to start a war if it is not a superpower. If, however, Allison's prediction of Pyongyang comes to existence and of the military taking power, they might decide to demonstrate a force greater than that of their leader by firing a nuclear missile at one of America's allies. Thus, I think that instead of dividing countries into superpowers and great powers, which will obscure our rational attitudes towards the post-pandemic system, it is better to look at how many of them have the destructive potential to start World War III. After all, after the signing of the Versailles-Washington system, a few imagined that in a century of the League of Nations, defeated Germany could recover so quickly. Excluding nuclear-weapon states from the model means recognizing that the US and China superpowers can defeat them without risking nuclear war.

Objection 7: Mathematical calculations reduce the scenarios

I do not claim that the pyramid of balance and the four worlds are the only explanations of the post-pandemic security architecture. My assumption stems from both the behavior of states and the post-pandemic structure of international politics. The worlds I have outlined are a guide for the future of international relations, so I did not hesitate to include the nuclear war scenario among them. It is possible that more scenarios will be developed based on whether the pyramid will not change its walls at some point if the world becomes unipolar again with China at the apex or if some of the nuclear powers collapse. I noted that the pyramid is adapted to the post-pandemic structure, though it can also serve as a template for future scenarios related to the structure of the international system. Nuclear weapons will not disappear unless humanity discovers another tool of self-destruction. However, as countries seek to acquire or develop their nuclear capabilities, the pyramid of balance will operate, regardless of possible scenarios and the number of poles in the system.

With the present objection, I do not claim to end the self-criticism of my explanation. I believe that scholars will be found to revise it better or identify its weaknesses so that it can be used in a clearer way as a tool for analyzing the international system in the future. My assertion is that the model will be incorporated into the framework of the academic debate, as I have already listed the shortcomings and limits of the pyramid models that have been used so far. Having already set out my theory in detail, I move on to the final part of my study.

Three-Check Chess: The Grand Chessboard Revisited

I will finish this chapter with a brief conclusion on how the pyramid of balance would affect the chessboard that Brzezinski envisions in his notable book *The Grand Chessboard: American Primacy and Its Geostrategic Imperatives*. The purpose of my concept is not to challenge Brzezinski's theory but merely to adapt it to the post-pandemic world. Therefore, I summarize several conclusions that will be, I assume, essential to the transformation of Brzezinski's chessboard. Most of the conclusions concern Russia's place on the chessboard. As Robert Jervis states the very fact that the essays are such insightful leaves Brzezinski somewhat of an enigma – and extends an invitation to further research (Jervis 2021).

Conclusion 1: Eurasia becomes Asia

I assume that Brzezinski is right in his assumption that for America, Eurasia is the geopolitical prize (Brzezinski 2016, 30). However, it is arguable that Eurasia is the heartland of the chessboard, on which the struggle for geopolitical primacy continues to be played. I believe that Merschheimer is also right in assuming that the geopolitical race is more likely to shift from Europe to Asia. Indeed, the Eurasian continent is rich in resources, and if the United States maintains control over Eurasia, China will find itself in a very difficult position. Russia, quite the opposite, is a loyal partner of Beijing and it is unlikely, even under Vladimir Putin's successor that Russian foreign policy will turn against the Chinese. Nuclear power with enormous destructive capabilities, Moscow will not allow being controlled by either America or China. Instead, Russia will maneuver between the two powers, trying to act as a balancer. Only if Eurasia unites politically, militarily and economically will Russia once again become a superpower, as it was in the Soviet Era. My prediction is that the Kremlin will pursue a policy of manipulation to keep Europe in check with gas policy, America deterred by its nuclear weapons, and China closer to restraining Japan. There is even talk that Russia could collapse, giving the West absolute control over its resources. My concern is that such scenarios are far from realistic. History shows that Eurasia transforms periodically into a form that rejects foreign influence or at least allows it for a very short period. When Tsarist Russia began to modernize, a few conspirators assassinated Emperor Alexander II, and later the monarchy itself fell victim to attempts of the Provisional Government to Westernize Russia. For a long time, the USSR opposed the West until Gorbachev took over and initiated the Perestroika, which resulted in the Soviet collapse. Then, despite Yeltsin's presidency, which buried Russia's attempt to democratize, Eurasian politics has once again favored a centralized model of government in the face of Vladimir Putin. Therefore, even if the Russian Federation weakens due to domestic processes of decentralization, it will not transform into another political entity.

Conclusion 2: Soft power does not work in Eurasia

This book joins Brzezinski's claim that nuclear weapons will now allow the United States to gain control over Eurasia, due to the fear of MAD (Brzezinski 2016, 34). My concern is that other options such as soft power, alliances building, coercive diplomacy, and deliberate deployment are unlikely to work. If Moscow becomes more dialogical in the near future, it will be much more willing to cooperate with China than with Washington. Siberia and the Far Eastern regions of

Russia are sparsely populated but rich in natural habitats, which will certainly be of great interest to Chinese investors. Beijing needs to increase its strategic presence in the region to contain Tokyo. The Western dream of transforming Russia is as bold as the attempts to liberalize China. Yeltsin's experiment in the 1990s did not work because Russian society refused to recognize liberal democracy as an alternative to communism but preferred strong leadership and centralized government. These attitudes are a reflection of the Eurasian political culture, which combines the Tatar heritage of the Golden Horde with the Orthodox spirit of Byzantium.

Although Brzezinski foresaw China's rise and Ukraine's strategic importance to Russia, he failed to predict that a unified Europe would increasingly become an important political player on the Eurasian chessboard. Although the European Union is trying to maintain a constructive relationship with Russia, European leaders realize that the European project is now much more dependent on Beijing than on the United States. Robert Jervis points out that only if Europe really unites can we talk about a real competitor to the United States (Jervis 2006, 6). However, the creation of European armed forces is unlikely to happen in the coming years for two reasons. First, Europe cannot allocate enough resources to fund and build military capabilities similar to those of the United States, Russia and China. The European Rapid Reaction Forces project might be successful and Brussels might be in possession of limited ability to act within NATO. However, dependence on the United States can hardly be a question, at least until Germany has the right to rearm. This brings us to the second dilemma that France and the other EU member states will inevitably face if they want Europe to create an army – military coordination. My assertion is that the rearmament of Berlin is a crucial precondition for Europe's security architecture. Germany has always been central to European security and the European military identity. This leads to the third problem facing Europe's defense identity – the future of NATO. My claim is that the most plausible option for Europe is to design its future armed forces within the Alliance. It will eliminate America's fears of European nationalism and bring the old continent one step closer to the legacy of the EU founding fathers.

Conclusion 3: The Soviet decline was China's rise

The historical prophecy of Brzezinski that America should focus on the rise of potential regional hegemons was neglected as many policymakers disregarded the warnings of Kissinger about China. Brzezinski's strategy for gaining control over the Eurasian chessboard involves short-term, middle-term, and long-term politics of consolidating and perpetuating Eurasian pluralism, creating strategically important partners to prompt American leadership, and eventually – transforming Eurasia into a global core of shared responsibility (Brzezinski 2016, 40). Such an approach would have been successful had it not been for China's rise. Throughout the post-Cold War period, Beijing reached the status of regional power in a remarkably silent manner, while America was preoccupied with the war on terror and its efforts to halt the resurgence of the Soviet Union. It was only in recent years that China began to be talked about as the next superpower, as if people had never known the prophecies of Morgenthau and Kissinger, which warned that the heart of the board was increasingly shifting to Asia. Brzezinski is right in his conclusion that the United States should not allow another power to displace Washington from the region, but this has already happened because the main power there is Russia. Even if, under Putin's successors, Moscow loses its great influence in Eurasia, the vacuum will be occupied by China. Then, the consequences for American influence will be even more disastrous, because with the establishment of control over the whole of Eurasia, Beijing will gain political and military access to America's European allies.

Conclusion

At the beginning of this book, I purported to present a new explanation of what the world would look like after the Pandemic. By "after the Pandemic," I do not refer to COVID19 as the limit of my research. Dealing with the virus may take years or decades. For the purpose of my research, I began with a critical reading of the basic neorealist theories that I took as the starting point of my research, and then moved on to an analysis of American and Chinese foreign policy after the end of the Cold War. Finally, I introduced a structural concept of the post-pandemic world order. To summarize, my explanation of coercive realism has three elements: a theoretical framework that draws inspiration from realism; a methodological framework that I derive from the foreign policies of America and China, and finally, an empirical part in which I shape the pyramidal structure of international politics. In the final part of my research, I find it reasonable to test my approach through reminding the realist legacy of Kenneth Waltz, who defines three basic conditions, which I believe my concept meets.

First, coercive realism is an edifice of truth and reproduction of reality. This book does not deal with conspiracies that accuse China of releasing the virus and avoids assumptions that are inclined to claim the world as unipolar just because it rests on liberal hegemony. Coercive realism, most of all deals with three realities that will dominate the post-pandemic system of international relations: anarchy, power, and politics. Therefore, my concept joins the realist consensus that the ultimate truth about the international system lies in: the conflicts that arise from its anarchic structure; the desire of states to maximize their power, and the behavior of state actors towards each other. Therefore, the problem of power and peace in the twenty-first century will be solved by those countries that are actively involved in conflicts and thus manipulate the balance of power, that have the resources to maximize their capabilities, and that can afford to challenge the most powerful nations on the earth. Therefore, I find the division of great powers and superpowers too provisional and less rational. Although the United States and China are emerging as the strongest nations in the post-pandemic world, power and peace will still be a privilege of nuclear powers.

Second, coercive realism sets three variables, which I believe, correspond to the geopolitical realities, and predetermine the post-pandemic structure of international politics: power, politics, and anarchy. Analyzing the dependence between the variables, my concept follows Morgenthau's explanation of the forces that determine political relations among nations. With regard to the United States and China, these forces relate to the resources they have and their behavior toward each other, which I discussed in Chapters Two and Three. The rest of the nuclear actors, which occupie the lateral faces of my model, will seek to maximize their power and benefit from international conflicts. Nuclear weapons will remain the ultimate source of destruction in the bipolar world, dominated by the US-China rivalry.

Third, coercive realism offers a systematic approach, through which, in the first chapter of this book, I posed three questions. The first discusses the dilemma of whether anarchy is still central to international politics. The answer to the book is yes. Only state actors have the sovereignty and the resources to act independently in the international system. Moreover, under nuclear bipolarity, states are merely in condition to acquire nuclear weapons. International organizations such as the United Nations and NATO are an expression of the collective will of the nuclear powers, and so far there is no precedent in which a country has delegated its nuclear sovereignty to an international organization. Some would argue that the EU is more than an international organization, namely a unique integration community. Although I do not deny this claim, I reject the possibility of a united Europe gaining nuclear sovereignty, as this is a privilege only for the Member States. Iran's attempts to get nukes and Pyongyang's nuclear program also demonstrated that WMD plays a substantial role in world politics and that agreements to limit them cannot be a barrier to countries pursuing an independent foreign policy. The second question concerns how the struggle for power determines the problem of peace in the first half of the twenty-first century. My explanation joined the neorealist consensus that the lust for power alone is not enough to allow us to understand the international system, so I decided to move on to building my model. However, I believe that Morgenthau's theory is a starting point for realism, because if our equation consists only of its structure and the foreign policy of states, then the question of micro-level attitudes remains open, among the political elite that tends to sacrifice national interests in the struggle for global domination. The third dilemma deals with how great powers competition will reshape the post-pandemic world order. The concept presented me with a structural explanation, which I called the pyramid of balance, and which is based on my model. Using both international relations and mathematics, I have come to the conclusion that the state of the dilemma will be a situation of constant confrontation in which the United States and China, together with the nuclear concert, will decide the future of world politics.

Finally, I will highlight again that this book does not pretend to introduce a new theory of international relations for various reasons I discussed in the first chapter. However, I have employed the standard methodological approach to IR studies by defining the variables in my research and by testing my assumptions.

To test whether the pyramid of balance is applicable to other geopolitical realities will require another book, which could be more likely to deal with theories.

The struggle for power and peace in international relations cannot express the nature of the system with the simple formula of history's end, which, under the guise of Hegelianism, has fired the sparkle of hope for future generations. Although the liberal paradigm is a unique attempt to solve the puzzle of international politics, its absolute conclusions about realism, being insufficient and one-sided, expose the greatest weakness of liberalism, which is its optimism. The promise of a universal solution of war and peace, for the last time, is as elegant as misguided. It is a grandiose legacy with a glamorous and inspiring message, similar to that of Kant's hope for eternal peace. Our world made it to the end of the liberal world order, which presupposes the emergence of a post-pandemic one that is yet to be constructed. As the rise of China, and its quest for power continue to shape the geopolitical realities of our time, so the United States and its allies should adapt to a bipolar world, where interdependence, obtaining power through attraction, and smart strategies will be secondary to the pure hard power, the ultimate expression of which is nuclear diplomacy.

If reading this book, liberal scholars might object that realism failed to predict the end of the Cold War. To such a challenge, I would say that the realist paradigm rather won the bipolar confrontation Soviet Union than misjudged it. Yet, there are liberal scholars who claim the opposite and even realists who tend to make realism *softer*. Both approaches would have been praiseworthy if it had not been for the rise of Chinese Communism, twenty years after the USSR had collapsed. Realism has not failed to predict the end of the Cold War, though liberalism did not succeed in its task to preserve the New World Order. Realists might sometimes fail when a few policymakers follow the optimistic predictions of liberalism about a world where democracy and human rights secure peace and prevent the possibility of war. When Alexander the Great invaded the Persian Empire and took over Alexandria Arachosia, none presumed that the future great powers could only dream of his conquests. The trouble with the liberal paradigm is that it still lives in the times of Alexander when Ancient Greek culture pretended to shape the universal attitudes of humanity. When Emperor Pu Yi abdicated, China turned back its Imperial past, but kept its legacy to inweave later it in the Communist ideology, transforming it into Chinese *realpolitik*.

If reading this book, realist scholars might object that the revival of obsolete theories would lead my brave explanation to the point of a dead end. To such objection, I would answer that my appraisal of realism is not absolute. When state actors have adopted a policy in defense of their national interest, they have not always succeeded. This logic applies to American policymakers, who pretend to defend the U.S. national interests, but instead benefit China with their policy of intransigence. During the Cold War, the conflict between the United States and the Soviet Union threatened to destroy the world, which forced both superpowers to deter each other. Yet, twenty years after the collapse of the USSR, tensions between Washington and Beijing over Taiwan could trigger another military conflict, which would be far hotter than the Cuban missile crisis. Thus, the basic efforts for the preservation of peace and the struggle for power must revise the strategies of the Cold War and adapt them to the post-pandemic security architecture. Only if the United States enters another competition, similar to the U.S.-Soviet bipolar confrontation, would Washington have a chance to deter China effectively. For Beijing, the competition with the United States is the path to the restoration of Chinese leadership. A true realist, however, would ask, has the world not lived too long in peace?

References

Allen, John, Nicholas Burns, Laurie Garrett, Richard N. Haass, G. John Ikenberry, Kishore Mahbubani, Shivshankar Menon et al. "How the world will look after the coronavirus pandemic." Foreign Policy 20, no. 20 (2020): 97–103.

Allison, Graham. *Destined for war: Can America and China escape Thucydides's trap?*. Houghton Mifflin Harcourt, 2017.

Allison, Graham T. "The Cuban missile crisis." In *Foreign Policy: Theories, Actors, Cases*, ed. by Steve Smith, 263–291. Oxford: Oxford University Press, 2008.

Allison, Graham. *Nuclear terrorism: The ultimate preventable catastrophe*. Macmillan, 2004.

Allison, Graham T., and Robert Blackwill. "America's national interests." *United States: The Commission on America's National Interests* (2000).

An, Jiang. "Mao Zedong's "Three Worlds" Theory: Political Considerations and Value for the Times." *Social Sciences in China* 34, no. 1 (2013): 35–57, https://doi.org/10.1080/02529203.2013.760715.

Antoniades, Andreas. "Recasting the Power Politics of Debt: Structural Power, Hegemonic Stabilisers & Change." *Rising powers and the future of global governance* (2014): 1–246, https://doi.org/10.1080/01436597.2013.775780.

Art, Robert J. *A grand strategy for America*. Cornell University Press, 2013.

Art, Robert J. "The United States and the rise of China: implications for the long haul." *Political Science Quarterly* 125, no. 3 (2010): 359–391.

Art, Robert J. "American foreign policy and the fungibility of force." *Security Studies* 5, no. 4 (1996): 7–42, https://doi.org/10.1080/09636419608429287.

Art, Robert J., and Patrick M. Cronin, eds. *The United States and coercive diplomacy*. US Institute of Peace Press, 2003.

Bader, Jeffrey A. *How Xi Jinping sees the world & and why*. Washington, DC: Brookings Institution, 2016.

Bell, Daniel A. *The China Model*. Princeton University Press, 2016.

Bell, Daniel A. "Reconciling socialism and Confucianism?: Reviving tradition in China." *Dissent* 57, no. 1 (2010): 91–99, https://doi.org/10.1353/dss.0.0114.

Biden Jr, Joseph R. "Unholy symbiosis: Isolationism and anti-americanism." *Washington Quarterly* 23, no. 4 (2000): 5–14, https://doi.org/10.1162/016366000561222.

Bieber, Florian. "Global nationalism in times of the COVID-19 pandemic." *Nationalities Papers* (2020): 1–13, https://doi.org/10.1017/nps.2020.35.

Boer, Roland. "Xi Jinping on Marx and Engels." In *Socialism with Chinese Characteristics*, ed. by Roland Boer, pp. 273–307. Springer, Singapore, 2021, https://doi.org/10.1007/978-981-16-1622-8_10.

Brecher, Michael. "International relations and Asian studies: the subordinate state system of Southern Asia." *World Politics* 15, no. 2 (1963): 213–235, https://doi.org/10.2307/2009374.

Brzezinski, Zbigniew. *The grand chessboard: American primacy and its geostrategic imperatives*. Basic books, 2016.

Burgess, Stephen F. "Rising bipolarity in the South China Sea: the American rebalance to Asia and China's expansion." *Contemporary Security Policy* 37, no. 1 (2016): 111–143, https://doi.org/10.1080/13523260.2016.1149968.

Buzan, Barry. "Polarity." In *Security Studies*, ed. by Paul D. Williams and Matt McDonald, pp. 177–191. Routledge, 2012.

Campbell, Kurt M., and Ely Ratner. "The China reckoning: how Beijing defied American expectations." *Foreign Aff.* 97 (2018): 60.

Campbell, Kurt M., and Michael E. O'Hanlon. *Hard power: The new politics of national security.* Basic Books (AZ), 2006.

Cesa, Marco. "Realist visions of the end of the Cold War: Morgenthau, Aron and Waltz." *The British Journal of Politics and International Relations* 11, no. 2 (2009): 177–191, https://doi.org/10.1111%2Fj.1467-856X.2008.00357.x.

Cheung, Ching-yuen. "The Problem of Evil in Confucianism." In *Probing the Depths of Evil and Good*, ed. by Jerald D. Gort, Henry Jansen and Hendrik M. Vroom, pp. 87–99. Brill Rodopi, 2007, https://doi.org/10.1163/9789401204620_007.

Chifu, Iulian, and Teodor Frunzeti. "Trump Doctrine. The 'Principled Realism'." *Strategic Impact* (2018): 7–17.

Cho, Young Chul, and Yih-Jye Hwang. "Mainstream IR theoretical perspectives and rising China Vis-À-Vis the west: The logic of conquest, conversion and socialisation." *Journal of Chinese Political Science* 25, no. 2 (2020): 175–198, https://doi.org/10.1007/s11366-019-09620-3.

Christensen, Thomas J. "Chinese realpolitik." *Foreign Affairs* (1996): 37–52.

Confucius. *The Analects,* ed. by D. C. Lau. Columbia University Press, 2000.

Creel, Herrlee Glessner. "Confucius and Hsün-Tzŭ." *Journal of the American Oriental Society* (1931): 23–32, https://doi.org/10.2307/593216.

Deng, Yong. "The Chinese conception of national interests in international relations." *The China Quarterly* 154 (1998): 308–329, https://doi.org/10.1017/S0305741000002058.

Dîrdală, Lucian-Dumitru. "After Vilnius: the European Union's smart power and the Eastern Neighbourhood." *Eastern Journal of European Studies* 4, no. 2 (2013): 123–136.

Dugin, Alexander. *Last war of the World-Island: the Geopolitics of contemporary Russia.* Arktos, 2015.

Dugin, Alexander. *Eurasian Mission: An Introduction to Neo-Eurasianism.* Arktos, 2014.

Dunne, Michael. "Kennedy's Alliance for Progress: countering revolution in Latin America Part II: the historiographical record." *International Affairs* 92, no. 2 (2016): 435–452, https://doi.org/10.1111/1468-2346.12080.

Elman, Colin, and Michael Jensen. *The realism reader.* Routledge, 2014.

Fa, Zhang. "The Concept of Universe in Chinese Philosophy." *Journal of Social Sciences* 1, no. 1 (2014): 4–10.

Fairbank, John K. "Tributary trade and China's relations with the West." *The Journal of Asian Studies* 1, no. 2 (1942): 129–149, https://doi.org/10.2307/2049617.

Feng, Huiyun. *Chinese strategic culture and foreign policy decision-making: Confucianism, leadership and war.* Routledge, 2007.

Friedberg, Aaron L. "Hegemony with Chinese characteristics." *The National Interest* 114 (2011): 18–27.

Fukuyama, Francis. "The pandemic and political order." *Foreign Aff.* 99 (2020): 26.

Fukuyama, Francis. *The end of history and the last man.* Simon and Schuster, 2006.

Fukuyama, Francis. "The end of history?." *The national interest* 16 (1989): 3–18.

Garver, John W. "China's Decision for War with India in 1962." In *New Directions in the Study of China's Foreign Policy,* ed. by Alastair Iain Johnson and Robert S. Ross, pp. 86–150. Stanford University Press, 2006.

Garver, John W. "China's push through the South China Sea: the interaction of bureaucratic and national interests." *The China Quarterly* 132 (1992): 999–1028, https://doi.org/10.1017/S0305741000045513.

George, Alexander L. "Knowledge for statecraft: the challenge for political science and history." *International Security* 22, no. 1 (1997): 44–52, https://doi.org/10.1162/isec.22.1.44.

Gilpin, Robert. *War and change in world politics.* Cambridge University Press, 1981.

Goldberg, J. "The Obama Doctrine, RIP The Atlantic." 3 no. 1 (2017): 1–3.

Greener, B. K. "Liberalism and the use of force: Core themes and conceptual tensions." *Alternatives* 32, no. 3 (2007): 295–318, https://doi.org/10.1177%2F030437540703200302.

Guang, Lei. "Realpolitik nationalism: International sources of Chinese nationalism." *Modern China* 31, no. 4 (2005): 487–514, https://doi.org/10.1177%2F0097700405279355.

Guzman, Andrew T. *How international law works: a rational choice theory.* Oxford University Press, 2008.

Hegel, Georg Wilhelm Friedrich, and John Sibree. *The philosophy of history.* Courier Corporation, 2004.

Heisbourg, François. "From Wuhan to the world: How the pandemic will reshape geopolitics." *Survival* 62, no. 3 (2020): 7–24, https://doi.org/10.1080/00396338.2020.1763608.

Holmes, Colleen K. *What the Chinese learned from Sun-tzu.* Army War Coll Carlisle Barracks, PA, 2001.

Holubnychy, Vsevolod. "Mao Tse-tung's Materialistic Dialectics." *The China Quarterly* 19 (1964): 3–37, https://doi.org/10.1017/S0305741000042090.

Huang, Yasheng. "Why China will not collapse." *Foreign Policy* 99 (1995): 54–68, https://doi.org/10.2307/1149005.

Ikenberry, G. John. "The end of liberal international order?." *International Affairs* 94, no. 1 (2018): 7–23.

Ikenberry, G. John. "Liberal internationalism 3.0: America and the dilemmas of liberal world order." *Perspectives on politics* 7, no. 1 (2009): 71–87, https://doi.org/10.1017/S1537592709090112.

Ikenberry, G. John, Stephen Walt, and Christopher Lydon. "Offshore balancing or international institutions? The way forward for US foreign policy: A debate at the Watson Institute for International Studies 8 May 2007." *The Brown Journal of World Affairs* 14, no. 1 (2007): 13–23.

Ivanov, Iskren. "Understanding Russian Smart Power: Perceptions and Ideology." *Academy of Public Service Under the President of Kazakhstan,* (2021): 51–59, https://doi.org/10.52123/1994-2370-2021-76-1-65.

Ivanov, Iskren. "Reshaping US Smart Power." Journal of Strategic Security 13, no. 3 (2020): 46–74, https://doi.org/10.5038/1944-0472.13.3.1829.

Jervis, Robert. "1. President Trump and International Relations Theory." In *Chaos in the Liberal Order,* ed. by Robert Jervis, Francis J. Gavin, Joshua Rovner, and Dianne N. Labrosse, pp. 3–7. Columbia University Press, 2018, https://doi.org/10.7312/jerv18834-002.

Jervis, Robert. "President Trump and International Relations Theory" *In Chaos in the Liberal Order: The Trump Presidency and International Politics in the Twenty-First Century*, ed. by Robert Jervis, Francis J. Gavin, Joshua Rovner and Diane N. Labrosse, pp. 3–7. Columbia University Press, 2018. https://doi.org/10.7312/jerv18834-002.

Jervis, Robert. *Perception and misperception in international politics*. Princeton University Press, 2017.

Jervis, Robert. *Deterrence and perception*. Princeton University Press, 2014.

Jervis, Robert. "Getting to Yes with Iran: The Challenges of Coercive Diplomacy." *Foreign Aff.* 92 (2013): 105.

Jervis, Robert. *American foreign policy in a new era*. Routledge, 2013.

Jervis, Robert. *Why intelligence fails*. Cornell University Press, 2010.

Jervis, Robert. "Unipolarity: A structural perspective." *World Politics* 61, no. 1 (2009): 188–213, https://doi.org/10.1017/S0043887109000070.

Jervis, Robert. "The remaking of a unipolar world." *Washington Quarterly* 29, no. 3 (2006): 5–19, https://doi.org/10.1162/wash.2006.29.3.5.

Jervis, Robert. "The compulsive empire." *Foreign Policy* (2003): 83–87, https://doi.org/10.2307/3183700.

Jervis, Robert. "Understanding the Bush doctrine." *Political Science Quarterly* 118, no. 3 (2003): 365–388, https://doi.org/10.1002/J.1538-165X.2003.TB00398.X.

Jervis, Robert. "An interim assessment of September 11: what has changed and what has not?." *Political Science Quarterly* 117, no. 1 (2002): 37–54, https://doi.org/10.2307/798093.

Jervis, Robert. "Mutual assured destruction." *Foreign Policy* 133 (2002): 40.

Jervis, Robert. "Was the cold war a security dilemma?." *Journal of Cold War Studies* 3, no. 1 (2001): 36–60, https://doi.org/10.1162/15203970151032146.

Jervis, Robert. "War and misperception." *The Journal of Interdisciplinary History* 18, no. 4 (1988): 675–700, https://doi.org/10.2307/204820.

Jervis, Robert. "Cooperation under the security dilemma." *World politics* 30, no. 2 (1978): 167–214, https://doi.org/10.2307/2009958.

Johnston, Alastair Iain. *Cultural realism: Strategic culture and grand strategy in Chinese history*. Vol. 178. Princeton University Press, 1998.

Jones, Bruce. "China and the return of great power strategic competition." *Global China: Assessing China's Growing Role in the World. Washington, DC: The Brookings Institution* (2020).

Kaltenmark, Max. *Lao Tzu and Taoism*. Stanford University Press, 1969.

Kennedy, John F. "A Democrat looks at foreign policy." *Foreign Affairs* 36, no. 1 (1957): 44–59.

Kerr, Gordon. *A Short History of China*. Oldcastle Books, 2013.

Khan, Muqtedar, and Isa Haskologlu. "Fear as Driver of International Relations." *Special report. Center for global policy* (2020).

Khan, Muqtedar. "Five American perspectives on Islam: An analytical guide." *Special Report 01. Center for global policy* (2018).

Khan, MA Muqtedar, and Sara J. Chehab. "American Foreign Policy and the continuing struggle against Anti-Americanism in the Muslim world." In *National Security under the Obama Administration*, ed. by Bahram M. Rajaee and Mark J. Miller, pp. 179–195. Palgrave Macmillan, New York, 2012, https://doi.org/10.1057/9781137010476_11.

Khan, M. A. "Postmodern Empire: The United States' New Foreign Policy and Its Global Challanges." *Brown J. World Aff.* 10 (2003): 271.
Kirkey, Sharon. "Is Donald Trump's "principled realism" a real doctrine?'." *National Post* 26 (2018): 1–3.
Kissinger, Henry. *World order*. Penguin Books, 2014.
Kissinger, Henry A. "The future of US-Chinese relations: conflict is a choice, not a necessity." *Foreign Affairs* (2012): 44–55.
Kissinger, Henry. "China: containment won't work." *Washington Post* 13 (2005): A19.
Kissinger, Henry A. "Domestic structure and foreign policy." *Daedalus* (1966): 503–529.
Kuang, Qizhang. "Pragmatism in China: the Deweyan influence." PhD diss., Michigan State University, 1994.
Lake, David A. *Hierarchy in international relations*. Cornell University Press, 2011.
Layne, Christopher. "This time it's real: The end of unipolarity and the Pax Americana." *International studies quarterly* 56, no. 1 (2012): 203–213, https://doi.org/10.1111/j.1468-2478.2011.00704.x.
Layne, Christopher. "The unipolar exit: beyond the Pax Americana." *Cambridge Review of International Affairs* 24, no. 2 (2011): 149–164, https://doi.org/10.1080/09557571.2011.558491.
Lebow, Richard Ned. "The long peace, the end of the cold war, and the failure of realism." *International Organization* 48, no. 2 (1994): 249–277, https://doi.org/10.1017/S0020818300028186.
Lebow, Richard Ned, and Janice Gross Stein. "Rational deterrence theory: I think, therefore I deter." *World politics* 41, no. 2 (1989): 208–224, https://doi.org/10.2307/2010408.
Leffler, Melvyn P. "From the Truman Doctrine to the Carter Doctrine: Lessons and Dilemmas of the Cold War." *Diplomatic History* 7, no. 4 (1983): 245–266, https://doi.org/10.1111/j.1467-7709.1983.tb00394.x.
Legro, Jeffrey W., and Andrew Moravcsik. "Faux realism." *Foreign Policy* (2001): 80–82.
Legro, Jeffrey W., and Andrew Moravcsik. "Is anybody still a realist?." *International security* 24, no. 2 (1999): 5–55, http://doi.org/10.1162/016228899560130.
Leidig, Eviane Cheng. "Immigrant, nationalist and proud: A Twitter analysis of Indian diaspora supporters for Brexit and Trump." *Media and Communication* 7, no. 1 (2019): 77–89, https://doi.org/10.17645/mac.v7i1.1629.
Lenin, Vladimir Ilich. *What is to be Done?*. Wellred Books, 1935.
Litwak, Robert S. *Détente and the Nixon doctrine: American foreign policy and the pursuit of stability, 1969–1976*. CUP Archive, 1986.
Locke, John. *Locke: political writings*. Hackett Publishing, 2003.
Lovejoy, Arthur O. "The Chinese origin of a romanticism." *The Journal of English and Germanic Philology* 32, no. 1 (1933): 1–20.
MacAskill, Ewen, and Julian Borger. "Iraq war was illegal and breached UN charter, says Annan." *The Guardian* 16 (2004): 1–3.
Maher, Richard. "Bipolarity and the Future of US-China Relations." *Political science quarterly* 133, no. 3 (2018): 497–525.
Mansfield, Edward D. "Concentration, polarity, and the distribution of power." *International Studies Quarterly* 37, no. 1 (1993): 105–128, https://doi.org/10.2307/2600833.
Mattis, Jim. *Summary of the 2018 national defense strategy of the United States of America*. Department of Defense Washington United States, (2018).

McFate, Sean. *The new rules of war: Victory in the age of durable disorder.* William Morrow, 2019.

Mearsheimer, John J., and Stephen M. Walt. "The Case for Offshore Balancing: A Superior US Grand Stategy." *Foreign Aff.* 95 (2016): 70.

Mearsheimer, John J. "Can China rise peacefully?." *The National Interest* 25, no. 1 (2014): 1–40.

Mearsheimer, John J. "Taiwan's dire straits." *The National Interest* 130 (2014): 29–39.

Mearsheimer, John J. "Why the Ukraine crisis is the West's fault: the liberal delusions that provoked Putin." *Foreign Aff.* 93 (2014): 77.

Mearsheimer, John J. "Imperial by design." *The National Interest* 111 (2011): 16–34.

Mearsheimer, John J. "Kissing Cousins: Nationalism and Realism", unpublished paper prepared for the Yale Workshop on International Relations, 2011. Available online at https://www.mearsheimer.com/publications/.

Mearsheimer, John J. "The gathering storm: China's challenge to US power in Asia." *The Chinese journal of international politics* 3, no. 4 (2010): 381–396, https://doi.org/10.1093/cjip/poq016.

Mearsheimer, John J. "Structural realism." *International relations theories: Discipline and diversity* 83 (2007): 77–94.

Mearsheimer, John J. "China's unpeaceful rise." *Current History* 105, no. 690 (2006): 160–162.

Mearsheimer, John J. "The Future of the American Pacifer." *Foreign Aff.* 80 (2001): 46.

Mearsheimer, John J., and Glenn Alterman. *The tragedy of great power politics.* WW Norton & Company, 2001.

Mearsheimer, John J. "A realist reply." *International security* 20, no. 1 (1995): 82–93, http://doi.org/10.2307/2539218.

Mearsheimer, John J. "The false promise of international institutions." *International security* 19, no. 3 (1994): 5–49, https://doi.org/10.2307/2539078.

Meiser, Jeffrey W. "Power and Restraint: Liberal Foreign Policy Theory and America's Rise: 1904–1912." In *APSA 2010 Annual Meeting Paper.* 2010.

Moore, John Bassett. "The Monroe Doctrine." *The ANNALS of the American Academy of Political and Social Science* 96, no. 1 (1921): 31–33, https://doi.org/10.1177%2F000271622109600106.

Moravcsik, Andrew. "Liberal theories of international law." *Interdisciplinary Perspectives on International Law and International Relations* 83 (2013): 1–65.

Moravcsik, Andrew. "Europe: The quiet superpower." *French politics* 7, no. 3 (2009): 403–422, https://doi.org/10.1057/fp.2009.29.

Moravcsik, Andrew. "Taking preferences seriously: A liberal theory of international politics." *International organization* 51, no. 4 (1997): 513–553, https://doi.org/10.1162/002081897550447.

Moravcsik, Andrew. *Liberalism and international relations theory.* Center for International Affairs, Harvard University, 1992.

Morgenthau, Hans J. "Six principles of political realism." *Classic Readings of International Relations* (2006): 34–38.

Morgenthau, Hans J. "The United States and China." *International Studies* 10, no. 1–2 (1968): 23–34, https://doi.org/10.1177%2F002088176801000102.

Morgenthau, Hans J. "US Misadventure in Vietnam." *Current History* 54, no. 317 (1968): 29–34.
Morgenthau, Hans J. "To intervene or not to intervene." *Foreign Aff.* 45 (1966): 425.
Morgenthau, Hans J. "War with China? The New Republic 3 April 1965." *Survival* 7, no. 4 (1965): 155–159, https://doi.org/10.1080/00396336508440539.
Morgenthau, Hans J. "The Roots of America's China Policy." *The China Quarterly* 10 (1962): 45–50, https://doi.org/10.2307/651773.
Morgenthau, Hans J. "The primacy of the national interest." *The American Scholar* (1949): 207–212.
Morgenthau, Hans Joachim. *Politics Among Nations: The Struggle For Power and Peace.* A. A. Knopf, 1948.
Mueller, Karl P., Jasen J. Castillo, Forrest E. Morgan, Negeen Pegahi, and Brian Rosen. *Striking first: preemptive and preventive attack in US national security policy.* Vol. 375. Rand Corporation, 2006.
Nathan, Andrew J., and Andrew Scobell. "How China Sees America: The Sum of Beijing's Fears." *Foreign Aff.* 91 (2012): 32.
Neher, Clark D. "Asian style democracy." *Asian Survey* 34, no. 11 (1994): 949–961, https://doi.org/10.2307/2645346.
Nye, Joseph S. "Soft power: the evolution of a concept." *Journal of Political Power* 14, no. 1 (2021): 196–208, https://doi.org/10.1080/2158379X.2021.1879572.
Nye Jr, Joseph S. "Smart power." *New Perspectives Quarterly* 26, no. 2 (2009): 7–9.
Nye Jr, Joseph S. "The decline of America's soft power-Why Washington should worry." *Foreign Aff.* 83 (2004): 16.
Nye Jr, Joseph S. "US power and strategy after Iraq." *Foreign Aff.* 82 (2003): 60.
Nye, Joseph S. "Soft power." *Foreign policy* 80 (1990): 153–171.
Osiander, Andreas. "Sovereignty, international relations, and the Westphalian myth." *International organization* 55, no. 2 (2001): 251–287, https://doi.org/10.1162/00208180151140577.
Paterson, Thomas G., ed. *Kennedy's quest for victory: American foreign policy, 1961–1963.* New York: Oxford University Press, 1989.
Peidong, Yang, and Tang Lijun. "'Positive Energy': Hegemonic Intervention and Online Media Discourse in China's Xi Jinping Era." *China: An International Journal* 16, no. 1 (2018): 1–22.
Peng, Yan Qin, Chao-Chuan Chen, and Xin Hui Yang. "Bridging Confucianism and Legalism: Xunzi's philosophy of sage-kingship." In *Leadership and management in China: Philosophies, theories, and practices*, ed. by Chao-Chuan Chen and Yueh-Ting Lee, pp. 51–80. Cambridge University Press, 2008, https://doi.org/10.1017/CBO9780511753763.004.
Pillet, A. "The Monroe Doctrine." *The ANNALS of the American Academy of Political and Social Science* 54, no. 1 (1914): 131–133, https://doi.org/10.1177%2F000271621405400116.
Powell, Robert. "Anarchy in international relations theory: the neorealist-neoliberal debate." *International organization* 48, no. 2 (1994): 313–344, https://doi.org/10.1017/S0020818300028204.

Qin, Yaqing. "Development of International Relations theory in China: progress through debates." *International Relations of the Asia-Pacific* 11, no. 2 (2011): 231–257, https://doi.org/10.1093/irap/lcr003.

Qin, Yaqing. "Why is there no Chinese international relations theory?." *International Relations of the Asia-Pacific* 7, no. 3 (2007): 313–340, https://doi.org/10.1093/irap/lcm013.

Renatus, Flavius Vegetius. *Vegetius: epitome of military science*. Vol. 16. Liverpool University Press, 1996.

Ricard, Serge. "The Roosevelt Corollary." *Presidential Studies Quarterly* 36, no. 1 (2006): 17–26, https://doi.org/10.1111/j.1741-5705.2006.00283.x.

Robertson, Christopher J. "The global dispersion of Chinese values: A three-country study of Confucian dynamism." *MIR: Management International Review* (2000): 253–268.

Robinson, Thomas W., and David L. Shambaugh, eds. *Chinese foreign policy: theory and practice*. Oxford University Press, 1995.

Rose, Gideon. "Neoclassical realism and theories of foreign policy." *World politics* 51, no. 1 (1998): 144–172, https://doi.org/10.1017/S0043887100007814.

Rupp, Richard. "NATO 1949 and NATO 2000: From collective defense toward collective security." *The Journal of Strategic Studies* 23, no. 3 (2000): 154–176, https://doi.org/10.1080/01402390008437804.

Schweigler, Gebhard. "Carter's détente policy: change or continuity?." *The World Today* 34, no. 3 (1978): 81–89.

Scobell, Andrew. *China and strategic culture*. Strategic Studies Institute, 2002.

Shih, Chih-yu. *The spirit of Chinese foreign policy: a psychocultural view*. Springer, 1990.

Smith, James M., and Paul J. Bolt, eds. *China's Strategic Arsenal: Worldview, Doctrine, and Systems*. Georgetown University Press, 2021.

Snyder, Jack. *Myths of empire*. Cornell University Press, 2013.

Snyder, Jack. "One world, rival theories." *Foreign policy* 145 (2004): 52, https://doi.org/10.2307/4152944.

Snyder, Jack. "Imperial temptations." *The National Interest* 71 (2003): 29–40.

Snyder, Jack. *Myths of Empire: Domestic Policies and Strategic Ideology*. Cornell University Press, 1991.

Snyder, Richard Carlton, Henry W. Bruck, Burton Sapin, V. Hudson, D. Chollet, and J. Goldgeier. *Foreign policy decision making*. Palgrave Macmillan, 2002.

Stanger, Roland J. "Appendix XI Japan. Agreement Under Article VI of the Treaty of Mutual Cooperation and Security." *International Law Studies* 52, no. 1 (1965): 16.

Strukov, Vlad. "Russian 'Manipulative Smart Power': Zviagintsev's Oscar nomination, (non-)government agency and contradictions of the globalized world." *New Cinemas: Journal of Contemporary Film* 14, no. 1 (2016): 31–49, https://doi.org/10.1386/ncin.14.1.31_1.

Tang, Shiping. "From offensive to defensive realism." In *China's Ascent: Power, Security, and the Future of International Politics*, ed. by Robert S. Ross and Zhu Feng, pp. 141–162. Cornell University Press, 2008.

Tow, William T. "Sino-Japanese security cooperation: Evolution and prospects." *Pacific Affairs* 56, no. 1 (1983): 51–83, https://doi.org/10.2307/2758770.

Tu, Wei-Ming. "Confucius and confucianism." *Confucianism and the family* (1998): 3–36.

Tzu, Sun. *Sun Tzu's The Art of War: Bilingual Edition Complete Chinese and English Text*. Tuttle Publishing, 2012.

Tzu, Sun. *The art of war: Translated by Lionel Giles*. Ricardo Cebrián Salé, 2008.

Van Hoften, Derek. "Declaring War on the Japanese Constitution: Japan's Right to Military Sovereignty and the United States' Right to Military Presence in Japan." *Hastings Int'l & Comp. L. Rev.* 26 (2002): 289.

Von Goethe, Johann Wolfgang. *Faust,* translated by Martin Greenberg. Yale University Press, 2014.

Wah, Sheh Seow. "Confucianism and Chinese leadership." *Chinese management studies* (2010), https://doi.org/10.1108/17506141011074165.

Walker, Christopher, and Jessica Ludwig. "A Full-Spectrum Response to Sharp Power." In *Sharp Power and Democratic Resilience Series*, ed. by Christopher Walker, pp. 2–21. International Forum for Democratic Studies, 2021.

Walt, Stephen M. "The end of hubris and the new age of American restraint." *Foreign Aff.* 98 (2019): 26.

Walt, Stephen M. "US grand strategy after the Cold War: Can realism explain it? Should realism guide it?." *International Relations* 32, no. 1 (2018): 3–22, https://doi.org/10.1177%2F0047117817753272.

Walt, Stephen M. *The origins of alliances*. Cornell University Press, 2013.

Walt, Stephen M. "Alliances in a unipolar world." *World politics* 61, no. 1 (2009): 86–120, https://doi.org/10.1017/S0043887109000045.

Walt, Stephen M. "International relations: one world, many theories." *Foreign policy* (1998): 29–46, https://doi.org/10.2307/1149275.

Walt, Stephen M. "Why alliances endure or collapse." *Survival* 39, no. 1 (1997): 156–179, https://doi.org/10.1080/00396339708442901.

Walt, Stephen M. "Testing theories of alliance formation: the case of Southwest Asia." *International Organization* 42, no. 2 (1988): 275–316, https://doi.org/10.1017/S0020818300032823.

Waltz, Kenneth. *The myth of national interdependence*. Routledge, 2019.

Waltz, Kenneth. *Man, the state, and war*. Columbia University Press, 2018.

Waltz, Kenneth N. "Anarchic orders and balances of power." *Realism Reader* 113 (2014).

Waltz, Kenneth N. "Why Iran should get the bomb: Nuclear balancing would mean stability." *Foreign Affairs* (2012): 2–5.

Waltz, Kenneth N. "Globalization and American power." *The National Interest* 59 (2000): 46–56.

Waltz, Kenneth N. "Structural realism after the Cold War." *International security* 25, no. 1 (2000): 5–41, https://doi.org/10.1162/016228800560372.

Waltz, Kenneth N. "NATO expansion: A realist's view." *Contemporary Security Policy* 21, no. 2 (2000): 23–38, https://doi.org/10.1080/13523260008404253.

Waltz, Kenneth N. "Policy Paper 15: Peace, Stability, and Nuclear Weapons." In *Policy Papers*, ed. by Institute on Global Conflict and Cooperation, pp. 3–19. UC San Diego Press, 1995.

Waltz, Kenneth N. "The emerging structure of international politics." *International security* 18, no. 2 (1993): 44–79, https://doi.org/10.1162/isec.18.2.44.

Waltz, Kenneth N. "America as a model for the world? A foreign policy perspective." *PS: Political Science & Politics* 24, no. 4 (1991): 667–670, https://doi.org/10.2307/419401.

Waltz, Kenneth N. "The origins of war in neorealist theory." *The Journal of Interdisciplinary History* 18, no. 4 (1988): 615–628, https://doi.org/10.2307/204817.

Waltz, Kenneth N. "The spread of nuclear weapons: More may be better: Introduction." (1981): 1–1, https://doi.org/10.1080/05679328108457394.

Waltz, Kenneth N. *Theory of international politics*. Waveland Press, 1979.

Waltz, Kenneth N. "The stability of a bipolar world." *Daedalus* (1964): 881–909.

Wang, Yiwei. "Public diplomacy and the rise of Chinese soft power." *The Annals of the American Academy of Political and Social Science* 616, no. 1 (2008): 257–273, https://doi.org/10.1177%2F0002716207312757.

Weigert, Hans W. "Haushofer and the Pacific." *Foreign Aff.* 20 (1941): 734.

Wilkinson, Endymion Porter. *Chinese history: a manual*. Vol. 52. Harvard Univ Asia Center, 2000.

Wong, Chack-kie. "Comparing social quality and social harmony from a governance perspective." *Development and Society* 38 (2009): 237–257.

Woolf, Greg. "Romanization 2.0 and its alternatives." *Archaeological Dialogues* 21, no. 1 (2014): 45–50, https://doi.org/10.1017/S1380203814000087.

Wuthnow, Joel, and Phillip Charles Saunders. *Chinese military reform in the age of Xi Jinping: Drivers, challenges, and Implications*. Government Printing Office, 2017.

Xiaogan, Liu. "Naturalness (Tzu-jan),"The Core Value in Taoism: Its Ancient Meaning and Its Significance Today,"." In *Lao-tzu and the Tao-te-ching*, ed. by Livia Kohn and Michael Lafargue, pp. 211–228. State University of New York Press, 1998.

Xuetong, Yan. "Chinese values vs. liberalism: What ideology will shape the international normative order?" In *Globalizing IR Theory*, ed. by Yaqing Qin, pp. 102–123. Routledge, 2020.

Xuetong, Yan. "The age of uneasy peace: Chinese power in a divided world." *Foreign Aff.* 98 (2019): 40.

Xuetong, Yan. "For a new bipolarity: China and Russia vs. America." *New Perspectives Quarterly* 30, no. 2 (2013): 12–15, https://doi.org/10.1111/npqu.11366.

Yan, Xuetong. *Ancient Chinese thought, modern Chinese power*. Princeton University Press, 2013.

Xuetong, Yan. "Xun Zi's thoughts on international politics and their implications." *Chinese Journal of International Politics* 2, no. 1 (2008): 135–165, https://doi.org/10.1093/cjip/pon005.

Xuetong, Yan. "The rise of China in Chinese eyes." *Journal of Contemporary China* 10, no. 26 (2001): 33–39, https://doi.org/10.1080/10670560123407.

Yahuda, Michael B. "Chinese foreign policy after 1963: The Maoist phases." *The China Quarterly* 36 (1968): 93–113, https://doi.org/10.1017/S0305741000005622.

Yang, Shih-ying, and Robert J. Sternberg. "Conceptions of intelligence in ancient Chinese philosophy." *Journal of Theoretical and Philosophical Psychology* 17, no. 2 (1997): 101, https://psycnet.apa.org/doi/10.1037/h0091164.

Yeh, Kuang-Hui. "Relationalism: The essence and evolving process of Chinese interactive relationships." *Chinese Journal of Communication* 3, no. 1 (2010): 76–94, https://doi.org/10.1080/17544750903528872.

Youlan, Feng. *A short history of Chinese philosophy*. Vol. 91098. Simon and Schuster, 1948.

Zakaria, Fareed. *Ten lessons for a post-pandemic world*. Penguin UK, 2020.

Zedong, Mao. "On contradiction." *Chinese Studies in Philosophy* 19, no. 2 (1987): 20–82, https://doi.org/10.2753/CSP1097-1467190220.

Zhang, Feng. "Confucian foreign policy traditions in Chinese history." *The Chinese Journal of International Politics* 8, no. 2 (2015): 197–218, https://doi.org/10.1093/cjip/pov004.

Zhang, Feng. "Rethinking China's grand strategy: Beijing's evolving national interests and strategic ideas in the reform era." *International Politics* 49, no. 3 (2012): 318–345, https://doi.org/10.1057/ip.2012.5.

Zhang, Qianfan. *The constitution of China: A contextual analysis*. Bloomsbury Publishing, 2012.

Zhao, Suisheng. "The US–China Rivalry in the Emerging Bipolar World: Hostility, Alignment, and Power Balance." *Journal of Contemporary China* (2021): 1–17, https://doi.org/10.1080/10670564.2021.1945733.

Zhao, Suisheng. "The China Model: can it replace the Western model of modernization?." *Journal of contemporary China* 19, no. 65 (2010): 419–436, https://doi.org/10.1080/10670561003666061.

Zhimin, Chen. "Nationalism, internationalism and Chinese foreign policy." *Journal of Contemporary China* 14, no. 42 (2005): 35–53, https://doi.org/10.1080/1067056042000300772.

Zhou, Xueguang. "The separation of officials from local staff: The logic of the Empire and personnel management in the Chinese bureaucracy." *Chinese Journal of Sociology* 2, no. 2 (2016): 259–299, https://doi.org/10.1177%2F2057150X16639194.

Zhou, Xueguang, Nancy Brandon Tuma, and Phyllis Moen. "Stratification dynamics under state socialism: The case of urban China, 1949–1993." *Social forces* 74, no. 3 (1996): 759–796, https://doi.org/10.1093/sf/74.3.759.

Zhou, Xueguang. "Unorganized interests and collective action in communist China." *American Sociological Review* (1993): 54–73, https://doi.org/10.2307/2096218.

Index

Alliance 12–18, 21, 24, 27, 31f., 36f., 40, 43, 45f., 48–53, 56, 72, 76–78, 80, 83–85, 91, 93, 95–97, 112, 119, 132, 146, 150, 156, 160, 175–178, 180, 184, 191–194, 197–199, 216, 222f.
Anarchic 7, 11, 31, 33, 39, 42, 55, 60, 69, 90, 95, 130, 161–163, 173, 204, 225
Anarchy 7, 9, 23, 26–29, 31, 35f., 38, 42, 44, 52, 57, 63f., 67, 69, 82, 90–93, 101, 115, 118, 130, 135f., 156, 161–163, 166, 168, 174, 204, 207, 209, 211, 214, 225f.
Apothem 172–174, 205f., 210, 212
– Apothem of defensive postures 173, 205–209, 212, 214

Bandwagoning 16f.
Base 20, 83, 154, 165, 169, 173f., 203, 205–212, 214
– Base area 162, 166–168, 171, 173f., 203, 206, 208f., 212, 214
– Base edges 171, 203, 207, 209, 211, 214
– Base side of defense 205f., 208f., 212, 214
Bipolar 4, 7f., 13, 22, 25, 30, 34f., 39, 45, 52, 80, 83, 88, 93f., 110f., 116, 138, 144, 159, 163, 165, 167, 172, 175f., 179, 185f., 188, 192–194, 197f., 202f., 226–228
Bipolarity 7, 29, 32, 34, 57, 65, 67f., 83, 93, 108–110, 130, 158f., 161, 164–166, 175, 188, 190, 192, 202

Coercion 20, 31f., 43–45, 51–53, 60, 62, 67, 80, 93f., 165
Cognitive 85, 116, 139, 184f.
– Cognitive delusion 85
Communism 9f., 18, 20, 24, 34f., 42, 52, 75, 80, 82, 90, 100, 102f., 105, 109f., 112–114, 116–118, 122f., 128f., 131, 137–140, 142–145, 149, 152, 161, 189, 200, 223, 227

Concave 214
– Concave polygon 214
Confucian 8, 13, 23, 103, 108, 115, 117, 119–121, 123, 142, 155–157, 199
Containment 21f., 26, 41f., 54, 58, 68, 75, 77, 80f., 99, 111, 149, 151, 161, 180f., 183–185, 207, 209
Continuity 102, 105, 108f., 129, 201
Convex 211f.
– Convex hexagonal pyramid 211
– Convex polygon 211
Cooperation 2f., 9–11, 13–16, 23, 36f., 43, 45, 50, 52f., 68f., 72, 75, 78, 81, 85, 91, 95f., 98, 100, 112, 126, 133, 145, 154, 159–161, 164, 178, 182, 189, 200, 203f., 206, 209, 211
Corollary 62
– Roosevelt Corollary 15, 61f.
Coronacrisis 6, 14, 89, 188
Coronavirus 1f., 5–7, 11–14, 18, 23, 26, 28, 30, 82, 87, 89, 135, 188
Cultivation 114, 116–121, 124, 128f., 134, 139, 145, 148, 157, 198
– Strategic cultivation 13
– Silent cultivator 4, 26, 102, 115, 152, 161, 175

Democracy 2f., 9, 18, 27f., 35f., 39f., 42, 45–47, 51f., 54, 57, 63–67, 69, 71f., 75, 78, 83f., 86f., 89–94, 96, 98, 100, 105, 117, 122, 127–130, 140–143, 145, 151, 153, 158, 184, 190, 192–197, 223, 227
– Oil diplomacy 67f
Destruction 41, 53, 96, 119, 150, 162, 182f., 221, 226
– Mutual assured destruction 7, 23, 25, 29, 31, 42, 68, 80, 82, 110, 162, 179
Détente 68, 109, 111f.
Deterrence 20–22, 41, 77, 150, 159, 179, 182–186
Dialectics 4, 103–105, 113f., 117, 119, 200

Dilemma 16, 18, 20, 45, 50, 62, 66, 78 f., 90, 95, 142, 145, 193, 198, 202 f., 206, 223, 226
Diplomacy 2, 12, 15, 26, 44 f., 47, 58, 69, 111, 118 f., 131, 167, 170, 194, 197, 213, 222

Endurance 32, 70, 197
Eurasian 3, 8, 19, 43, 47, 51, 72, 88, 103, 114, 124, 191, 222–224

Gongfu 121

Harmony 106, 115, 118, 120, 129, 142, 147, 156, 186, 189, 199, 213
Hawkism 36, 39, 47, 53, 65, 196
Hegemony 3 f., 10 f., 14 f., 35 f., 39–41, 44, 46–51, 53, 55, 60 f., 65 f., 69, 75, 77, 85 f., 88, 91–94, 99, 101, 105–109, 113, 115, 121, 124 f., 129, 131, 140 f., 143, 158, 161, 165, 186 f., 190, 194 f., 199, 225
Height 14, 173 f., 203, 205 f., 208 f., 212, 219
– Height of offense 205–207, 209, 212, 214
– Slant height of offensive postures 202, 205–209, 212, 214

Imperialism 23, 59, 61, 77, 107 f., 112, 152 f.
Institutionalism 3, 70, 98
Interdependence 7, 23, 38, 52, 89, 91 f., 95 f., 98, 100, 106, 119, 131, 149, 186, 189, 193, 200, 219, 227
Isolationism 2, 48, 59, 71 f., 105, 107, 109

Lateral 169 f., 173, 206, 218
– Lateral edges 167, 169, 171, 173, 203, 207, 209, 211, 214
– Lateral faces 169–171, 174, 180, 207, 209, 211 f., 214, 226
Leadership 4, 8, 16, 24, 30, 36, 52, 61, 68, 79, 81 f., 93, 98, 100, 102, 107 f., 112–116, 118, 120 f., 123, 128 f., 134, 139, 142–144, 147, 151, 156 f., 167, 183, 186 f., 191, 198 f., 201, 223 f., 228

– Pragmatic leadership 102, 122, 143, 158, 161, 196, 201
Legalism 119–121
Liberal 2–7, 9, 14 f., 18, 27, 31, 34–46, 48 f., 51–53, 55, 60–63, 65 f., 69–72, 75, 82 f., 86 f., 89–100, 102, 105 f., 109, 117, 121 f., 125, 127–130, 133, 135–138, 140–143, 145, 147, 149 f., 152 f., 156, 158, 161, 165 f., 169, 178 f., 186–190, 192, 194–197, 200–202, 217 f., 223, 225, 227
– Liberal institutionalism 70, 98
Liberalism 2–4, 18, 36, 65 f., 93–95, 98, 120, 127, 135 f., 156, 194, 227

Maoism 105–109, 112 f., 140
Meritocracy 129, 134, 142 f., 145, 157, 161, 201
Military 2 f., 7, 9–24, 26–28, 30 f., 33, 35–46, 48, 50 f., 53–60, 63 f., 66 f., 71–86, 88–99, 104, 108–111, 113, 115 f., 118 f., 121, 124–127, 131–133, 137 f., 141–144, 146, 149–152, 154, 160, 162–164, 167, 170 f., 173, 175, 178, 181, 183 f., 187 f., 190, 192–199, 201, 210, 213, 215–217, 220, 223 f., 228
– Military paternalism 123, 131
Mohist 103
Moralpolitik 39, 83, 122
Multipolar 8, 12, 14, 35, 45, 58, 86, 93 f., 118, 125, 141, 172, 203

Nationalism 14 f., 29, 47, 53–55, 58, 61, 76, 79, 82, 95, 134 f., 151 f., 156 f., 177 f., 217 f., 223
– Principled nationalism 55–57, 65, 95
Neoconservatism 20
Neo-Eurasian 77, 93, 135
Neo-liberalism 6
Neo-realist 4, 14
Nuclear 16, 18, 23, 25 f., 32, 41, 47–49, 55, 60, 66–69, 72–76, 82, 85, 95, 97, 99, 107 f., 110 f., 114, 125, 130, 133 f., 146, 149–151, 154, 159 f., 163, 166–176, 179–188, 194, 202, 206, 208–211, 213 f., 216, 218, 220–222, 225 f.

- Nuclear apocalypse   23, 67, 86, 99, 179–183, 213–215
- Nuclear bipolarity   29, 35, 74, 159, 177, 186, 188–190, 200, 202f., 214, 226
- Nuclear concert   29, 169, 174, 208, 226
- Nuclear diplomacy   20, 48, 68f., 73f., 97, 133, 169f., 181, 210, 216, 227
- Nuclear holocaust   12, 25, 32, 41, 49, 68, 74, 80, 191
- Nuclear war   11, 68, 76, 87, 180, 182, 187, 202, 212, 214, 217, 220f.
- Nuclear weapons   4, 29, 32, 46, 66f., 69, 74, 99, 168, 170, 172, 179–181, 183, 186, 200, 203, 205f., 213f., 220–222, 226

Offshore-balancing   15, 58, 78, 131

Pandemic   1–3, 5–7, 9, 11f., 14–17, 22f., 26–28, 30, 33f., 41f., 82, 87f., 90f., 98f., 135, 159, 163, 171, 180, 186, 188f., 203, 218, 220, 225
Parabellum   143, 152, 155
- Parabellum paradigm   13, 42, 86, 103, 115, 119, 124, 153
Peace   3, 6, 9, 11, 20f., 26–29, 31, 35f., 39, 43, 46f., 50, 52, 54, 58, 62, 64–66, 70, 73f., 82–84, 91–97, 129, 133, 141, 147, 156f., 164–167, 169, 175f., 183, 186, 190f., 196, 200, 209f., 213, 225–228
Personalism   128
Polarity   2, 9, 30, 32, 60, 66, 130, 202
Politics   1–7, 9, 11, 19, 23, 25–31, 33, 35, 41–44, 47, 49, 52f., 56–65, 69f., 74, 77, 79, 87, 91, 93–95, 98–100, 102, 104–106, 108f., 115, 118–122, 124, 126, 128f., 132, 134–137, 140f., 143f., 146, 148f., 156f., 159–167, 169–172, 174, 176–179, 185, 191, 193, 195, 206f., 209, 211, 214, 217–222, 224–227
Polygon   162, 172, 203
- Irregular polygon   209–211, 214
- Regular polygon   174, 203, 207
Post-pandemic   1f., 4, 6–18, 20–25, 27–30, 33–35, 42, 69, 74f., 79, 82f., 99, 108f., 149, 159–163, 165f., 168–176, 178f., 181–183, 185f., 188, 191, 193, 202–204, 206f., 209, 211, 214, 219–221, 225–228
Power   1–13, 17, 19, 21–48, 50–67, 69–75, 77–80, 82–84, 86, 89–91, 93–100, 102–105, 107–109, 111, 113–116, 118–125, 127–135, 137–139, 141–152, 154, 159–176, 179, 181–188, 190–200, 202–204, 206–211, 213–222, 224–228
- Hard power   4, 11, 24f., 44, 99, 116, 118f., 124, 132f., 149, 160, 165, 167, 170, 193, 213, 227
- Sharp power   152
- Smart power   1, 20, 22, 44, 46, 92f., 124f., 132, 170
- Soft power   2f., 8, 41, 44f., 63, 70, 73, 75, 118–120, 124f., 132, 139, 141, 148f., 152, 160, 164–167, 170, 175, 186–188, 193–197, 201, 213, 219f., 222
Powershifting   33, 82, 85f., 96
Preemption   3
Preemptive   46, 67, 183, 206, 215
- Preemptive strike   2f., 12f., 18, 31, 39, 48, 63, 70, 78, 146f., 154, 170, 194, 215
Pyramid   159, 161–167, 169–174, 179f., 198, 202–214, 218, 221
- Oblique hexagonal pyramid   202, 207, 209
- Pyramid of balance   2, 4, 27, 162, 167–170, 172–175, 179, 186, 193, 202, 204–206, 208f., 211, 219, 221, 226f.
- Regular hexagonal pyramid   202

Rationality   184
- Imperfect rationality   29, 171, 207, 209, 211, 214
Realism   2, 5, 7, 16, 19, 27, 29, 35, 37, 44, 46, 53, 55f., 60–62, 70, 74, 83, 92f., 95f., 98, 100, 102, 118, 127, 132f., 136–138, 143f., 146–151, 156, 160f., 164, 166, 169, 189f., 202, 205, 218, 225–227
- Classical realism   5, 120, 147, 149, 218
- Coercive realism   1, 4, 25–27, 31f., 159, 167, 219, 225f.
- Cultural realism   153

Index — 243

- Defensive realism   25, 144–146, 148 f., 219
- Offensive realism   11–13, 25, 144, 148, 151
- Principled realism   53, 55, 57 f., 95
Realpolitik   4, 26, 39, 55, 57, 94 f., 99, 102 f., 113, 116, 123–127, 131 f., 134 f., 141, 143 f., 146–148, 152, 155 f., 158, 169, 190, 227

Security   1 f., 6–18, 20 f., 23, 25, 32, 36, 38, 41, 43, 45, 48–50, 52–55, 60, 62, 66, 68 f., 72 f., 75 f., 78–80, 83–85, 94 f., 97, 100, 102, 116, 118, 126, 130, 133, 145–147, 149, 151, 154, 159 f., 164, 170, 176–179, 182, 185, 191, 196, 204, 210, 212, 216, 218, 220 f., 223, 228
- Security dilemma   1, 4, 9 f., 23, 32, 50, 52, 100, 145, 160, 165 f., 174, 202–206, 208
Sinocentric   35, 136, 138, 153, 155–157, 169, 192, 199
Socialism   109, 120, 130, 136, 138, 141 f., 144 f., 156, 200 f.
Sovereignty   16, 29, 32, 41, 51, 53 f., 69 f., 72, 133 f., 164, 168, 175, 179, 200, 218, 226
Strategy   1, 3 f., 9–15, 17, 20–22, 24 f., 27, 30, 32, 34–42, 46, 48, 50, 53 f., 58 f., 64, 66, 68, 71–73, 77 f., 80 f., 83, 85–89, 92 f., 97, 99 f., 102, 107 f., 110–115, 118, 120 f., 123–125, 127, 131 f., 134–136, 138, 140, 144, 146–154, 156, 161, 175, 179, 183, 187, 193, 196–200, 205 f., 217, 223
Syndrome   42, 65 f., 77, 90, 96, 200
- Unipolar syndrome   60–64, 66, 96

Taoism   4, 104, 113, 117–121
Tributary   34, 100, 106, 115, 120, 131, 186, 192, 217
- Tributary diplomacy   4, 123, 131 f., 149, 153, 155, 175, 184, 187, 192 f., 196, 198–200, 208, 210, 217

Unipolarity   2, 9, 30, 33 f., 39, 41, 47, 53, 60–64, 83, 86, 91–93, 95–97, 99, 130, 166, 193

Vozhdizm   114

War   1–3, 7–11, 13–15, 18–31, 33–36, 38–48, 50–54, 56–75, 77 f., 80, 82–85, 87–100, 106–111, 113–117, 119, 121–123, 126, 128, 130, 133, 137–139, 141–146, 149–152, 154 f., 157–161, 163–170, 172, 174–177, 179–188, 190–195, 197, 199 f., 202–204, 211, 213–217, 220, 224 f., 227 f.
- Hegemonic war   23–25
- Scorch war   186, 193, 211 f.
Warfare   1, 11, 13, 19, 22–25, 32, 61, 86 f., 96, 110 f., 115, 152, 160, 177
- Conventional warfare   31, 74, 110, 160
- Hybrid warfare   44, 75, 124, 152, 160

www.ingramcontent.com/pod-product-compliance
Lightning Source LLC
Chambersburg PA
CBHW050522170426
43201CB00013B/2045